Donated to
The Camas Public Library
By:

JANICE SAUNDERS

KNOW YOUR
SINGER

KNOW YOUR
SINGER

JACKIE DODSON

CHILTON BOOK COMPANY

RADNOR, PENNSYLVANIA

Published in Radnor, Pennsylvania 19089, by Chilton Book Company
No part of this book may be reproduced, transmitted or stored
in any form or by any means, electronic or mechanical,
without prior written permission from the publisher

Designed by William E. Lickfield
Manufactured in the United States of America

Library of Congress Cataloging in Publication Data
Dodson, Jackie.
    Know your singer/Jackie Dodson.
        p.   cm.—(Creative machine arts series)
    Bibliography: p. 194
    Includes index.
    ISBN 0-8019-7886-6
    1. Machine sewing. 2. Sewing machines. I. Title. II. Series.
TT713.D643 1989
646.2′044—dc20   88-43311
                                                             CIP

1 2 3 4 5 6 7 8 9 0   8 7 6 5 4 3 2 1 0 9

Contents

Foreword

Recently I've been on an anti-clutter rampage, cleaning out closets, boxes, shelves, and files with a vengeance. I call it Playing the Game of Condominium—if I had to move to a condominium and compress all my belongings, what could I give away? The level of clutter surrounding me parallels the messy state of my brain: clean surfaces, clean mind. So I'm ruthlessly cleaning; if I haven't used it, worn it, thought of it for a year or more, out it goes.

But I cannot bring myself to throw away my bulging file of letters from Jackie Dodson, author of this book. Jackie and I met 10 years ago by accident on a tour bus in Chicago. Since then she has showered me with wacky, inspiring letters. This is a woman who is brimming with laughter and ideas, sharing both freely. Most of the letters arrived with swatches of machine-embroidered fabric pinned to them. "Have you tried this?" she'd ask, again and again.

Over the years I have learned about her machine-embroidery classes, her work with the Hinsdale Embroiderers' Guild, her ongoing family escapades. But always her letters have inspired me to run to my machine and play around with new ideas.

When it came time to revise my machine-embroidery book, I knew who to ask for help as a designer and critic: Jackie.

Now you, too, can participate in the output of this creative woman, whether or not you own a Singer. She has developed a series of lessons that will introduce you to the full range of what you and your machine can accomplish as partners. By the end of the book, you will truly know your machine. Enjoy the trip!

Robbie Fanning

Series Editor, Creative Machine Arts, and co-author
The Complete Book of Machine Embroidery

Are you interested in a quarterly magazine about creative uses of the sewing machine? Robbie Fanning and Jackie Dodson are planning to start one. For more information, write:

The Creative Machine
PO Box 2634
Menlo Park, CA 94026

Preface

When our children were small, we took long car trips. I remember one that took longer than planned. We all grumbled about being lost, but one of our boys said, "It's just one of Dad's long-cuts."

We loved that new word, so we came up with dictionary meanings.

Long-cut (noun): When it takes longer, but Dad convinces everyone he wanted it that way. A "little something extra." An adventure. An educational side-trip. You are happier when you finally reach your destination. And so on.

What does this have to do with the Singer sewing machine? This book contains long-cuts, those adventurous techniques that help you and your sewing machine create something special, something out of the ordinary.

Most of us learned basic techniques of sewing when we bought our machines—how to thread it, wind a bobbin, make a buttonhole, sew a straight seam. We were shown each presser foot and how to use it . . . and, I'll bet, except for the zipper and buttonhole feet, you haven't looked at those other feet again.

But there's so much more to learn. Join me on an educational side-trip. By the time you're done with this book, you'll truly know your Singer.

Let's begin by exploring how we can change a piece of fabric: we can add texture to it, appliqué it, quilt it, stitch across

holes in it, draw thread out of it, gather it up and decorate it. We can stitch in space with our sewing machines, make cording; more importantly, once we understand the machine, it makes all our stitching easier.

As we explore these effects, presented in 38 lessons, we'll make small samples for a notebook; make finished 6" squares to fit in a tote bag, displaying what we've learned; and make 32 projects. In the process of stitching the samples and projects in the book, you'll take an educational side-trip as well. You'll learn to adjust and manipulate your Singer until you can use it to its full potential.

This workbook of ideas does not take the place of your basic manual or Creative Sewing Guide. Instead, it is to be used as a reinforcement and supplement to what you already know. By working through the lessons, you will come to know your machine better.

Yes, there is much more to sewing than straight stitching. And wouldn't you rather go that long-cut route—to make your stitching more interesting and original?

In my classes I often hear this progression: "I can't do that" to "Can I really do that?" to "I can do that!" I hope this book is the next best thing to having me prompting, prodding, patting you on the back in person.

Jackie Dodson
La Grange Park, Illinois

Acknowledgments

Thank you.

To the following: Gail Schwindeman, Zoe Graul and Becky Hanson from Singer and to the Singer Sewing Machine Co.

To friends who answered questions when I needed help: Ed Perk and Sherry Karasek.

A special thank you to Ed and Flo Perk, who let me work out these lessons with students at their shop.

To Carol Ahles, Caryl Rae Hancock, Nora Lou Kampe, Gail Kibiger, Pat Pasquini and Marcia Strickland for sharing ideas; Ladi Tisol who helped me before I had to ask; and Marilyn Tisol, critic, sounding-board, and special friend.

To Chuck, who took the photos and to the rest of my family, who learned to accept decorative clothing in place of mended clothing.

To Robbie Fanning, for her optimism, encouragement, and endless support.

And to my students, who kept telling me to write it all down.

KNOW YOUR SINGER

CHAPTER **1**

Getting Started

This book is organized by the changes you can make to a piece of fabric—add stitches, add texture, subtract threads, and so on. Following this introductory chapter, each chapter consists of several lessons and some projects. Each lesson asks you to stitch up practice samples for a notebook or for finished projects. The largest project in the book is the tote bag (directions for making it are in Chapter 12). It was designed to show off interchangeable decorative squares, which you'll make as you proceed through the lessons.

For the practice samples, you will want to set up a three-ring notebook—the kind with the largest rings—to keep track of your stitching (Fig. 1.1). Buy plastic pockets and blank notebook paper (both available at office supply stores). Write the settings you've used directly on the stitched samples and slip them into the plastic pockets for future reference.

Clip pictures from magazines that trigger ideas. Ask yourself: Could I get that effect if I loosened or tightened the tension? Which presser foot would I use for

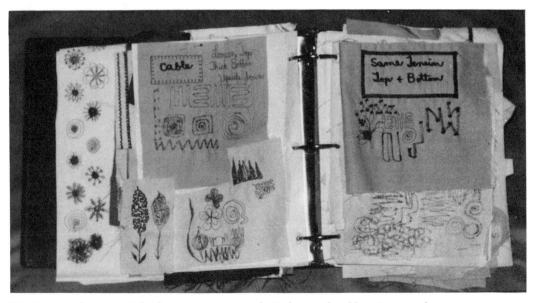

Fig. 1.1 A reference notebook, open to a page of stitch samples. Notations on the stitchery will help you reset the machine.

that? Which thread would produce loops like that? Write notes to yourself with ideas to try and add these to the notebook along with the magazine pictures.

Love your Singer

When I first learned to use a sewing machine, I didn't enjoy sewing the apron or quilted potholder we were required to finish for the next semester's cooking class. Not until years later when I constructed clothing that fit, gifts that were creative, upholstery that was a challenge, did I have fun with my machine. I think that you'll have fun, too, once you understand all the wonderful things you can do with your Singer.

I bought my first sewing machine with never a thought that the blind hem stitch could be used for more than putting in a blind hem. I'd expected to use my machine for clothing construction and repair, so it didn't occur to me that many of the built-in stitches I was using for sewing could also be used decoratively, and I could sew freely, with feed dogs covered to create laces, embroidery and much, much more. However, once I discovered books on machining, I began to see the sewing machine in an entirely new way: I had found a type of stitchery that suited the way I worked and had the look I loved. I've concentrated on learning everything I can about machine stitchery ever since. Notice that I did not say "machine embroidery." Embroidery is only one part of machine stitchery, which also includes making lace, needleweaving, appliquéing in creative ways, to name a few we'll touch on in this book.

If you use your machine for clothing construction, consider the possibilities of binding a pocket with your own decorated bias, hemstitching a baby bonnet, topstitching to make a seam lie flat, embroidering the edge of a placket. This book will show you the best, fastest way of accomplishing all that.

I'm assuming you attended basic lessons when you bought your machine or, if you purchased your machine at a garage sale, that you have read and worked through the basic manual and Creative Sewing Guide, if you have one. If not, do this first. But even if you've taken the basic lessons and memorized the manual, that is just the jumping-off place. There is so much more. A blind hem is taught in the manual, but did you know you can use it to attach elastic cord to the edge of a garment for button loops, couch down yarns and cords, attach appliqués and patch pockets? That is the type of information I've included in this book.

Let's begin by talking about your machine. First, be sure that it is in good working order: cleaned, oiled, and tuned up if it needs it. I've sewn long enough to know that if it isn't, stitches may be uneven or skipped, thread may break, the

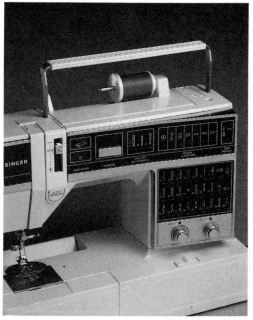

Fig. 1.2 Control panel of the Singer 6268 Ultra Unlimited.

machine may be sluggish or sound like a truck.

I'm from a family of Singer owners. That's not an earth-shaking admission: I'll bet most of you watched your mothers and grandmothers sew on Singers. Over the years I also sewed on Singers in home economics classes, and later I familiarized myself with the newer models when my students brought their Singers to classes. When asked to write this book, I was excited about learning the new Singer computer machine, the 6268 Ultra Unlimited (Fig. 1.2). This machine has unique Sew Ware cartridges that add designs, monograms, alphabets and numbers to what is already built into the machine. Being able to add cartridges to the two included with the machine means you're able to update your 6268 whenever a new cartridge is introduced.

The machine itself contains three buttonholes, and 24 built-in stitches, a memory so you can combine stitches, mirror image, reverse image, a button to push if you wish a stitch to be twice as long as standard, and another to narrow stitches when using the double needle. Of course it includes the all-important zigzag, blind stitch, overlock stitch, and stretch stitches for clothing construction.

The one-step buttonhole foot L is sensational. Place a button into the slot in the attachment and the machine automatically stitches a buttonhole the correct size for that particular button.

I also found that with auto-tension on the 6268, I could sew on the thickest, most tightly woven fabric made, and it would stitch over sheers or in open spaces without balking or needing a tension change. Actually, I rarely change the auto-tension on the 6268, but I know it can be changed easily if I want to tighten or loosen it for embroidery. The tension setting is included with each project. If a change is indicated, I'll show it as a tension setting (auto) and then tell if the setting is 1, 2,

or 3 dots into the negative (loosened) or positive (tightened). These are examples of how it may look: auto − 2 or auto + 3. See Figure 1.3.

Another new Singer computer machine, the 2210 Microcomputer, has over 100 decorative stitches, but without the Sew Ware capability. It fits between the top mechanical machine and the top 6268 Ultra Unlimited.

Of course not everyone needs or wants a computer machine, so Singer makes seven other models, each mechanical. How can you find one that's right for you? First decide how you use a sewing machine now; then ask yourself how you want to use one in the future: mending? clothing construction? embroidery? If you've never embroidered or monogrammed, perhaps you would if you had a machine that would do it for you. Ask for a comparison and demonstration at the dealer's and talk to friends who own Singers. Then make your decision.

Fig. 1.3 The auto-tension panel on the 6268.

3

Even though I used the 6268 computer machine when writing this book, I haven't left out any of you who have different models. If your machine will zigzag and blind stitch, this book is still for you. Stitch widths and lengths will be the same and I'll describe the presser feet I use so you can use the matching foot on your machine. The monogramming I show is exclusive with the 6268, but I hope you'll also be able to substitute free machine monogramming by the time you finish working through all the lessons.

Presser feet and attachments

Look at the presser feet and accessories included with your machine, as well as those extras you've purchased (Chart 1.1). Do you know how they are used? Turn each over and look at the bottom—it's the most important part. If it's the plastic buttonhole foot L (not the one-step), it will have two deep grooves to keep the fabric moving freely and in line as the beads of satin stitches are stitched in. The special purpose foot J is used for embroidery when feed dogs are up. It has a wide groove cut out to allow the fabric to feed through more freely as decorative stitches are sewn in place. The blind stitch foot K allows you to keep the fold of the stitching line exactly at the inside edge of the foot while stitching a straight line. The overedge foot has a wire to stitch over so the fabric being overcast won't tunnel (curl). The list goes on.

What presser feet and accessories do you own? Work with them and do a sample for each. Write on the fabric which foot you've used, and file it in your notebook. Though

Chart 1.1
Singer Presser Feet and Attachments

	Owner's Record
INCLUDED WITH SINGER PURCHASE	
A—general purpose needle plate	———
B—general purpose presser foot	———
C—straight stitch needle plate	———
D—straight sewing foot	———
E—zipper foot	———
F—feed cover plate	———
G—darning and embroidery foot	———
H—button sewing foot	———
J—special purpose foot	———
K—blind stitch foot	———
L—buttonhole foot	———
M—even-feed foot	———
T—mending foot for sideways sewing	———
AVAILABLE AS SEPARATE PURCHASE	
quilting guide	———
ruffler	———
roller foot	———
narrow hem foot	———
gathering foot	———
overedge foot	———
fringing and tacking foot	———

I'll include some of the basics in this book, you'll learn new ways to use them as well. You can't use your machine to its full potential until you understand what the presser feet can do and then take advantage of that knowledge. With every project in the book, I suggest the presser foot to use, so by the time you finish the book, the feet and accessories will be familiar to you and you'll understand which ones can be substituted for others.

So let's begin. Get out the box of attachments and presser feet that came with your machine, as well as the basic manual of instructions. If you can't find the manual, contact the dealer and arrange to purchase another.

When you purchased your machine, you probably asked what built-in stitches were included, but didn't think of asking about the presser feet. Most sewers don't look beyond the zigzag and zipper feet, even though presser feet expand the capabilities of the machine.

First you should know what type of presser foot fits your machine: vertical or slant shank. All Singer models today are slant if the number of the machine is *above* 6233, and vertical if the number is *below* 6217. One exception to this rule is the Singer model 2210 microcomputer, which has a slant shank.

Don't be limited by using only the five or ten different presser feet that came with your machine. Once you know the type of shank your machine has, check for other feet available that weren't included when you purchased it.

Generic feet are available for all sewing machines. Again, you must order a slant or short, vertical shank. If you buy only the clip-on part of the foot, be sure it fits the Singer shank (check the width of the metal bar on top of the foot to see that the shank will hold the foot securely). If not, generic shanks for generic feet can also be purchased.

Check the Sources of Supply at the end of the book for mail-order catalogues where you can purchase generic presser feet—available for almost every machine. I've also discovered that sewing machine repairmen and some mail-order houses will modify presser feet to fit your machine if you can't find exactly what you need.

Use Chart 1.1 to keep a record of the presser feet and attachments you have. When you come to know your sewing machine well, you will quickly realize that a zipper foot is not for zippers only, a blind hemmer is not only for hems alone, and many feet can do the same job.

The foot I use most often is the special purpose, plastic J foot. Although it is see-thru, I want to see better, so I bought a second one and customized it by cutting out the center with a small wire cutter; the center should be $\frac{1}{4}''$ (6.4mm), wide—the same as the width of the groove at the back of the presser foot, then I filed down the rough plastic with an emery board (Fig. 1.4). This became my "open embroidery foot." I like to see precisely what I'm doing, as I often match motifs or want to stop exactly on a certain stitch. When hemstitching, I must see where my needle has penetrated the fabric so I can place the wing needle in the same hole on the return

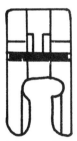

Fig. 1.4 To create an open embroidery foot, cut out $\frac{1}{4}''$ (6.4mm) from the center of the special purpose J foot.

pass. I use this foot when attaching $\frac{1}{8}''$ (3.2mm) or $\frac{1}{4}''$ (6.4mm) flat elastic. I also use it when I want to hold a half-dozen pearl cotton cords together while I stitch over them. The inside edges of the open J foot keep the elastic or pearl cotton cords in place as I guide them.

I modified another J foot by clipping out the center up to and including the black line found in the center (Fig. 1.5). With this foot I can roll and whip fabric easily for French machine sewing (see Chapter 8). Also, I use it to keep cord in place when I want to stitch over it. Included throughout the book are many other uses for these two altered feet. I'll call one the open J foot and the other the modified J foot. I never hesitate to do this when using any of my machines—if a foot that will make my stitching easier is not included, I'll either change an existing presser foot of the same brand as my machine, or I'll find a generic foot (see Sources of Supply) to use. This doesn't mean that a foot included with the machine can't be used—for example, I can use the J foot as is to couch down cord, but if that tiny bit of plastic is taken out of the center, I can hold the cord next to that cut and the cord doesn't have the tendency to travel back and forth under the presser foot.

I love the even-feed foot M for matching

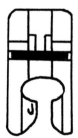

Fig. 1.5 To make the modified J foot, clip out the left center up to and including the black line.

plaids and stripes and for quilting: all the puckers and pleats you don't want in the backing are eliminated. Use it also to stitch on plastics, leather, slippery and thick fabrics.

If you don't have an even-feed foot, and sometimes even if you do, on certain projects you'll opt instead for the quilting foot in combination with the seam guide to help you stitch evenly spaced lines. Don't ignore the seam guide for other jobs as well. Use it in combination with other presser feet for exact seams and for topstitching.

Another foot that helps sew over leathers, vinyls, and napped fabrics is the roller foot. The rollers are covered with tiny points that grip the fabric so it is fed evenly.

A narrow hemmer is not included with the 6268, but it is one of the first feet I added to my collection. I use it for hemming—it was intended for that—but also to guide cords, elastic and yarn when I want to couch them down (instead of using the modified J foot).

The gathering foot is used for shirring (tiny gathers) and is another foot I purchased. I like to do waffle shirring on children's clothing with it.

When I want to sew deep gathers or pleats, I use the ruffler attachment. The ruffler ruffles fabric and also pleats it. It is adjustable and you determine how full you want your ruffle or pleats to be. Always do a sample first, using the fabric you plan to use on your finished project, so you can determine how much fabric you will need. The ruffles, or pleats, are not adjustable once they are sewn in.

I'm still having fun experimenting with the mending or directional sewing foot T, which I use for sideways sewing. It works well for attaching scout or armed forces patches to uniforms. Try it for topstitching in hard-to-reach areas such as pants legs or sleeves. Slip the pants leg or sleeve on the free arm, then stitch in any direction you wish—no twisting and wrestling fabric into position. Especially use the foot to sew on patch pockets!

The button sewing foot H permits you to sew on buttons quickly and easily (see Chapter 2). I don't agree with anyone who thinks buttons have to be sewn on by hand. Try the machine method and never waste another minute tediously hand stitching buttons in place.

The overedge foot is a must for overcasting the edge of fabric in clothing construction. Stitching over the metal pin allows play in the stitch so the fabric doesn't tunnel at the edge.

The tailor tacking or fringing foot is used for fringing on fabrics or at the edges, and fagoting between fabrics for an open, decorative seam. Of course it's also used for tailor tacking. Buttons are attached using this foot if an extra long shank is desired. Experiment.

The darning or embroidery foot G is used often throughout the book, because that is the foot used for free-machine embroidery (feed dogs are usually covered). Although a feed cover F (sometimes called a darning plate) is included with the machine, and is simple to slip into place and remove, I often leave it off (dial down to stitch length O). I find that unless there's a huge buildup of threads underneath my embroidery (which normally doesn't happen) then I can stitch without the protective cover. Try it both ways and use the one you prefer.

The straight stitch foot D and plate C are used for quilt piecing precision, and for seaming fine fabrics. The needle plate prevents fabric, no matter how flimsy, from being pushed down into the bobbin area. Use it also for topstitching (place the edge of the foot on the edge of the fold).

I like to experiment, finding new uses for presser feet or old stitches, to make my sewing easier and more fun. Though many old sewing methods are still valid, we've come a long way: we've entered the computer age of sewing machines.

I love to sew. One of the reasons my enthusiasm never wanes is because I have a group of friends who also love to sew. We exchange sewing advice, pass on our creative discoveries, recommend books to each other, and sometimes meet to try new ideas. If you don't have such friends already, you'll find them in classes at your dealer, where new ideas are taught regularly.

While at the store, check out the books and magazines there, especially those about the Singer.

Supplies

In addition to your sewing machine and a good supply of threads, here's a shopping list of what you'll need for the lessons. (Each lesson will give you a detailed materials list). You probably have many of the supplies in your sewing room.

1. Scissors and shears: sharp embroidery scissors, plus shears for cutting fabric and paper-cutting scissors
2. Water-erasable markers for light fabrics; vanishing markers—lines disappear after 24 to 48 hours (if you live in a humid area, as I do, the lines disappear more quickly); white opaque permanent marker for water-soluble stabilizer; slivers of soap or light-colored chalk pencils for dark fabrics
3. T square or 6″ × 24″ (15.2cm × 61.0cm) plastic ruler; 6″ (15.2cm) and 12″ (30.5cm) see-through rulers are also helpful
4. Wood and spring-type hoops in varied sizes, maximum, 7″ (17.8cm) for ease
5. Rotary cutting wheel and board

Have fabric ready for stitching samples. A handy size is a 9″ (22.9cm) square. It will fit in the 7″ (17.8cm) hoop and can be trimmed slightly for your notebook. Cut up a variety of fabrics from extra-lightweight types like organdy, lightweights like calicos, medium-weight poplins, and heavy-weight denim. Extra-heavy-weight canvas scraps will be left over from your tote bag and can be used for experiments.

In the projects, you'll also use felt, transparent fabrics, bridal veil, $\frac{1}{8}''$ (3.2mm) and $\frac{1}{2}''$ (12.7mm) satin double-faced ribbon, lace insertion, scalloped lace, lace beading, beads and buttons, Battenberg tape, fleece, batting, stabilizers and fusibles. If you can't buy these locally, see the Sources of Supply for mail-order companies who sell these materials. Now let's discuss your choices of threads, needles, and other supplies.

Threads

One of the most useful charts I have in my notebook is a piece of doubled fabric with line after line of satin stitches on it. Each row is stitched using a different type of thread. I recommend that you make one, too. More important than telling you which thread to use, your chart will graphically convince you that what is called machine-embroidery cotton is usually more lustrous and covers an area more quickly and more beautifully than regular sewing thread. It's easy to compare differences among threads.

Generally, sewing threads are not used for machine embroidery. Ordinary sewing threads are usually thicker, stretch more (if polyester), and do not cover as well as machine embroidery threads. However, for durability or when you need a certain color, try using a high quality sewing thread. I never use thread from the sale bin—the ones that are three spools for 88 cents. This thread does not hold up to heavy use; it breaks, shrinks, knots, and, after all the time spent stitching with it, looks sloppy. If I am going to take the time to sew or embroider anything, then it deserves quality thread.

Machine embroidery rayons and cottons are more lustrous and have a softer twist than ordinary sewing thread. Rayon embroidery threads are silky and loosely twisted, but if you use a #90/14 needle and sew evenly and at a moderate speed, they are easy to use. However, don't use rayons or any other machine embroidery threads for clothing construction because they aren't strong enough.

Besides regular sewing threads and those used for machine embroidery, there are others to become acquainted with. The fine nylon used for lingerie and woolly overlock used for serging are just a couple of them. Another is darning thread: It's often used on the bobbin for machine embroidery because it's lightweight and you can get so much more of it wound on. It comes in only a few colors, so it cannot always be used should you want the bobbin thread to be seen on the surface.

Monofilament, another popular thread, comes in two shades. One blends into light-colored fabrics, the other darks. It is not the wild, fish-line type anymore, so don't be afraid of making it work. I use it on the top and bobbin constantly.

If you use silk and silk buttonhole twists as well as fine pearl cottons, crochet and cordonnet, the needle must be large enough to keep the threads from fraying against the fabric and the eye large enough to enable the thread to go through smoothly. Sometimes topstitching needles are called for. Or you may have to use a needle larger than you normally would embroider with.

Waxed or glacé finished quilting thread should never be used on your machine, as the finish wears off and does your machine no good.

Chart 1.2 is a handy guide, showing which needles and threads to use with which fabrics. More about where to purchase threads can be found in Sources of Supplies at the end of the book.

Needles

It is important to choose the right needle for the job. Match fabric weight, thread, and needle size, as well as type of material. The lighter the material, the smaller

Chart 1.2
Needle and Thread Chart

Fabric	Thread	Needles
Very heavy (upholstery, canvas, denim)	Heavy-duty cotton; polyester; buttonhole twist; cordonnet	18 (110)
Heavy (sailcloth, heavy coating)	Heavy-duty cotton; polyester	16 (100)
Medium weight (wool, poplin, velvet)	Ordinary sewing cotton and polyester; machine-embroidery cotton and rayon	12, 14 (80, 90)
Lightweight (shirt cotton, dress fabrics, silk)	Extra-fine to ordinary sewing cotton and polyester	9, 11 (65, 75)
Very lightweight (lace, net, organdy, batiste)	Extra-fine sewing cotton and polyester	8, 9 (60, 65)

the needle and finer the thread should be. The heavier the fabric, the larger the needle should be (Chart 1.3).

Like presser feet, needles come in different sizes and shapes and produce different effects. I once had a student in quilting class who struggled to get a needle out of her machine—it was rusted in. "I don't do much sewing," she said. (Why didn't that surprise me?) No matter how mind-boggling this sounds, I know that few sewers change needles unless they break, even though a new needle keeps thread from fraying, fabric from being damaged, and your stitches from skipping. The correct size and shape enables you to stitch through the heaviest or the flimsiest materials with ease. Also, hemstitching and double needles allow you to create unique, decorative work.

But all needles do not fit all machines.

Chart 1.3
Needle Sizes

	Very Fine	Fine	Med.	Strong	Large	Very Large
U.S.	8,9	10	11,12	14	16	18
Euro.	60,65	70	75,80	90	100	110

Check your manual to find out which needle system to buy for yours. Singer needles are available and are color coded. Red bands are standard points and available in sizes 9, 11, 14, 16. Yellow bands are ballpoints and come in the same sizes.

Needles are available in pierce point, used for woven fabrics; and ball point, used for knits to minimize cutting threads and causing runs in the fabric. The universal-point needle is all-purpose and can be used for knits, as well as woven fabrics. Instead of cutting through the fabric, the slightly rounded point deflects off the threads and slips between them. Because of its versatility, it is the needle in greatest use today.

Following is a list of needles and their uses:

Universal Needles: All-purpose sewing.
Fine Ballpoint Needles: Fine fabrics, including knits and wovens.
Medium Ballpoint Needles: Heavier knitted fabrics.
Medium Ballpoint Stretch Needles: Special needles for problem stretch fabrics.
Extra-Fine Point Needles: Used to

pierce closely woven fabrics such as canvas or denim; often called jeans needles.

Topstitching Needles: Equipped with an eye and thread groove larger than a regular needle of the same size. Use buttonhole twist or double thread when topstitching. Use them for embroidery, too.

Double and Triple Needles: Used for sewing with more than one thread on top. Double needles come in 6 sizes (1.6mm, 1.8mm, 2mm, 2.5mm, 3mm, 4mm).

Hemstitching Needles: Double and single types.

Leather Needles: Often called wedge needles because of their cutting points. Use them on real suede and leather. Or use a regular #110/18 needle in place of a leather needle.

To keep your machine running trouble-free, change the needle often. Be sure the needle is straight and has no burr on the point. Damaged needles damage fabric and machines.

If your machine is noisy and is skipping stitches, change the needle (assuming the machine is oiled and clean). Be sure you've used the correct needle system for your machine and be certain you've placed the needle in the machine correctly. Most of the time a damaged needle is the only problem—and an easy one to rectify.

To make it easier for you to prepare appropriate supplies before beginning the lessons, let's discuss items often called for and the terms I'll use.

Batting, fleece, and fiberfill

Batting, both cotton and polyester, is used between fabric layers for quilting. Different weights and sizes are available, as well as different qualities. For our use, most of the projects can be quilted with bonded batting, which holds together firmly, or with fleece, which is a filler that's thinner than bonded batting and about as thick as a heavy wool blanket. Alternative fillers can be flannel, when only a light garment is desired, or a wool blanket. Fiberfill is the shredded batting used to fill toys. Or stuff toys with batting.

Fusibles

Fusibles are used to hold appliqués to background fabrics so edges are held firmly for the final step of stitching them in place. Plastic sandwich bags or cleaner's garment bags can be used. Stitch Witchery, Fine Fuse, Magic Polyweb and Jiffy Fuse are commercial fusible webbings. To use, place them between two pieces of fabric and press with a hot iron until the webbing melts and holds the two fabrics together. Use a Teflon pressing sheet to protect your iron and also to allow you to press the fusible to one fabric at a time. The Applique Pressing Sheet or Teflon sheet has eliminated any problem with the fusible melting on your iron: it looks like opaque wax paper, is reusable, and comes in handy sizes.

A fusible webbing already backed by paper, which saves one step in application, is called Wonder-Under Transfer Fusing Web. Draw your design directly onto the paper and place it against the underside of the appliqué fabric. Press for a few seconds, which fuses the webbing to the fabric. Then cut out the pattern and pull the paper away from the webbing. Place a damp cloth over the appliqué and press it to the background fabric for a few seconds.

Appliqué papers are paper-backed products that look very much like freezer wrap, but act like the transfer web. One side of the paper has a glue finish.

See Chapter 4 for more about fusibles.

Stabilizers

Stabilizers are used behind fabric to keep it from puckering when you embroider. At one time, we used typing paper, but today we have more choices of stabilizers, available at fabric and quilt shops and through mail-order (see Sources of Supplies).

The old standby, typing paper, still does the job. Or, use shelf paper when stitching large pictures and adding-machine tape for long strips of embroidery. A problem with paper is that it dulls machine needles faster than tear-away stabilizers do. It's also harder to remove from the back of the embroidery, although dampening the paper will help.

Another stabilizer you probably have in the cupboard is plastic-coated freezer wrap. I find I'm using it more and more. If I'm embroidering a fabric that could be damaged by the hoop, I back it instead with freezer wrap, which I iron to the back of the fabric. The freezer paper adheres to the fabric and stiffens it. When I finish my embroidery, I peel off the freezer paper. I like using it if I have a small piece of fabric to embroider. I iron the small piece to a larger, easier-to-manipulate piece of freezer paper.

Tear-away stabilizers come in crisp or soft finishes and some are iron-ons. When embroidering, place them between the fabric and machine. When the embroidery is completed, they tear away from the fabric easily.

Don't confuse stabilizers with interfacings. Interfacings are permanent and don't tear away. They can be used, of course, and so can fabrics like organdy, but they are usually used when you plan to leave the stabilizer on the back of the embroidery after it's completed.

One of the newest stabilizers is a thin film of plastic, available by the sheet or the yard, that will dissolve when wet. I'll refer to it as water-soluble stabilizer. Clamp it into the hoop along with the fabric. It is transparent, and can be used on top of the embroidery, too. It can be marked on, but choose a water-erasable marker or permanent white opaque marker that will not leave ink on your embroidery when the plastic is dissolved. When your em-broidery is completed, rinse out the stabilizer. It will become gooey, then disappear.

Helpful hints for sewing

Before beginning to sew, check out the following general helpful hints:

1. Every machine has its own idiosyncracies, so the settings I recommend for each lesson are only suggestions; your machine may prefer different ones.
2. Take your sewing machine in for regular check-ups whether you think it needs it or not. Between checkups, keep it clean and oil it if it is not self-lubricating. It should be oiled after every 10 or 12 hours of use. Or, if your machine starts clacking instead of humming, get out the oil can, but take it easy. There are more problems with over-oiling than with too little. To be sure the oil works its way through the areas that need lubricating, oil *before* sewing rather than when your sewing is completed. Check your manuals to learn all the spots on your machine that need oil.
3. No matter what model you have, you must keep the inside free of lint and threads. Clean the bobbin area by first removing the bobbin, then wiping out all the lint. A Q-tip works well and so does canned air. It's used for cameras and is wonderful to blow out lint from hard-to-reach areas. I sometimes vacuum out lint from inside the machine. Remember to clean the feed dogs whenever you finish sewing or during a long period of stitching nappy fabrics such as corduroy, fur, or velvets.

After the inside has been freed of lint, put a drop of oil in every spot that needs lubricating.

CHAPTER 2

Adding Stitches to Your Fabric

- Lesson 1. Using built-in stitches
- Lesson 2. Using free machining

In this chapter you'll become acquainted with the range of stitches your machine can produce. By the end of it, you'll easily switch back and forth from stitching with the feed dogs uncovered to stitching with feed dogs covered. To demonstrate your new facility, you'll make a beautiful small button, pendant, and gift card.

Lesson 1. Using built-in stitches

The first thing I did to learn my Singer was to try all the built-in stitches and those on Sew Ware cartridge 4. (I saved learning the embroidery unit until I was thoroughly familiar with the machine.) I wanted a reference, so I sewed stitches in rows at different widths and lengths and put them in a notebook, along with notations from the Basic Manual. I was determined to know my sewing machine, and this has been so helpful to me that I've made it your first lesson, too.

To save you time, Singer engineers have built practical and decorative stitches into their sewing machines. I classify these stitches as either "closed" or "open." "Closed" refers to those where the beauty is in stitching it close together (stitch width: wide; stitch length: $1\frac{1}{4}$ or $1\frac{1}{2}$), like the satin stitch or crescent stitch. "Open" built-in stitches, like the multi-zigzag stitch #4, blind stitch #3 built in the machine, or flowers #17 and vines #18 are sewn at a stitch length longer than $1\frac{1}{2}$.

But how did I come up with stitch length numbers when there are none on the 6268? On this machine, the stitch widths and stitch lengths are regulated by two dials located beneath the decorative stitch panel. On the edge of each dial is a notch. By turning the dials, the notch moves from one black line to the next. The black lines are printed directly on the machine surrounding the dial. Each line is an increment of stitch width or length. No, the black lines aren't numbered, but I've numbered them to clarify my directions in this book (Fig. 2.1). On the 6268 machine, starting at the lower lefthand side, each black line is numbered 0 to 7 in a clockwise direction. In other words, if the stitch width dial is on 0, it is a straight stitch; if it is on 7, then it is the widest zigzag possible. If the stitch length dial is on 0, then the stitch is so short you actually stitch in one place (use it for anchoring threads); if the length is on 7, then the stitch is the longest (use it for basting).

To change widths and lengths, push the button on the dial and turn it. If the red light is on above the dial, the machine accepts and stitches your changes. If you change from one stitch to another—for example, from straight stitch #1 to the fa-

Tote Bag Squares: (upper left, clockwise) Chapter 4, Lesson 19—Applique and Quilting; Chapter 4, Lesson 10—Straight Stitch Applique; Modified Reverse Applique; Chapter 3, Lesson 4—Cabling.

*Paper earrings
and stitching from
Chapter 11.*

*Chapter 2, Lesson
2—Pendants and
a greeting card are
a fast way to
practice free
machining and
satin stitches.*

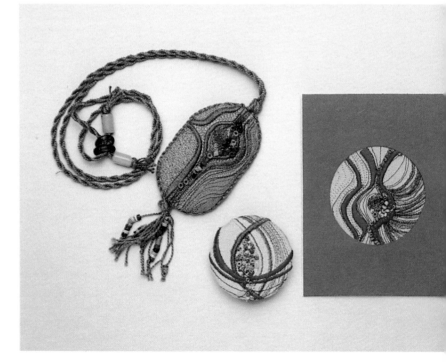

From Chapter 11, a necklace made by zigzagging over cord and attaching small worry dolls.

Framed messages using the Floral Motifs, Decorative Borders, and Holiday Cartridges.

A lightly quilted wall piece using the Animal Menagerie Cartridge.

Old laces, ribbons, decorative stitches, and messages embellish a Victorian stocking which can stay out all year.

Irene Stocker, England (student of Joy Clucas)— worked on a Singer Futura 2000

Fabric collage by Margaret Cusack, Brooklyn, NY— "Asparagus With Hollandaise Sauce," 11" × 14"

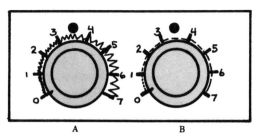

Fig. 2.1 Numbered stitch dials on the 6268. A. Stitch width dial. B. Stitch length dial.

goting stitch #9, the machine returns to its normal stitch width and length (the light over the dials will go out to indicate this). If you want to change the width and length of the new stitch, you must push the dials again and either leave them where they were for the last stitch, if that is your preference, or change one or both for the new stitch.

When feasible, I leave the dial on "0" width and length (red light off) when sewing with the normal settings. When I want to anchor my thread at beginning and end, and don't want to use the reverse button, I push the dial buttons and my needle stitches in one place. After several anchoring stitches, I can clip my threads.

If I push the reverse button to anchor threads, then the machine sews backward. I can press it again to sew forward. I use this often to anchor threads at the beginning and end of seams. But when stitching shows and I want a clean look to my anchoring stitches, without the doubled-back look, I dial the machine to 0 to stitch in one place.

Before I had a machine that dialed down stitch length, I anchored threads by lifting up the presser foot lever slightly to take pressure off the fabric and sewed several stitches in one place. This is a good trick to learn—I still use it in many sewing situations.

Other Singer models have sliding dials with numbers marked on the machine for stitch length (some go from 0 to 4; others, 0 to 5). Remember to practice the satin stitch to find the correct setting for stitch length. Make a note on your sample so you remember it. As with any machine, stitch up samples to find the correct settings for each project you do.

For stitch width, your machine may have zigzag lines of different widths marked above the dial. Stitch each width so you'll have a sample to refer to when planning projects.

Fig. 2.2 shows a sample of stitch widths and lengths found on my 6268 machine. They are numbered for you, so you can compare them to those on your own machine. They will also give you a base when reading the directions for each project. Also, it's helpful to know that when I refer to stitch width 2, it means the stitch width is 1mm wide; 3 is 2mm, 4 is 3mm, 5 is 4mm, 6 is 5mm, and stitch width 7 is 6mm wide. If you own a different model Singer, make a stitched sample like Fig. 2.2. Write the settings for your machine directly on the fabric. Then compare your settings to mine. When I tell you to set your machine to stitch width 5, you may have to translate for your machine to stitch width 4.

If you have a machine with decorative stitches, try them in new ways—different widths and lengths, stitch each singly, narrow them with the double needle button if you have one, lengthen them with the 2X button if your machine includes one. Check out all the possibilities for each stitch.

To practice the built-in stitches and make a record of them, first set up your machine as indicated at the beginning of the lesson.

Stitch width: varies
Stitch length: varies
Needle: #90/14
Feed dogs: uncovered
Presser foot: special purpose J
Tension: normal

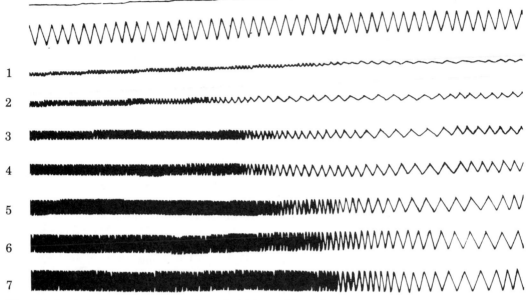

Fig. 2.2 A stitched sample, actual size, of widths and lengths.

Fabric suggestion: medium-weight striped cotton

Thread: machine-embroidery to contrast with fabric, different colors in top and bobbin

Accessories: fine-point marker

Stabilizer: tear-away or iron-on freezer paper

Back your striped cotton with stabilizer. Stitch lines of the built-in stitches found on your machine (Fig. 2.3). The striped fabric will help you keep them straight. Start by using the settings suggested in the manual. Vary the settings as you stitch, making the stitches wider and narrower, longer and shorter. If there is a setting you find particularly useful, mark it right on the fabric with a marker to show where that setting begins.

This is a good time to determine the precise width and length settings for the best-looking closed, decorative stitches.

Using different colors of thread on top and bobbin will help you adjust the ma-chine to find the perfect stitch. Adjust tension by loosening the top tension slightly. The top thread should be pulled down and show underneath the fabric and should mound slightly on top when making satin stitches.

Start by stitching the zigzag, with the widest stitch width and stitch length. Adjust the length as you stitch until the satin stitch is perfect. Be sure the fabric moves smoothly without your pulling or pushing it. This will be somewhere between $1\frac{1}{4}$ and $1\frac{1}{2}$ length. Write the setting on the sample.

When you finish your record of the built-in stitches, practice mirror images. This is as simple as pushing the mirror image button if you have a machine with this capability. If you don't have a machine with a mirror image, practice matching patterns as you stitch the second pass next to the first. Check your manual.

There are a number of variables with mirror images. Are you feeding the fabric through exactly? Don't pull on one side

14

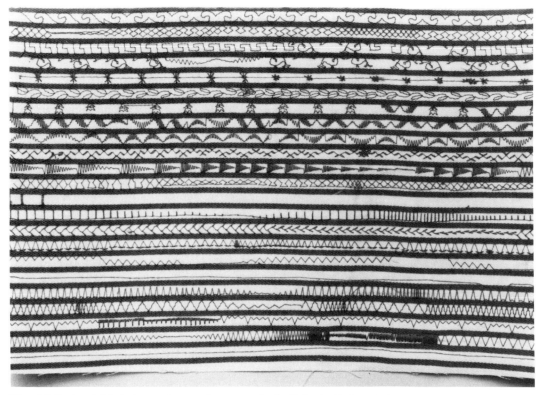

*Fig. 2.3 Striped fabric is used to make a record of all the built-in stitches on my
Singer 6268.*

when the other has been fed through freely. Did you start the second row at exactly the right spot? Just one stitch off will make a difference. Do you have the same thickness of fabric under both sides of the design? If you're stitching on top of a seam allowance, the needle may go off the two layers.

Not only can you make a mirror image by pushing a button, but you can also program the machine to stop after the last stitch of a single design. Also, the design can be elongated (2X) and narrowed (double needle button). Make a record of the possibilities of your machine, whether you have a computer or mechanical model.

As you sew line after line of practical and decorative stitches, imagine how they can be used. For example, the blind-hem stitch is used for blind hems and as an invisible way of stitching on a patch pocket or an appliqué, or the stitch to use when couching down heavy cords.

Lesson 2. Using free-machining: darning, whipping, feather stitching

Singer was a pioneer in free-machine embroidery. As early as 1911, it published a wonderful book called *Singer Instructions for Art Embroidery,* which showed how to make lace, appliqué, beading on a treadle machine—even how to sew on wood veneer. Since the machine did not zigzag, the operator moved the hoop sideways to make a close satin stitch. Similarly, in free machining, you—not the presser foot—control the movement of the fabric, which in turn determines the length of the stitch. With fabric stretched tightly in a hoop, it is easy to move your work forward, backward, in circles, whatever way you wish.

I suggest working with a wooden hoop when first learning machine stitchery.

Choose one that has a smooth finish, and slips easily under the darning foot. But whatever wooden hoop you use, be sure it is the screw type, as that will hold the fabric tightly. To be sure that it does, the inside ring of the wooden hoop should be wound with narrow twill tape. This keeps the fabric from slipping. Take a few hand stitches at the end of the tape to hold it firmly.

If your needle will not clear the hoop you've chosen, turn the hoop on its side and slip it under the darning foot or put the hoop together and carve out a small wedge to make it easier. Then wrap the inside part with tape.

Fabric is placed in the hoop upside-down from the way you would put it in a hoop for hand embroidery (Fig. 2.5). Pull the cloth as tightly as you can. Tighten the screw; pull again; tighten. Tap on the fabric. If it sounds like a drum, it is tight enough. You may or may not want to use a stabilizer under a hoop, depending upon the effect you want and the weight of the fabric.

You can stitch with a darning foot on or without a presser foot (but keep your fingers a safe distance from the needle!).

It is possible to stitch freely without a hoop if you use your fingers to hold the fabric taut while stitching. If you don't use a hoop—or if you use a spring-type hoop—use a darning foot to prevent skipped stitches. It will hold the fabric down each time the machine makes a stitch so the threads interlock correctly underneath. Also, use a stabilizer under the fabric to keep the stitches from puckering.

Fig. 2.4 Free-machine darning stitches were used to make a picture.

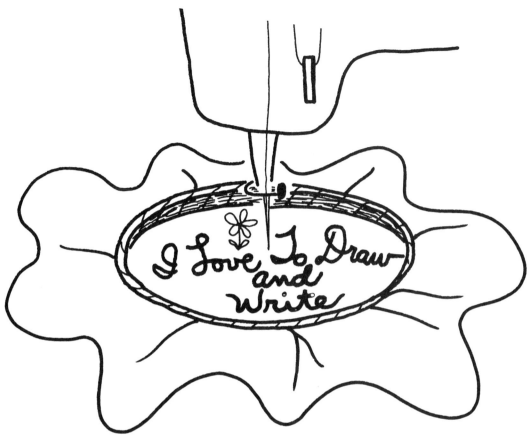

Fig. 2.5 Tighten fabric in a hoop. The fabric rests against the bed of the machine, with the material topside up for machine embroidery.

Stitch width: 0–widest
Stitch length: 0
Needle: #90/14 and double needle
Feed dogs: covered
Presser foot: darning foot G or none
Tension: slightly loosened
Fabric: light-colored, medium-weight fabric, such as poplin—scrap for practice; 18″ × 18″ (45.7cm × 45.7cm) square for your notebook
Thread: one color for top, another for bobbin; both should contrast with fabric
Accessories: wrapped wooden hoop no larger than 7″ (17.8cm), fine-point marker
Stabilizer: tear-away or freezer paper

The two samples in this lesson will give you practice in control and coordination. One sample will be for practice; the other, for your notebook. Keep a record of the newfound stitches you create with your machine and your imagination.

Free machining such as darning, whipping and feather stitching (also called "spark stitching" in old Singer embroidery books) takes practice, but it is worth every minute. It opens up a new world of stitchery to you.

First, you are going to learn to draw, write, and sketch with your machine. It's called the darning stitch.

Set up your machine for darning. After placing your fabric in the hoop, slip stabilizer between it and the bed of the machine. Always begin by dipping the needle into the fabric and bringing the bobbin thread to the top. Hold both threads to the side while stitching in one place several stitches to anchor the thread. Clip off the ends. When you begin your stitchery, start slowly. Practice moving the hoop slowly, as well. You must coordinate the speed at which you move your hoop and your sewing speed. It is not necessary to stitch at top speed—moderate speed is fine. You'll soon learn how fast is right for you and for the particular stitching you are creating.

Move the hoop back and forth, then in circles—remember the old Palmer Method exercises for handwriting? Stitch faster; move your hoop faster. Then write your name, draw a picture of a tree, your dog, an old flame. It doesn't matter how well you draw; you are really practicing control.

Change to zigzag and try it all over again. Yes, it will take awhile to gain absolute control, but don't give up. Stitch tiny fill-in spirals, figure eights and jigsaw patterns.

Fig. 2.6 Whipping and feather stitching.

18

Now stitch, hesitate, stitch. The bobbin color may come to the top. Good! That's what we want. To make sure it does, tighten the top tension slowly. When you see the bobbin thread, note where the tension dial is set and write this on the sample. This type of stitchery is called whipping. If the hoop is moved slowly and the machine run very fast, a nubby, thickened line of bobbin thread will appear on the surface. This may be easier to accomplish if the stabilizer is eliminated. It can be used in place

Fig. 2.7 Draw 36 squares on a piece of fabric, then fill them in with the new stitches and techniques you've learned and will learn. Be sure to record machine settings.

of the darning stitch when embroidering—or used with it for variety. Whipping can be seen in the tiny circles of dark bobbin thread in Fig. 2.6.

With the top tension very tight, stitch straight lines, circles and spirals. Move the hoop quickly. The top thread is visible as a straight line on top of the fabric. Covering it are looping, feathery bobbin stitches. This is an exaggeration of whipping, which is called feather stitching. I've even bypassed the bobbin tension and stitched freely, which brings long loops of bobbin thread to the top. Though not acceptable for garment embellishment, this can be used for wall hangings, embroideries, anywhere that would not get wear and tear.

To do this, place the bobbin in the machine, but hold the thread to the side back with your left hand. Dip the needle down and pull up the bobbin thread through the plate. In other words, don't slip the bobbin thread under the two numbers as you normally do when threading the bobbin. Feather stitching can be seen in the hoop in some of the small circles as I went from tight to tighter top tension (Fig. 2.6).

Practice is the only way to learn control. When you feel you have accomplished coordination between moving the hoop and the speed of the machine, make the following record of what you've learned: On the 18″ × 18″ (45.7cm × 45.7cm) square of fabric, draw a grid of 3″ (7.6cm) squares, six across, six down (Fig. 2.7). Then fill in your squares with examples of free machining—darning, whipping and feather stitching. Use both straight stitches and zigzag stitches in your squares. Try built-in stitches, too. You can stitch your own designs or use mine. But as you practice, write the machine settings on the fabric. Slip this into your notebook. Add new stitches as you discover them and refer to your notebook regularly for stitches you want to use on a project.

For variety, thread your needle with two

colors, or try a double needle. But remember to check that your double needle will fall inside the hole of the plate when setting it on zigzag. If there's a double needle button on your machine, push it down.

Project
Button, Pin, Pendant, and Greeting Card

The following one-of-a-kind projects include free machining and stitching with feed dogs up. Get to know your Singer by stitching up these small embroideries.

You have a choice of stitches on the designs and they can be finished as large pins or buttons. The round design in Fig. 2.8 is suitable for either. Buy button forms at fabric or needlecraft shops. I use a size 75, which is about 2″ (5.1cm) in diameter or finish the button as you do the pendant, but hand-stitch a pin to the back fabric before stretching it around the cardboard backing.

Fig. 2.8 Use button forms or cut shapes from heavy cardboard to make a machine-embroidered pin or button. See color section.

20

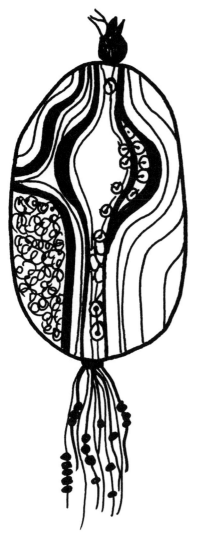

Fig. 2.9 Pattern for embroidered pendant.

I was inspired by Mary Ann Spawn of Tacoma, Washington, to finish the design in Fig. 2.9 by attaching a cord and tassel to make a pendant. Use them for greeting cards, too. I slip them into cards with round cutouts (see Sources of Supply). The patterns provided in this project have been finished several different ways—see pen-

dant, gift card, and button/pin in the color section.

If you use a round design, draw two circles with the same center point on your fabric. One is the area to be embroidered; the other circle, $\frac{1}{4}''$ (6.4mm) outside the first, is the cutting line. It's important to keep the area between the lines free from stitching. Use a piece of fabric large enough to go into a spring hoop and place a piece of tear-away stabilizer underneath.

Embroider, using free machining such as whipping and darning, as well as satin stitches. Leave a $\frac{1}{4}''$ (6.4mm) margin on the other designs as well. For each, trace the designs on linen fabric. The threads are rayon because I liked the contrast between the linen and the shiny threads.

Stitch width: 0–3
Stitch length: 0–1$\frac{1}{2}$
Needle: #70/10 sharp
Feed dogs: covered and uncovered
Presser foot: special purpose J, darning foot G
Tension: loosen
Fabric suggestion: medium-weight, tightly woven linen

Fig. 2.10 This pattern can be used for a button, pendant or greeting card.

Thread: rayon embroidery in many colors

Accessories: wood or spring hoop, button forms or cardboard, batting, craft glue, cord, water-erasable or vanishing marker, small beads (optional), colored markers, tracing paper, dressmaker's carbon, empty ball-point pen

Stabilizer: tear-away or ironed-on freezer paper

What do I like best about making pendants and buttons? They're fast, of course, but more importantly, they give me a chance to experiment with colors and stitches. I like taking a line drawing, then filling it in with my own ideas.

I often give the same designs to a class of embroiderers and ask them to invent stitches; use built-in stitches free-motion, as well as old-faithfuls like satin stitches.

Before stitching the pendants, they make stitch samples on a piece of the same fabric they'll use for their finished product. They also experiment with color on the sample fabric. After choosing five or six thread colors for their linen, they stitch with them to see the effect of one color next to another. This may result in their adding or eliminating colors. *Helpful hint:* Choose a spool of variegated thread, then use the same colors in that thread for the whole embroidery.

Every pendant starts with the same design, but every pendant ends up as a unique piece of art. No matter how many students are in class, no two results are ever the same. That's what I like the best.

On small embroidered pendants, I find it much easier to imitate the decorative built-in stitches than to actually use them. This way I can fudge a little on the designs, either shortening or lengthening them, or making them wider or narrower to fit the space. Of course you can use built-in decorative stitches if you prefer.

First, find the colored threads you'll need and then wind bobbins for all the spools of colors you'll use. If you want to add small beads to any of the pendants, keep them well within the outline and attach them after all the embroidery is completed.

Either back your linen with ironed-on freezer paper or place it tightly in a hoop and slip stabilizer under the hoop before you embroider. For each of these embroideries, I drew the design within the outline, using a water-erasable or vanishing marker. Instead of tracing it from the original, I sketched it in free-hand, as these are simple line drawings. It's your stitching that takes them from simple to exciting. This is an excellent opportunity to be creative.

Instead of changing threads many times, I try to stitch everything I can with one color before I switch to another.

First I fill in the free-motion embroidery. I use a scribbling that looks like small circles strung together, stitched layer upon layer, or in the case of variegated thread on the pendant and greeting card, I stitched in the centers by traveling from side-to-side as I moved from top to bottom of the area. I often tighten the top tension slightly to use a whipstitch in place of satin stitches—sewing lines of them close to each other, or filling in space with them. Or I tighten the tension even more to produce spiky bobbin stitches on top of a straight line of top thread (feather stitches). Knots and blobs can also be used as I did behind the beads on the pin. Satin stitches of different widths separate sections of the design or emphasize an area. Two built-in stitches I use are: (1) the triple straight stitch (on the 6268 use stitch #9, stitch width 0, or cartridge 4, stitch #8, stitch width 0); and (2) the triple zigzag or rick-rack stitch (cartridge 4, stitch #8, stitch width and length adjusted as needed). If your Singer doesn't have these stitches, then use two threads through your needle and use the straight stitch or zigzag setting. I use rickrack stitches on top of satin stitches, and triple straight stitches on both sides of them.

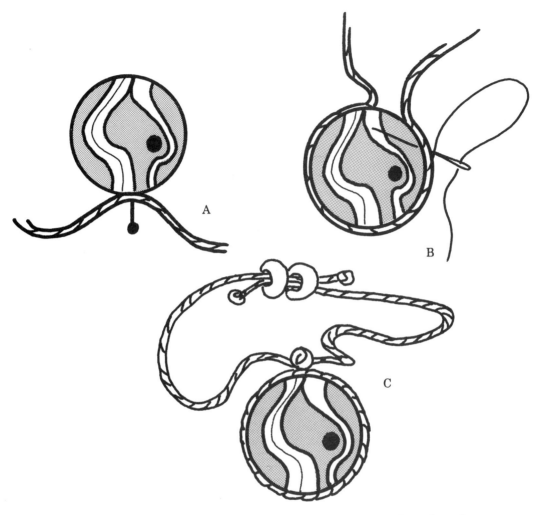

Fig. 2.11 A. Pin center of cord to center bottom of the pendant. B. Attach cord at edge of the pendant by hand, laying the thread in the twist of the cord as you stitch. C. Make an adjustable cord by threading both ends through two beads.

If you use beads, apply them using one of the methods described in this chapter, or stitch them on by hand.

When using a button form, it's advisable to reduce the texture. Instead, keep the stitches flat and close to the fabric or you'll have difficulty later when trying to cover the forms and snap the backs in place. Instead of using a button form for the pin,

I made the pin like a pendant, but finished it by sewing a pin (found in craft stores) to the backing fabric before I covered the cardboard. Large safety pins can also be used.

Finish the pendant and pin by cutting out two cardboard shapes, then cutting fleecy Pellon the same size as the cardboards. Place a dot of glue between Pellon

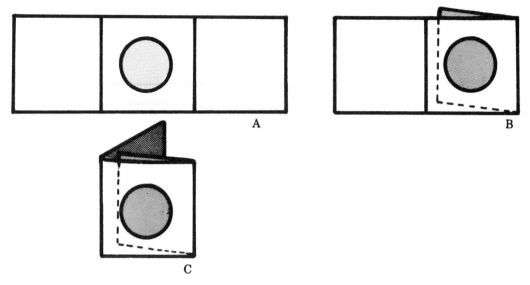

Fig. 2.12 A. To make a double-fold card, cut out a circle in the center and score the two fold lines. B. Fold the right side behind the center. C. Fold the left side back behind the front of the card.

and cardboard to hold the Pellon in place when stretching the fabric around the cardboard. Next, cut out the front and back of the pendant and pin from the fabric. Remove any stabilizer you can, especially from the outside $\frac{1}{4}''$ (6.4mm) allowance that will be turned under. Use a hand running-stitch $\frac{1}{8}''$ (3.2mm) inside the cut edge, then draw up the thread as you cover the cardboard and fleecy Pellon. Clip out any bulky folds. An alternative method is to clip up almost to the inside line around the entire pendant, then place the fabric over the batting and cardboard and glue the edges to the back of the cardboard. Follow either one of those methods to finish the back of the pendant and pin. Then glue the two halves together with a dot of glue and hand-stitch the edges together.

Make enough cord (see Chapter 10) to encircle the pendant, make a tassel, and hang it the length you wish. One simple way to finish the pendant is to mark the center of the cord and the middle of the pendant. Pin together. Stitch around the cord by hand, laying the thread in the twist, and stitching through the side of the pendant while attaching the cord (Fig. 2.11). When completed and the cords meet at the top, tie an overhand knot at the center. Then determine the length of the pendant and tie the ends of the cords together in an overhand knot. Clip back to the knot and dot the ends with glue.

To make the length of your pendant adjustable, use the finish that resembles a fisherman's knot. Thread the cord ends through two beads as shown in Fig. 2.11C. Tie knots at each end. Cut cords off back to the knots and dot with glue. Attach beads to the cord for decoration if you wish. Add a tassel with beads also.

If you make buttons with button forms, you will eliminate the back fabric-covered cardboard and finish them as described in the button kit.

Slip these small embroideries into greeting cards and glue in place. I made a simple double-fold card, as shown in Fig. 2.12. I like these because one side of the card is folded back over the back of the embroidery, hiding the tangled threads. If the card is a single fold, then cut back the embroidery so a margin of card shows around it when it is glued in place. Cut out your own backing to fit the card and glue it over the back of the embroidery.

I can now make my own cards with the Olfa circle cutter (see Sources of Supply) and colored construction paper. But the stiffer Bristol-weight colored paper is my favorite greeting card medium. I buy it at school supply stores. Local print shops will sell it to you, too.

Pendants, buttons, pins and greeting card inserts are small enough to do quickly and, if you make a mistake, they're easily disposable. What a delightful way to spend an afternoon—stitching and getting to know your Singer.

CHAPTER **3**

Adding Texture to Your Fabric

- **Lesson 3. Building up sewing stitches**
- **Lesson 4. Applying thick threads from top and bobbin**
- **Lesson 5. Fringing yarn and fabric**
- **Lesson 6. Adding buttons, beads, shisha**
- **Lesson 7. Smocking and gathering**
- **Lesson 8. Pulling threads together**

Add to or create texture on fabrics by building up sewing stitches, using thick threads, attaching fringe or objects like buttons and beads, gathering fabric for smocking or for utilitarian purposes—to stitch elastic on sleeves or bodices, or to make ruffles for curtains.

You'll make samples for your notebook; stitch up a fabric greeting card; cable stitch a tote bag square; make fabric fringe for rugs and doll hair; and make a framed picture. Both projects and samples will suggest numerous other ways to use these stitches.

Lesson 3. Building up sewing stitches

One of the simplest ways to build up texture is to sew in one place many times. Sounds simple and it is. But you can do this in so many ways that even though it is simple, the results aren't. Texture can look studied and exact or free and wild.

I use the following techniques for land-scapes, monograms, and flowers. Practice each one for your notebook, recording your machine settings and any notes on how you might use the stitches later.

Begin with my suggested settings, but change them if they are not to your liking.

Stitch width: 0 to widest
Stitch length: 0–1
Needle: #90/14
Feed dogs: covered or uncovered
Presser foot: darning G or special purpose J

Tension: loosened
Fabric suggestion: experiment with varied weights, types, and colors
Thread: practice with any type, but use machine embroidery thread for good; include several sizes of pearl cotton, cordonnet, yarns and $\frac{1}{8}''$ (3.2mm) ribbon
Accessories: 7" (17.8cm) spring hoop
Stabilizer: tear-away

Set up your machine by dialing length to anchor (stitch length 0). Leave red light on so length can be changed easily. Set stitch width to anchor (0) and leave red light on.

With the feed dogs uncovered and J foot on, anchor the threads first by stitching in place several times.

Fig. 3.1 Use satin stitches for flower centers or fill-in background stitches.

Fig. 3.3 Straight-stitching around blobs.

Change width to 7 (widest setting) and length to 1½. This is the satin stitch setting I use. You may want to adjust the length to suit your machine. The fabric should feed through easily as the satin stitches are stitched evenly and smoothly, without fabric seen between stitches.

Sew a block of 6 or 8 satin stitches. Anchor them by using 0 width and length again and stitch in place. Move the hoop and do another block of satin stitches. Keep them quite close together, but all at different angles (Fig. 3.1). Use these to fill in areas in designs.

For the next sample, lower or cover the feed dogs and use darning foot G. Anchor the threads by stitching in one place. Use the same wide zigzag, but sew in one place to build up 10 or 12 stitches. Move to another spot close to the first blob of stitches

and stitch again. If you wish to achieve the effect in Fig. 3.2, pull the threads into loops as you move from place to place and don't cut them off. You can make flower centers this way. Or finish by clipping between the satin stitches and then, using a different color on top, outlining with straight stitches (Fig. 3.3). Using variegated thread is especially effective.

In the next experiment, with feed dogs up, place the embroidery foot on, and set your machine on the widest satin stitch. Anchor the threads and sew a block of satin stitches at the left of the practice fabric. Pull the fabric down about three inches and over to the right slightly. Stitch another block of satin stitches. Pull up and over a bit to the right to stitch another block of satin stitches. Pull down and over for the third block. Continue across the

Fig. 3.2 Blobs and loops.

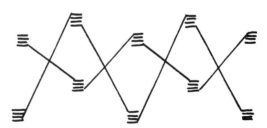

Fig. 3.4 Crossed threads and satin stitches.

fabric. Change threads and come back with another color. Cross the threads from the first pass as you do (Fig. 3.4). This is a good filler for garden pictures—the stitches become hedges of flowers—or use layers of these to crown trees (Fig. 3.5).

Speaking of flowers, try the ones in Figure 3.6, with feed dogs covered, using the same machine settings. Anchor the threads. Stitch one blob of about 10 or 12 satin stitches in one place and, ending on the left side, the needle still in the fabric, turn the hoop. Do another blob and end on the left side. Turn the hoop and do another and another. Lay in about five or six of these to create a satin-stitch flower. The satin stitches will all have that common center—at needle left.

Make the next satin stitch flower (Fig. 3.7) by first tracing around a drinking glass with a water-erasable marker. With feed dogs lowered, anchor the thread and make a satin stitch blob perpendicular to the edge of the circle. Pull the thread across to the other side of the circle and make another blob. Anchor it. Cut off the thread.

Fig. 3.5 This tree was stitched on cotton net. The trunk is encroaching zigzags, the crown of the tree is satin stitches and crossed threads.

Fig. 3.6 Zigzag star flowers.

Fig. 3.7 Create flowers using zigzag stitches and crossed threads.

Go to another place on, just within, or just without the circle and stitch another blob. Pull the thread over to the other side, make another satin stitch blob, anchor it, and cut off the thread. Begin again and continue until you have made a flower head.

Now you'll practice filling in shapes, another way to bring texture to your base fabric. Zigzagging is probably the most widely used method to fill in designs. You can use any stitch width, but the wider the setting, the looser the look. I feel I have more control if I use a 3 width—or better yet, I sew with straight stitches to fill in backgrounds. It is more like drawing with a pencil.

The drawback to straight-stitch filling is that the stitches are very tight to the fabric. Sometimes I want a lighter, loopier look, so I may start with zigzagging to fill in a design and then draw on top of that with straight stitches to emphasize a color, to outline, or to add shading to my embroidery. So I've included three ways to add texture to fabric by filling in designs with zigzag stitches.

Method A

In this method you will follow the contour of your design with zigzag stitches, changing a flat circle into a ball shape.

Stitch width: widest
Stitch length: 0
Needle: #90/14
Feed dogs: covered
Presser foot: darning foot G or use a wooden
    hoop with no foot
Tension: slightly loosened
Fabric suggestion: medium-weight cotton
Thread: sewing thread for practice
Accessories: large hoop at least 7″ (17.8cm);
    water-erasable marker
Stabilizer: tear-away

Using the marker, draw several circles on the fabric in the hoop (I drew around the base of a large spool of thread). Place

stabilizer under the hoop. Zigzag the first circle into a ball shape by stitching in curved lines. To make it easier, first draw stitching guidelines inside the circle (Fig. 3.8, method A, *left*).

Start at the top of the circle, stitching and moving your hoop sideways and back while following the curves you've drawn (Fig. 3.8, method A, *right*). Move from top

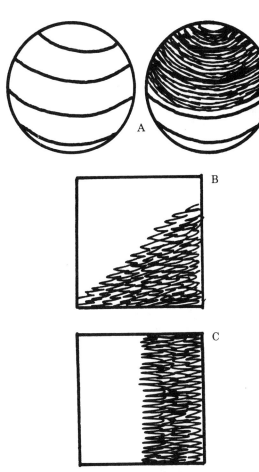

Fig. 3.8 Filling in designs with zigzag stitches. A. Draw guidelines in the circles, then move sideways and back, following the guidelines. B. Stair-step method. C. Encroaching zigzag.

to bottom, creating the ball shape as you stitch. Don't build up stitches too fast in one place. Move the hoop evenly, slowly, and practice coordination.

Try other stitch widths on the other circles you've drawn. Put the samples in your notebook.

Method B

This has been described as the stair-step method. Designs can be filled in by zigzag stitching from lower-left corner to upper-right corner and back again (Fig. 3.8, method B). To practice this, set up your machine as you did in method A. Draw several 1½″ (3.8cm) squares on your fabric. Although you will start with the widest stitch, experiment with other widths as you did before. Each line of zigzags blends into the one before it. Add your experiments to your notebook.

Method C

Encroaching zigzag is another way to fill in a design (Fig. 3.8, method C). Set up your machine as follows:

Stitch width: widest
Stitch length: 0
Needle: #90/14
Feed dogs: covered
Presser foot: darning foot G or no foot
Tension: slightly loosened
Fabric: medium-weight cotton
Thread: sewing thread for practice
Accessories: 7″ (17.8cm) hoop, tear-away
   stabilizer, water-erasable marker

This time, draw only one 2″ (5.1cm) square on the fabric in the hoop, and place stabilizer under it. Keep the hoop in the same position in front of you; don't rotate it. Instead, move it backward and forward as you stitch. Start at the top of the right side of the square you've drawn and stitch down to the bottom, moving the hoop slowly to keep the stitches close together. Move the hoop to the left a bit and stitch back up to the top, overlapping the first stitching slightly. Continue until you have covered the square. Go back and stitch on top of stitches for more texture. Do a sample for your notebook.

Lesson 4. Applying thick threads from the top and bobbin

We created texture with regular sewing threads in Lesson 3, but in this lesson we'll change sewing and machine-embroidery threads for thicker threads, such as pearl cotton, cordonnet, and crocheted cotton. We'll explore three different ways to create texture by attaching these thick threads to fabric, including using them on the top spool, couched down on top of fabric, and wound on the bobbin.

Adding texture adds interest to sewing and embroidery. Perhaps it's not essential—a dress is still a dress without textured decoration—but it is a long-cut, that something extra that takes your dress from ordinary to special. Adding cords, fringe, objects, and gathers to the background fabric are all easy techniques once you know your machine.

Applying thick thread through the needle

Thread as large as cordonnet can be sewn with a #110/18 needle. Topstitching needles also have eyes to accommodate double threads or thick threads like buttonhole twist, available in #90/14–#110/18 needles.

Whatever you use, the thread must slip

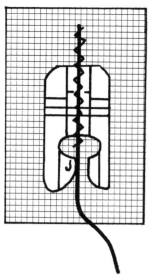

Fig. 3.9 Cord attached with modified J foot.

through the needle easily and the needle must make a hole in the fabric large enough to keep the thread from fraying.

Couching thread down on top of fabric

If thread is too thick for the needle, try couching it down on top of the fabric using the modified J foot (Fig. 3.9). Pull cord front to back, and guide the cord so it rides along the inside left edge of the presser foot. Satin stitch over it with a zigzag or other decorative stitch. Cover the cord as closely or sparsely as you wish, using different stitch lengths.

You can substitute other feet too, such as the narrow hemmer or invisible zipper foot. If you use the hemmer, hold the cord up slightly, letting it slip through the scroll as it is stitched down (Fig. 3.10).

Available at any fabric shop, you'll find

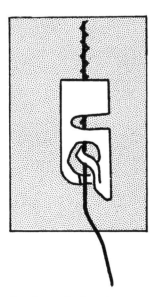

Fig. 3.10 Cord attached with narrow hemmer foot.

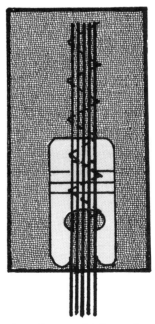

Fig. 3.11 Attaching multiple cords with an open J foot.

the unique zipper foot. (This is not a Singer foot, but it will fit.) Follow the directions for your machine (use shank C for the 6268 machine). Adjust the foot for zigzag, setting width to 3, length standard. Thread the cord through the groove and hold the cord up slightly as you zigzag over it. This is an excellent cording foot.

Try multiple cords as well. Use the J foot (the open J foot works best) and place the cords next to each other, within the cutout area from the back to the front of the foot (Fig. 3.11).

Stitching perfect circles

In the following project you'll stitch circles on a greeting card, using the tape-and-tack method. Let me explain what I mean by that. First you'll need transparent tape, a thumbtack and a hoop. Determine the radius of the circle you wish to stitch. Measure that distance from the needle to a place at the left of it on the machine bed. Place a tack there, point up. Hold the tack in place by pushing the tape over the point and sticking it onto the machine (Fig. 3.12A).

Then stretch your fabric into the hoop and place the center of the circle over the tack (Fig. 3.12B). Push a small cork or eraser over the point. When you rotate the hoop and stitch, you'll create a perfect circle.

Of course perfect circles can be stitched without the tape and tack, but it takes practice and confidence. It's not necessary to practice stitching one hundred circles. Rather, you gain confidence by using your machine often and by teaching yourself to precision-stitch, even if it is only a simple dress seam. This is a good time to explain how I stitch perfect circles without the help of the tape-and-tack method. You can apply the same methods to stitching satin-stitched curves.

Stabilize your appliqué fabric before drawing the circle and cutting it out. I use a fusible so there will be no creeping or

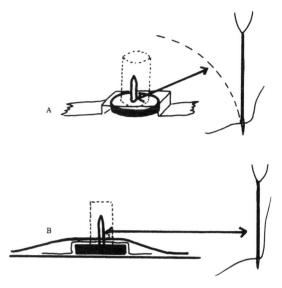

Fig. 3. 12 A. Make your own circle maker by taping a thumbtack upside-down on the bed of the machine a radius away from the needle. Tape it in place. B. Place material in a hoop and stick the fabric onto the thumbtack wherever you want the center of the circle to be. Secure the fabric with a cork. Keep the fabric taut between the thumbtack and the needle as you sew a circular design.

pleating when the circle is stitched down to the background fabric. With the sheers used in the following project, stretch the appliqué fabrics in a hoop along with the base fabric.

Be sure you start by drawing a perfect circle. I've used templates such as spools, cups and plates. If you plan to stitch a lot of circles, buy a plastic template at an art or office supply store (you'll need a fine-line marker or sharp pencil, too). The template is thick, but transparent, with cut-out circles that range from too-tiny-to-be-of-any-use to 3″ (7.6cm). Use the cups and plates for larger circles.

To get a more perfect edge when you stitch wovens, use a sharp, sometimes called a jeans, needle; to produce a more beautiful satin stitch, always use machine embroidery thread and back your work with freezer paper or tear-away stabilizer.

Large circles are easier to stitch than small ones, and it's easier to maneuver narrow satin stitches than wide ones. I usually prefer a satin stitch no wider than stitch width 3 for appliqué, but the special purpose J foot, which you'll use, will accommodate the width of your machine's satin stitch (on the 6268, it's stitch width 7).

Using the special purpose J foot, and stitch width 3, I experimented with where the appliqué edge should be placed under the presser foot and found out that if I place the inside edge of the left toe directly over the edge of the fabric I'm attaching when I stitch clockwise, then all the satin stitches are on the appliqué (Fig. 3.13A). On the zig, the stitches are within the appliqué, on the zag, they're just off the edge.

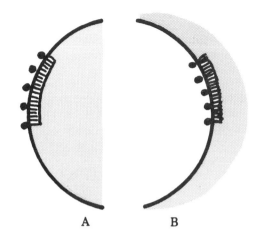

Fig. 3.14 A. When stitching convex curves, the pivot points are on the outside. B. When stitching concave curves, the pivot points are on the inside.

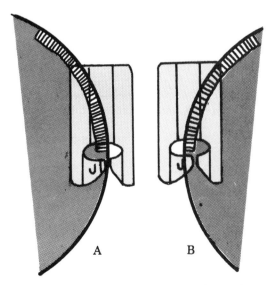

Fig. 3.13 Place the presser foot on the circle so all the stitches will be on the appliqué when stitching clockwise. B. Placement of the presser foot when stitching a circle counterclockwise so all stitches are on the appliqué.

Never satin stitch out beyond the appliqué, attaching the circle with stitches that barely catch the edge.

When stitching counterclockwise with stitch width 3, I place the edge under the long stroke of the letter J (Fig. 3.13B).

For a wider or narrower satin stitch, find a reference point on the presser foot by hand-walking your machine. Use a fine-point marker to indicate it on the foot: then watch your mark and the edge of the fabric as you stitch slowly around your perfect circle. Pivot as you satin stitch. The smaller the circle, the more pivoting and the harder it is to stitch a perfect circle. Keep this in mind: If the curve is an outside (convex) one your pivot points are on the outside of the circle (Fig. 3.14A). If the curve is inside (concave), then the pivot points are on the inside edge (Fig. 3.14B). Always pivot whenever you see the satin stitches slanting instead of radiating (imagine your circle has lines radiating from the center and you are stitching only the edges of those lines). You may have to go back to the same pivot point several times as you complete the continuous curve. Do this with needle down in the pivot point, turn the fabric slightly, stitch, needle down in the same pivot point, move the fabric again, and so on, until the curve is smooth and covered evenly with satin stitches. Yes, it is slow going, but never stitch a circle if you are in a hurry—it won't work. Circles are a stitch-by-stitch process and a slow one, if you want a perfect circle.

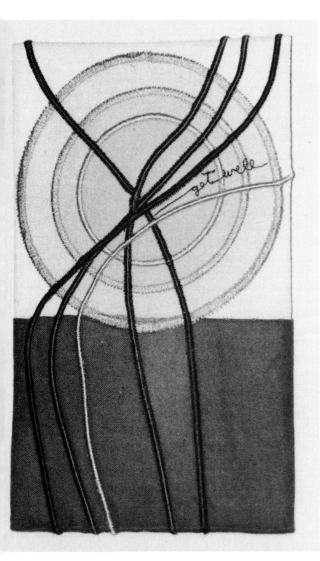

Practice stitching perfect circles with and without tape and tack and put your samples in your notebook.

Project
Greeting Card

Practice making perfect circles and applying thick threads on top of the fabric by making the greeting card shown in Fig. 3.15.

Stitch width: 0–3
Stitch length: 1–standard setting
Needle: #90/14
Feed dogs: covered and uncovered
Presser foot: appliqué or embroidery J, blind stitch K, open J, darning foot G
Tension: slightly loosened (auto − 1)
Fabric suggestions: 12″ (30.5cm) square of white polished cotton, 6″ (15.2cm) square of green polished cotton, 12″ (30.5cm) square of yellow organdy
Thread: rayon in rainbow colors—yellow, red, green, purple, blue; #3 pearl cotton in the same colors; monofilament
Accessories: 7″ (17.8cm) spring hoop; thumb tack, transparent tape, cork or eraser; water-erasable pen; greeting card folder (available at craft, art, and needlework shops) or picture frame; dressmaker's carbon; empty ballpoint pen
Stabilizer: tear-away

Use the pattern in Fig. 3.16 as a guide, changing measurements to fit the card folder or frame. Trace the pattern from the book, then place the drawing on top of the white background fabric, with dressmaker's carbon between. Transfer it, using the empty ballpoint pen.

Cut a piece from the green fabric large

Fig. 3.15 "Even the Rainbow is Upset" greeting card.

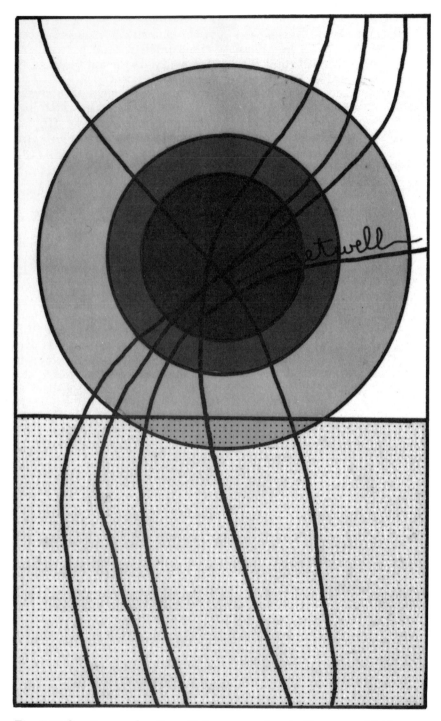

Fig. 3.16 Greeting card pattern. Enlarge or reduce to fit your card folder.

enough for the area at the bottom of the design, plus 1″ (2.5cm). Fold under the top edge of the green about ½″ (12.7mm) and press it. Hold it in place with pins and apply it using the J foot, with monofilament thread on the top and bobbin, and the machine set on a blind hem stitch—but push down the double needle button.

Adjust foot to sew on white background and zig into the fold of fabric, catching only one or two threads.

Next, stretch three layers of yellow organdy over the white and green fabric and put them all in a spring hoop. Back this with tear-away. Set up the tack on your machine (use the tape-and-tack method in Fig. 3.12). Poke the tack through at the center of the three layers of organdy. Place the open J foot on the line of the inner circle. Stitch on that line around the circle with a straight stitch. Take the fabric out of the hoop and cut back only the top layer or organdy to the stitching.

Place the greeting card back in the hoop, with the tack back in its original hole. Satin stitch with the machine set on a width of 3, length 1, or adjust the settings on your machine for smooth, close satin stitches.

Then move the tack so the line of the next circle will be centered under your presser foot. Straight stitch around the circle, cut back and satin stitch again as you did with the first. Do the same for the last layer of organdy.

Take the fabric out of the hoop while you stitch over the cords, but place tear-away stabilizer underneath. Each cord is a different color; use the narrow hemmer, modified J foot, or invisible zipper foot to guide the pearl cotton. Stitch over the cords, using close satin stitches. I prefer to stitch in two passes, attaching the cord first, then stitching in close satin stitches to cover it evenly and smoothly on the second pass.

When the last cord has been covered, change to the darning foot, feed dogs covered, straight stitch. Use the color you have

on your machine—unless it's yellow—to write a message along the top of one of the cords. I wrote "get well," and on the inside I'll write the message: "Even the rainbow is upset."

Finish the edge with a straight stitch. Trim close to stitches and slip into the card folder or finish it for a framed picture.

When sewing down bulky yarns or cords, try the blind stitch foot K (Fig. 3.17).

Stitch width: 3
Stitch length: standard setting
Needle: varies
Feed dogs: uncovered
Presser foot: blind stitch K
Tension: normal
Thread: monofilament on top, polyester on bobbin
Stabilizer: tear-away

Place the cord alongside the middle extension of the presser foot. Stitch alongside the cord. At the wide bite of the needle, the cord is sewn down with a tiny, almost unnoticeable stitch. When the line of stitching is completed, go back and gently nudge the cord over toward the stitching

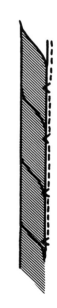

Fig. 3.17 Use the blind-hem stitch to attach cord invisibly.

line. Now your monofilament will be completely hidden.

Or using the open J foot, line up several threads of pearl cotton next to each other. Use the multistitch (#4) zigzag or another built-in stitch to attach them with monofilament or with a colored thread. Make colorful shoelaces or friendship bracelets this way.

Soutache is like a thick cord, and can be attached using the open J foot. Hold the braid in place by pulling it through the groove at the back of the foot so the needle will enter exactly in the center each time. It's possible to feed middy braid or rickrack through the groove in this foot. Stitch slowly to keep the decorative tapes and braids in the correct place for stitching perfection.

Corners of soutache are not impossible if you walk the machine around them. Stop at the corner, needle down, presser foot raised. Turn the fabric 45 degrees, lower the foot, take one stitch; then, needle down again, raise the presser foot, turn the fabric to complete the corner. You'll get a good angle. If you can, though, choose a design with undulating curves, which are easier to accomplish.

Use soutache and other braids down jacket and vest fronts, around sleeves, or to decorate belts and handbags.

Stitch ribbon in place using the blind stitch K foot, with the ribbon at the edge of the extension. Set on blind hem (stitch width 3, stitch length standard). If stitched with monofilament, it is almost invisible.

Here's another invisible way to attach thick, twisted cord or yarn to fabric (Fig. 3.18). Set up for free machining, but remove the presser foot or use a darning foot. Use monofilament thread on top. Iron a piece of freezer paper on the back of the fabric. Begin by drawing the bobbin thread to the top and anchoring the threads. Stitch the end of the cord down. Then move along one side of the cord with a straight stitch. When you reach a twist in the cord, follow

Fig. 3.18 Stitch alongside, then across the twist, to attach cord.

it to the other side by stitching in the twist. Once on the other side, follow along that side for a few stitches until you reach the top of the next twist. Cross over again, following the twist. Continue in this manner until the cord is attached.

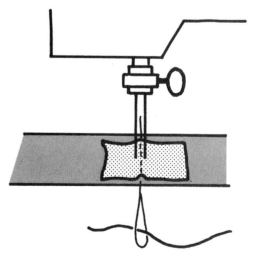

Fig. 3.19 Threading cord through double needles.

Use pearl cotton under the fabric, between double needles, for pintucking. Use your modified or open J foot to keep the pintuck ridge from being squashed. Tighten top tension slightly. It's preferable to use a lightweight fabric such as organdy so you can see that the cord is fed through in a straight line (Fig. 3.19).

Using thick thread from the bobbin

Cable stitching is an embroidery technique using thick thread on the bobbin. It is called *bouclé stitching* in old Singer books, where directions call for yarns wound on the bobbins. Singer books also refer to *cordonnet stitch,* which is done with stiffer, thick cordonnet thread on the bobbin instead of the fluffy yarn of bouclé embroidery. I'm lumping bouclé with cordonnet and calling it by its contemporary name: Cabling.

The topside of the fabric will be against the bed of the machine. It can be done with feed dogs uncovered, using the J or B foot for straight or built-in stitches, or it can be done freely with feed dogs covered, using a G foot or using no presser foot at all.

Cabling can look like a tightly couched thread or like fluffy fur, depending on the thread you choose. A hard-twist thread like crochet cotton will lay flatter, with less beading or looping than a soft, loosely twisted yarn like mohair. The effects you get will depend not only on tension, but on stitch width, stitch length, color and size of cord, color of top thread, feed dogs up or down, color, weight, and type of fabric, how fast you stitch and how fast you move the hoop.

When I say you can use thick threads, I'm not kidding. Did you know that you can use up to a four-ply yarn in the bobbin? Of course, the thicker the yarn, the less you can wind on the bobbin. With yarn or ribbon, you must fill the bobbin by hand. Be sure you wind clockwise and evenly,

without stretching it. Wind round elastic the same way.

After you place the bobbin in the machine, refrain from placing the bobbin thread in tension. Instead, dip needle down and pull up the thread. If you have trouble doing this, then take off the back plate and open the front plate. Hold the bobbin in your hand (it's easier this way) and thread the yarn or ribbon through the opening in the back plate (Fig. 3.20).

To make it easier, I use a loop of dental floss that serger owners are buying at pharmacies to use for looper threaders. Replace the plates and you are ready to cable stitch.

Practice cabling on a piece of scrap fabric. Set up your machine with feed dogs uncovered, using an embroidery thread on top or regular sewing thread. Place your fabric in a hoop and use an open embroidery foot. Stitch and then look under the fabric to be sure the tension is set correctly—do you want tight, stiff stitches or loosely looping ones? Manipulate the tension for different effects. It must be loose enough so the bobbin thread stays underneath the fabric; but if it is too loose, it may keep the stitches from staying neatly in place.

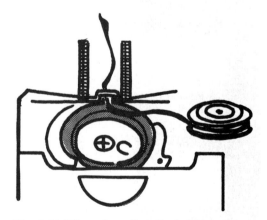

Fig. 3.20 When threading the bobbin with cord, bypass the bobbin tension.

Write on your sample fabric which is the topside, which the back. Also record the tension by using "auto +" or "auto −" and the number of dots into each position. Change tension, lengths, and widths and use your machine to its full potential. Get to know your Singer.

Now prepare a cabling sample for your notebook. Choose a medium-weight cotton or blend. Use several of the built-in stitches with #3, #5, and then #8 pearl cotton. If using #8 pearl cotton, you can place this thread in the bobbin tension. Any thicker (#3 or #5) must be left out of the tension as explained previously. Try ribbon and yarn as well. Keep the stitch long enough to prevent the cord from bunching up under the fabric. Open built-in stitches work best and simple zigzag is most effective. I like the zigzag stitched at a wide stitch length and long length. It gives a rick-rack effect. A rule of thumb is: the thicker the thread, the longer the stitch length. Always do samples first to find the correct settings.

Stretch a piece of fabric in a hoop, but don't use a stabilizer underneath. Instead, use a stabilizer on top to keep your stitches from pulling. Draw lines or designs on the stabilizer. This is actually the back of your work.

Dip the needle into the fabric, drawing the bobbin thread or cord to the top. Hold the threads to the side as you begin. If you can't bring the cord up through the fabric, then pierce the cloth with an awl or large needle and bring it up. Don't anchor the threads with a lockstitch at the beginning or end. Instead, pull the threads to the back each time you start; when you stop, leave a long enough tail to be able to thread it up in a hand-sewing needle and poke it through to the back. Later you can work these threads into the stitching by hand.

It is also possible to quilt with this technique. Using a white pearl cotton in the bobbin and a top thread to match the fabric, you can get an effect which looks much like Japanese Sashiko (Fig. 3.21).

Apply $\frac{1}{8}''$ (3.2mm) double-faced satin ribbon as shown in Fig. 3.22. Wind the ribbon onto the bobbin by hand, as explained pre-

Fig. 3.21 Stitching in the style of Japanese Sashiko.

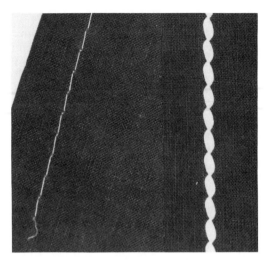

Fig. 3.22 The top and underneath of a ribbon attached by machine stitching.

straight lines. When your stitching changes direction, the tension is also changed, so practice how fast you should move your hoop for the effects you want. Often a design can be seen from the back of printed fabric. Take advantage of that to stitch a sample piece for your notebook. Stretch the fabric in a hoop. Water-soluble stabilizer can be used underneath if the fabric is washable. Otherwise, don't use a stabilizer. Instead, be sure your fabric is very taut, and use darning foot G. Embellish these prints by outlining the designs with pearl cotton or thick rayon thread on the bobbin.

Use bridal veiling as your fabric and create original lace. Or, decorate velveteen using velour yarn on the bobbin and monofilament thread on the top.

viously. Use the regular presser foot, stitch length about 7 or use the basting stitch #6. Tighten tension to auto + 3. Depending on your tension and stitch length settings, the applied ribbon looks loopy or flat.

When you start and stop in this type of couching, the ribbon is brought to the underside and finished off by hand. This technique is used on the infant's bonnet in Chapter 5.

Ribbon thread, available in many colors, is a soft, woven, $\frac{1}{8}''$ (3.2mm) ribbon for bobbins. Find it at dealers or in Sources of Supply. It is softer than satin ribbon, and has a different look, though it is handled the same way.

Next try cabling with free embroidery. Place a medium-weight fabric in a hoop with a stabilizer on top. Cover the feed dogs and, using the darning foot G or bare needle, freely straight stitch, then zigzag.

Plan the lines of stitching before you begin. As you work, sew and peek under your hoop so you can regulate the tension to your liking. Practice turning, pushing and pulling the hoop, sewing circles and

Project
Tote Bag
Square (Cabling)

Monograms and initials are found throughout this book, many of them sewn by using a cartridge. This initial (Fig. 3.23) is done so simply, you can stitch it from the top with machine embroidery thread, or top-side-down using thick thread in the bobbin as I've done here.

You'll want to design your own initial. To do this, draw a fat letter with rounded corners. Don't use a ruler; there are no straight edges. Or enlarge the initial in Fig. 3.24 that you want to use. Once the initial is drawn, add a flower-laden vine. Let it twist around the initial, but not overpower it.

Stitch width: 0 to wide satin stitch
Stitch length: varies
Needle: #80/12
Feed dogs: covered
Presser foot: darning

Fig. 3.23 Cabling design for tote bag square shown in color section.

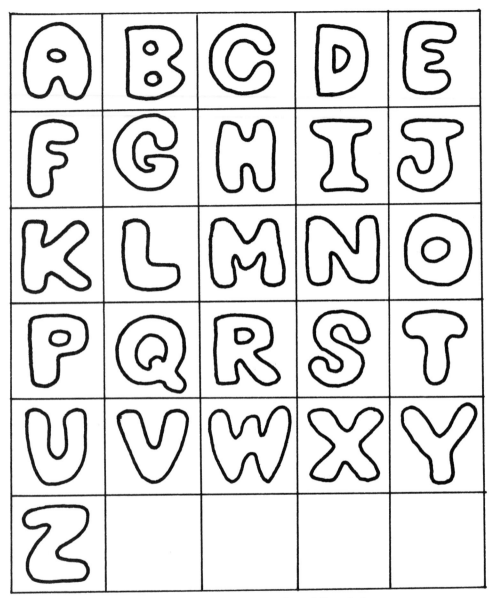

Fig. 3.24 Initials to enlarge for any monogram on the cabling design.

Tension: normal
Fabric suggestions: 9″-square medium-weight yellow
Thread: green, yellow, red, and purple sewing thread; #5 pearl cotton (yellow, turquoise, dark blue, red, dark lavender, light green, dark green (wind by hand on bobbins)
Accessories: tracing paper, dressmaker's carbon, empty ballpoint pen, water-erasable pen
Stabilizer: freezer paper

Transfer your design to tracing paper and then, using dressmaker's carbon and the ballpoint pen, transfer the design to freezer paper. Color in or mark each flower and vine to indicate color. Press this to the underside of your fabric. The initial has to be a mirror image. To do this, I draw the design, color it, then turn it upside-down (you can easily see through tracing paper) when transferring it to the freezer paper. Always do a sample first, using the same fabric, stabilizer and threads as you will be using on your finished copy. Peek under the sample and adjust the tensions as needed. When cabling, you always work with underside up.

With dark blue in the bobbin, straight stitch around the outside of the initial, then stitch around the inside several times freely (see color section). Stitch in the vine and leaves next. I used a light green, then I went over the same vine with dark green and added more leaves or outlined the ones already stitched in.

The flowers are stitched in next, changing colors as you wish. Top thread can be changed to match the bobbin thread or to contrast with it.

When you finish this square, you'll understand why this type of stitchery was once called bouclé.

When you've finished, pull off the freezer paper and work in the pearl cotton beginnings and ends by hiding them in the stitches on the underside. Finish as explained in Chapter 12.

Lesson 5. Fringing yarn and fabric

In this lesson you will learn to make fringe with a fringing fork, as well as with strips of fabric sewn together and clipped into fringe. Start by using a fringing fork to make yarn fringe. It can be used for wigs, costumes, rugs, and decorating edges of garments. Fringing forks are available in many different sizes. Or, you can make your own using wire, ranging from the thickness of a coat hanger to fine as a hairpin.

Wrap the fork as shown in Fig. 3.25, sew down the center, pull the loops toward you, and wrap some more. If making yards and yards of fringe, use Robbie Fanning's method of measuring. Robbie measures the length she wants from a roll of adding-machine tape and stitches her fringe right to the tape. This also keeps the fringe from

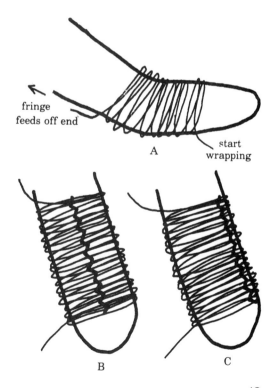

fringe feeds off end

start wrapping

A

B

C

Fig. 3.25 The fringe fork. A. Wrap with yarn or fabric strips. B. Sew down in the middle. C. Or sew at the side of the fork for wider fringe.

twisting. When you're finished, tear off the paper and apply the fringe.

Sometimes you may not want the fringe sewn in the middle. Stitch it at the edge of the fork to make fringe twice as wide as that made by sewing down the center (Fig. 3.25C). As you work with the fork, you will understand when to use each method. And don't limit yourself to yarn or string alone. Try fabric. I used it for doll hair for my denim doll.

Stitch width: normal
Stitch length: normal
Feed dogs: uncovered

Presser foot: open J foot
Tension: normal
Built-in stitch: zigzag #2
Fabric suggestion: 1"-wide (2.5cm wide) bias
   strips, several yards
Thread: polyester to match bias
Accessories: large fringe fork
Stabilizer: adding machine tape

I wrapped the fork with red denim and sewed down the center over adding-machine tape. When I had enough for hair, I tore the paper off the fringe and pinned the hair to her head in various ways to decide what hairdo I liked best. I sewed it

Fig. 3.26 The doll's hair is fabric fringe, her eyelashes are thread fringe done with the tailor-tacking foot.

on by hand; I could have left it as it was, but I decided to clip the loops (Fig. 3.26).

But you can achieve almost the same effect with fabric without using the fringing fork. Work with strips of fabric, but don't clip them into fringe until after they are sewn to the item you are making.

Project
Fringed Denim Rug

This fabric-fringe project, a little rug, ate up yards of old jeans and denim remnants I picked up at sales; I kept cutting $2\frac{1}{2}''$ (6.4cm) strips on the bias until I had finished the rug.

Stitch width: 0
Stitch length: 2
Needle: jeans needle #90/14
Presser foot: zipper
Tension: normal
Fabric suggestion: denim, cut into $2\frac{1}{2}''$ (6.4cm) bias strips of blues and red; use remnants and old jeans to cut quantity needed for rug size you want; heavy upholstery fabric for rug backing
Thread: matching polyester thread
Stabilizer: 1″-wide (2.5cm-wide) fusible webbing (measure circumference of rug)

You'll need a piece of heavy fabric the size of the finished rug, plus an inch all around. Measure the perimeter and cut a piece of 1″-wide (2.5cm-wide) fusible webbing. Using a Teflon pressing sheet, press the fusible webbing to the topside of all the edges and fold them back on the topside of the fabric, pressing again (Fig. 3.27). This is the top of the rug, so the edges will be finished when the last strip is stitched down.

Fold the first bias strip lengthwise to find the center, but open it again and place

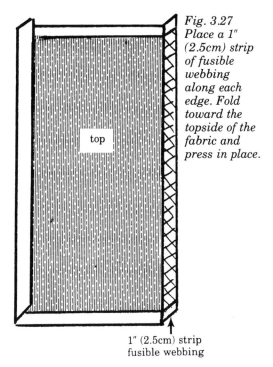

Fig. 3.27 Place a 1″ (2.5cm) strip of fusible webbing along each edge. Fold toward the topside of the fabric and press in place.

1″ (2.5cm) strip
fusible webbing

it $\frac{1}{8}''$ (3.2mm) from the edge of the upholstery fabric. Stitch down the center crease of each strip from top to bottom (Fig. 3.28). Fold the left side of the strip to the right. Push the next strip as close as you can get it to the first. Sew down the center again; Fig. 3.28 shows the first three fabric strips

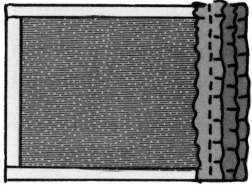

Fig. 3.28 Stitching bias strips onto the rug.

Fig. 3.29 The bias strips are clipped into fringe.

stitched down. If you run out of fabric for a strip, add another by overlapping the last strip at least 1″ (2.5cm).

When you're all done stitching, clip each strip every ½″ (12.7mm), staggering the clips for each row (Fig. 3.29). My rug went into the washer and dryer to soften.

Lesson 6. Adding buttons, beads, shisha

Attaching buttons

Once you've attached a button by machine, you won't want to do it any other way, it is so speedy.

To prevent a broken needle, I do a sample first. Using the button I'll use on my garment, I place it on a piece of scrap fabric, then poke the marker into the holes and mark the fabric.

The button is put aside, but I place the marked scrap under the needle and determine (by changing the stitch width dial) how wide the zigzag must be set to sew on the button.

After my machine is set up, I can sew on the button.

If you are applying buttons to a garment you've made, be sure the button area is interfaced. Dab glue stick on the underside of the button and position it.

Stitch width: space between holes in the button
Stitch length: 0
Needle: #80/12
Feed dogs: covered
Presser foot: button sewing H
Tension: normal
Thread: polyester
Accessories: button elevator or toothpick are optional, transparent tape, glue stick, scrap fabrics, buttons, beads and shisha mirrors (see Sources of Supply). Fray-check, marker, scrap fabric.

Place the button foot on top of the button and stitch with the settings used on the scrap fabric, stitching back and forth several times. When you have finished, pull threads to back and tie off. Then dot with Fray-check. That's all there is to it.

46

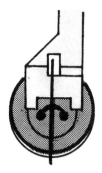

Fig. 3.30 To sew on a button with a shank, use the button foot and a toothpick.

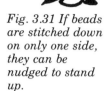

Fig. 3.31 If beads are stitched down on only one side, they can be nudged to stand up.

Fig. 3.32 Stitching down both sides to make beads lie flat.

If the garment fabric is thick, such as coating, you will need to make a button shank; otherwise, the buttonhole will pucker whenever the coat is buttoned. Raise the stitches to create a shank by taping a darning needle or round toothpick in the groove on top of the button sewing foot before you stitch (Fig. 3.30). When finished, pull off the tape and remove the darning needle. Leave a long thread to wrap around the shank and anchor with a hand needle, strengthening the shank.

Or use the button elevator. It is a gadget made to slip under the button to raise it off the fabric and create several shank heights. It's available at notion counters.

Attaching beads and baubles

Beads can be attached by machine if the hole in the bead is large enough and your needle fine enough. The thickness of the bead also matters. If in doubt, hand-walk the machine first to see if the needle will clear the bead, and if the sizes of the bead and needle are compatible. Attach the rim of the bead to the fabric by first holding it in place with a dot of glue from a glue stick. With feed dogs covered, anchor the thread in the center of the bead by stitching in place three or four times. Raise the needle. Move the fabric over to anchor the thread on the side of the bead. Go back to the center and anchor again. Repeat until the bead is securely sewn in place and will

stand up (Fig. 3.31). Nudge the bead to stand on its outside rim when you finish stitching. Wipe off the glue.

If you go back and stitch down the other side as well, your bead will lay flat, hole up (Fig. 3.32).

Attaching seed beads, or other fine or oddly shaped beads can be done in the following way. First string the beads onto a thread. Using monofilament, stitch one end of the beaded thread down on the fabric. Stitch along the thread the width of one bead. Push the first bead near that end and then stitch over the thread to keep the bead in place. Stitch again the distance of the next bead. Push the bead up to the first, stitch over the thread and repeat, as shown in Fig. 3.33.

Or sew beads down by stringing them singly on thick threads and stitching both ends of the threads down (Fig. 3.34).

You can attach beads invisibly, using monofilament thread to couch them down or to string the beads on. Or choose your thread wisely and use the stitching as a part of the decoration.

Another way to hold down beads is to first stitch strips of needlelace on water-soluble stabilizer. When the lace has been stitched, merely pull off the excess stabilizer and hold your work under a faucet to wash out most of what remains; leave a bit of the sticky residue. When it is almost dry, shape the needlelace strips and they will dry in that shape. Use two or

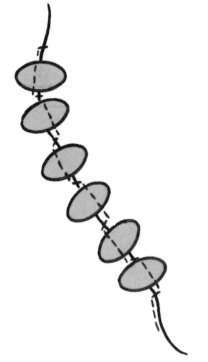

Fig. 3.35 Using needlelace to attach beads.

Fig. 3.33 A string of seed beads, attached by machine along dotted line (solid line is thread).

three of these strips to hold down beads or washers (Fig. 3.35).

Thread a strip through the object and stitch down one end. Move the bauble down over your stitching. Arrange the strip, twisting it if you wish. Then stitch down the other end freely and invisibly. Use this

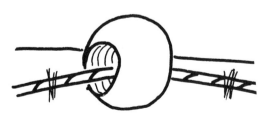

Fig. 3.34 Attach a large bead by threading a cord through it and stitching on either side of the cord.

method, as I have, on decorative box tops and collages (Fig. 3.36).

Another method of using stones and jewels for wall hangings or pictures is to cover them with net or transparent fabrics, and then stitch down the fabric. Then cut holes in the fabric large enough to let the objects show through and small enough so they don't fall out.

Or make needlelace in the center of wire bent into a circle, rectangle, or other shape. Stretch the lace over an object placed on a background fabric. Attach the lace to the fabric by stitching freely, close to the wire, around the inside of this frame, and cutting off the wire. Embroider the edges if you wish.

Attaching shisha mirrors

Shishas are small pieces of mirrored glass. They are about 1″ (2.5cm) in diameter, but are never exactly circular. It is possible to attach them to fabric if you follow the methods Caryl Rae Hancock of Indianapolis, and Gail Kibiger of Warsaw, Indiana, invented.

This is Caryl Rae Hancock's method, illustrated in Fig. 3.37. First, stretch organdy in a hoop. The shisha is placed on top of the organdy and its outline traced. The back of the shisha is dabbed with glue stick and placed on a background fabric, not the organdy.

Sew around—and about ⅛″ (3.2mm) inside—the drawn circle. Stitch around two

Fig. 3.36 "The Flop Box," made by Pat Pasquini, has a machine-embellished top by the author. It includes beads held down with needlelace, other beads strung with cord and porcupine quills and couched in place, textures created by stitching cords down, using a double needle to pintuck suede, and stitching blobs and satin stitches in the background. Photo by Robbie Fanning.

more times. Without taking the fabric out of the hoop, cut out the circle of fabric within the stitching. After anchoring threads, the machine should be set on a medium width zigzag and the circle stitched freely around the cut edge. Turn the hoop as you sew around it, letting the stitches radiate from the edge of the hole to about $\frac{1}{2}''$ (12.7mm) beyond. The organdy must be covered with stitches at this time. Anchor threads and take the organdy out of the

hoop. Cut very closely around the outside stitching.

With the machine changed back to straight stitch, place the piece of embroidery over the shisha and background fabric and pin organdy in place. Stitch around outside edge of the shisha. Be careful: if you stitch into the glass, the needle and probably the shisha will break.

Leave the machine as set or change to zigzag again and stitch over those straight

49

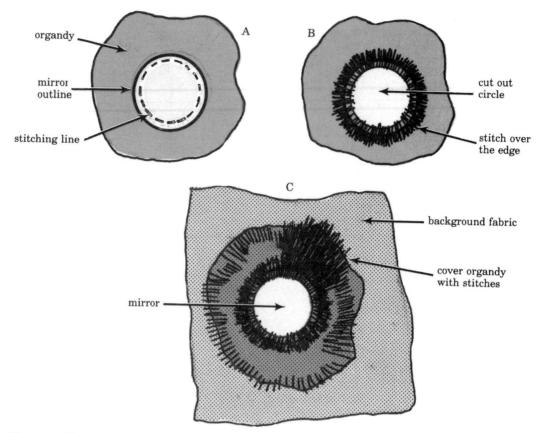

Fig. 3.37 Glue the shisha to the background fabric. A. On organdy, stitch around a circle slightly smaller than the shisha. B. Cut out the center and embroider over the edge. C. Place the organdy over the shisha and stitch it in place on background fabric by straight stitching. Embroider the background to conceal the edge.

stitches, following the radiating direction of the original zigzagging. Blend the outside edge of the organdy with the background fabric by radiating stitches onto the background fabric.

Gail Kibiger has a slightly different method. She applies shisha by first placing the mirror on the background fabric, not on organdy, and tracing around it. Removing the shisha, she stitches $\frac{1}{8}''$ (3.2mm) within this circle three times and cuts out the circle. Gail embroidered on the back-

ground fabric as Caryl Rae did the organdy.

The shisha is then glued to a piece of organdy and placed under the finished hole. After pinning it in place, she straight stitches around the mirror to hold it in place.

One of Gail's variations is to work a spiderweb across the hole before the edges are zigzagged.

Silver bangles, the large sequins found in craft and knitting shops, are an excellent substitute for shisha. Not only are they exactly round, unlike the uneven shape of shishas, but they are durable. If you sew into them, your needle doesn't break and neither do the shishas. Make a record for your notebook of how you have applied buttons, beads and shishas.

Project
Bird Collage

I work with transparent fabrics almost exclusively, so I collect them. Besides fabric stores, garage sales and thrift shops are wonderful sources. I check out the chiffon scarves, colored nylons, lingerie, curtains, as well as glitzy dresses—though it takes courage to buy some of these because of the double-takes at the checkout counter.

This is a beadwork project, which includes appliqué as well. Bird shapes are my favorites. I like them plump like baby chicks, sleek like soaring eagles, even whimsical like African Dahomey appliqués. I've used them on quilts, wall hangings, and in fabric collages.

In this small picture, shown in Fig. 3.38, I added small clay beads by machine to the appliquéd picture.

Fig. 3.38 Bird collage.

Stitch width: 0
Stitch length: 0
Needle: #90/14
Feed dogs: covered
Presser foot: darning foot G
Tension: slightly loosened
Fabric suggestions: green and gold suede or felt for bird's body and wings; transparent fabrics, such as organdy, chiffon, yellow mesh grapefruit bag, for the wings; moss green bridal veiling to cover the picture; 12″ (30.5cm) square of coarse beige upholstery linen for background; loosely woven taupe-colored fabric for the nest; gold lamé for the eggs; nude-colored nylon stocking; also needed are small clay beads
Thread: several strands of brown and beige coarse thread or string, cut into 1″ (2.5cm) pieces; brown, green and beige shiny rayon; monofilament
Stabilizer: ironed-on freezer paper

If this sounds overwhelming, you can substitute any colors you wish, and use only one, instead of a variety, of transparent fabrics. Although I used transparent thread for most of this collage, I added browns, greens and beiges in rayon stitches when my piece was almost complete.

Begin by pulling off a half-dozen threads from the square of background fabric. Cut these threads into small lengths of 1 and 2 inches (2.5–5.0cm) and add them to the other threads you've cut—you will need several dozen. Put them aside.

Iron freezer paper to the back of the linen fabric for stability, as you will not use a hoop for this project. Although not necessary, I always cut the background fabric at least 6″–8″ (15.2–20.3cm) bigger than the finished size so I can practice stitching or layering on the edges. Also, I plan my pieces so they look as if they go on beyond the frame. I don't want them to look as if they end inside it.

Fig. 3.39 shows the arrangement, and Fig. 3.40 provides the pattern pieces; cut out the fabric pieces as follows: Cut out the oval nest from the taupe fabric and place that slightly below the center on the background. When I cut fabric for col-

Fig. 3.39 Follow this design for assembling the bird picture.

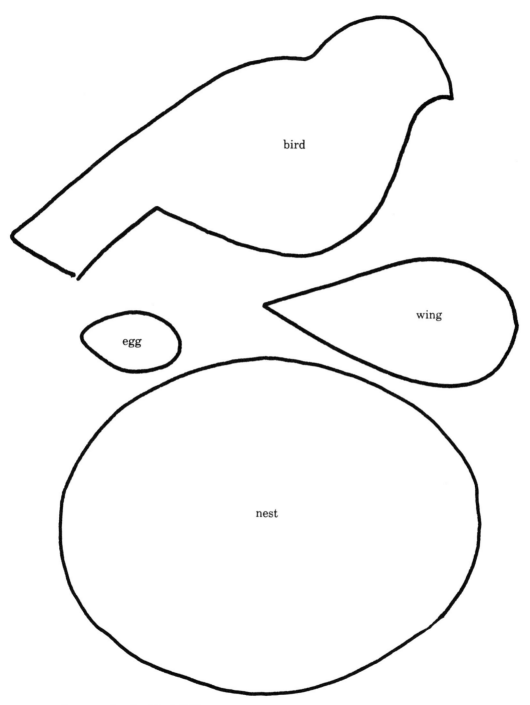

Fig. 3.40 Patterns for the Bird Collage.

lages, I use a cut/tear method. By pulling slightly on the fabric as I cut, I fray the material a bit to keep the edges soft. The bird should be cut from green suede or felt so it will not roll when you cut it out. Be sure to use fabric that has some body, so it will be easy to control. Place the bird on the nest (Fig. 3.39). Cut a gold wing from suede and position that on the bird. Cut out the transparent wings. Place one on top of the gold wing, but shift it a bit so it is not exactly in the same place as the first. Do the same with the other sheers. Your wings will cross, meet, blend, as if in a watercolor. Over the last wing you will use one cut from a yellow mesh grapefruit bag or a coarse yellow net. Rearrange until the wings look pleasing to you.

Cut the foot and top off a nude-colored nylon stocking and slit the stocking from top to bottom. Stretch it over the picture and pin it down just beyond the image area. As you stretch the stocking, it will lighten in color. It should be almost invisible, but not stretched so tightly it buckles the picture. This holds all the pieces in place, and softens, but does not change, the colors of your picture.

Lower or cover the feed dogs on your machine. Use a darning foot, as you will have many layers to stitch together. Begin by freely sewing around the bird with transparent thread. Stitch just off the edge of the body and wing pieces. It is not important to be completely accurate; it's fine if you stitch into the body or wings. You might want to stitch in a few feathers on the gold wing as well, giving the bird an attractive, padded look. Stitch to the outside of the nest and sew that down freely. Then sew all around the outside edge of your picture. Cut off the stocking from the outside edges.

Add three gold lamé eggs under the bird. Over the edge of the nest, scatter half the thread pieces you've cut. Hold all this down by laying a piece of moss green bridal veiling over the picture and pinning it in place.

Again, with transparent thread and a free machine, sew around the eggs, around the outside of the bird and around the nest, managing to catch threads to anchor them. Yes, you will be sewing in a haphazard manner around the nest—and you do not have to sew every thread in place. With a very fine embroidery scissors, cut out the veiling from in front of the bird and the eggs.

String the small clay beads onto some of the remaining "nest" threads. Arrange the threads around the nest on top of those you have already sewn in place. Be very careful as you sew these threads in place; you don't want to hit beads with the darning foot. With transparent thread, sew above and below the beads to hold them in place (see Fig. 3.34).

An alternative method is to remove the darning foot. Press the fabric firmly against the needle plate as you sew down the threads. Be careful of your fingers. Thread up with a shiny brown rayon thread. With your machine still set up for straight stitching, add texture and color to the nest by stitching a blob, lifting the presser foot lever and pulling the picture to stitch again in another spot. Cross and recross threads. I change colors several times (browns, beiges and greens). This also helps anchor the coarse threads.

The bird's eye can be added by sewing on a gold bead by hand, or with your machine, by building up a blob of thread. Your picture is complete. Pull off the freezer paper, or leave it in place. Cut off that extra margin from around your piece. Stretch the picture over a piece of batting and plywood and frame it. These pictures are so much fun to put together, and no two are alike.

Lesson 7. Smocking and gathering

Smocking

In hand smocking, fabric is gathered tightly into channels and embroidery is worked on top of the channels. Stitches chosen are open and stretchy.

Smocking by machine, on the other hand, will not be stretchy like hand smocking. After gathering with thread or cord, machine embroidery stitches usually hold the gathers in place. But if you use elastic, the gathering will stretch—but then, of course, you won't embroider over it.

There are at least a dozen ways to smock on your sewing machine, varying the method of gathering or embroidering, or varying the threads used. Here are several methods you can try. In each one, start with at least 2½ times the width needed for the finished pattern. For any garment, do the smocking first and then cut out the pattern.

Stitch width: 0–widest
Stitch length: varies
Needle: #90/14
Feed dogs: uncovered
Presser foot: open J foot or standard J foot

Built-in stitch: zigzag or open embroidery type
Tension: normal
Fabric: 2 or more 18″ × 45″ (45.7 × 114.3cm) pieces of medium-weight cotton; 1 yard (.9m) strip for gathering ruffles; several 12″ (30.5cm) or larger pieces of scrap fabrics
Threads: machine embroidery; monofilament
Accessories: water-erasable marker
Stabilizer: water-soluble, tear-away type

Simple gathered smocking

First draw at least four lines across the 45″-wide (114.3cm-wide) fabric with a water-erasable marker. The lines should be about ½″ (12.7mm) apart. Leave the seam allowances free of stitching. Anchor the threads, and then straight stitch along your drawn lines, leaving long ends of thread at the ends of the rows (Fig. 3.41). Pull on the bobbin threads to gather the fabric to 18″ (45.7cm) and knot every two threads together. Pin this to tear-away stabilizer.

Choose a decorative stitch and embroi-

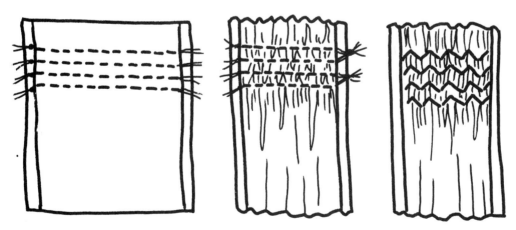

Fig. 3.41 One way to machine smock: Gather up rows of stitching. Embroider between them.

der across the fabric between the gathering lines of stitching as shown in Fig. 3.41. Then take out the gathering stitches and tear off the stabilizer.

Embroidering with thick thread in the bobbin

This may be used with the preceding method for gathering. First complete the gathering. Turn the fabric over, topside down on the bed of the machine. Place water-soluble stabilizer under the gathers.

Stitch width: widest
Stitch length: varies
Built-in stitch: zigzag or open embroidery type
Needle: #90/14
Feed dogs: uncovered
Presser foot: open J foot
Tension: normal
Fabric: medium-weight cotton
Thread: monofilament or sewing thread for top; #5 or #8 pearl cotton for bobbin
Stabilizer: water-soluble

When you stitch up the samples, sew, look underneath to see if the pearl cotton is attached evenly and smoothly. Adjust tensions as necessary.

Open built-in stitches look best—the simple zigzag is effective. Remove the stabilizer when your stitching is completed.

Smocking with elastic

Wind the bobbin with fine, round elastic. Do this by hand so it doesn't stretch. Again, stitch down rows $\frac{1}{2}''$ (12.7mm) apart, gathering as you sew. The thread on top will show, so choose the color carefully. You can use this for bodices of sun dresses, nightgowns or swimsuits. This works best on delicate to lightweight fabrics.

With $\frac{1}{8}''$ (3.2mm) or $\frac{1}{4}''$ (6.4mm) flat elastic, use either the zigzag stitch #2 (Fig. 3.42A), with normal width and length (or on cartridge 4, use stitches #8 and #9). Also use cartridge 4, stitch #3, enter, mir-

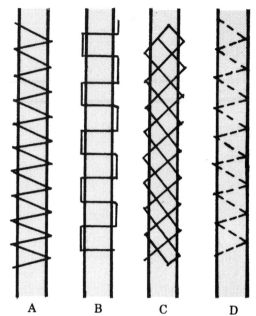

A   B   C   D

Fig. 3.42 Four ways to attach flat elastic. With the zigzag (A) or mirrored blanket stitch (B), the elastic can be adjusted. With the honeycomb (C) or multi-stitch zigzag (D) the elastic can't be adjusted later.

ror image, enter, memory (Fig. 3.42B). If the width is too wide for the $\frac{1}{8}''$ (3.2mm) elastic, adjust it. Once again, it's your choice. The width for $\frac{1}{4}''$ (6.4mm) elastic is perfect. Each of the previously mentioned stitches fall exactly outside the elastic. Use the open J foot.

With the honeycomb #22 or multistitch zigzag (#4) settings, the gathers can't be changed after they are sewn in, because the needle stitches into the elastic (C, D in Fig. 3.42). Stretch the elastic while sewing. The more you stretch it, the more gathers it will create.

Gathering
Using cord

To gather light to heavyweight materials, use this, my all-time favorite method (Fig. 3.43).

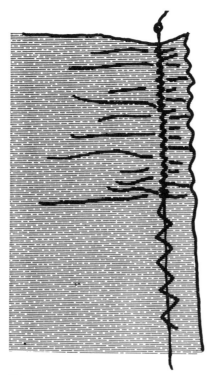

Fig. 3.43 Use an embroidery foot when zigzagging over cord to gather fabric.

Stitch width: 2
Stitch length: 2
Feed dogs: uncovered

Zigzag over a cord, such as gimp or cordonnet. To keep the cord in position while stitching over it, use the modified J foot and line up the cord to the inside edge of the left toe (Fig. 3.9). Other choices are the narrow hemmer (Fig. 3.10) or invisible zipper foot.

The cord is easily guided and covered. Pull up the cord to gather the fabric. Leave the cord in the fabric.

I use this for everything from skirts to dust ruffles to slipcovers. You won't break the gathering stitch as you often do when pulling on a basting thread. It saves hours.

Using elastic

Using the same settings as you did for cord, sew over it first to anchor it to the fabric. Pull on it from the front while sewing a zigzag over it. I use this for quick sleeve finishes for little girls' dresses. If sewn about 1″ (2.5cm) from the finished edge, it creates a ruffle.

Using the ruffler attachment

Gathering yards of ruffles is easy with the ruffler attachment. It simultaneously gathers and applies the gathers to another flat piece of fabric. The only drawback is that without seeing your fabric, I can't give you an iron-clad formula for how much fabric is needed to gather into, say, a 15″ (38.1cm) ruffle.

The key to your estimates is to stitch a sample. Work with the same material you're going to use for the ruffle. Finer materials need to be gathered more fully than heavy fabrics do. Gathering depends upon the position of the adjusting finger and screw. I admit I'm a coward and always add inches to be sure.

Even though this foot will gather a ruffle and apply it to fabric at the same time, I prefer gathering and attaching the gathers in two steps because of the difficulty in estimating the yardage I'll need for the ruffles. But, to do both steps at once, place the fabric to be attached to the ruffle under the fabric to be ruffled, and in the appropriate slot in the ruffler. Keep the edges of the fabrics even with each other. Right sides of fabric are placed together when the seam is to be inside.

Using a gathering foot

This foot is better known as a shirring foot, because that is what it does. Shirring is gathering, of course, but it looks more like easing fabric than gathering it. It can be used in the middle of fabrics as well as at edges for decorative waffle shirring. Draw a grid on your fabric, then stitch

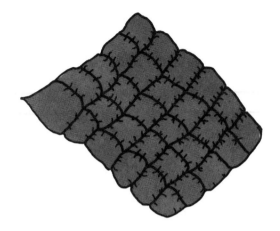

Fig. 3.44 Use the gathering foot to create waffle shirring.

down and across the grid, using the gathering foot for waffling (Fig. 3.44).

You can use this shirring as a form of smocking. Stitch with a heavy thread in the bobbin or on top for other interesting results.

This does not exhaust the methods of gathering and smocking on the machine. Check manual and other sewing books for others.

Lesson 8. Pulling threads together

Satin stitching on top of loosely woven fabric builds up texture quickly by drawing the threads of the fabric together into ridges. Then you can connect the ridges for even more texture. As you can see from the sample in Fig. 3.45, the result of this technique looks like lace.

If you're hesitant about stitching in open areas, stitch water-soluble stabilizer behind the fabric before stitching.

Stitch width: 0–5
Stitch length: 0
Needle: #90/14
Feed dogs: covered
Presser foot: darning foot G
Tension: slightly loosened
Fabric: loosely woven cheesecloth type
Thread: machine embroidery, desired color top and bobbin
Accessories: spring hoop, water-soluble stabilizer (optional)

To learn this technique, stitch an imaginary tree of satin stitches and lacy straight stitches. It's not necessary to trace my design as this is done freely.

Put the fabric in a hoop. It must be stretched tightly. Bring the bobbin thread

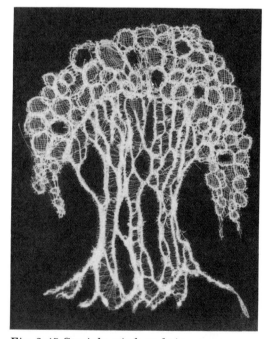

Fig. 3.45 Straight stitch and zigzag over loosely woven fabric produced both lacy and textured embroidery.

58

to the top and anchor the threads. Using the widest stitch setting, sew up and down in straight lines. At the down points, move the fabric over a bit and go up and down again. Continue until you have three or four rows of satin stitches. Then go back over them, zigzagging in between. This draws the previous lines together. Cut fabric threads if there is too much pulling and puckering.

Create branches on top and, when you come down to the bottom again, flare the line of stitching to resemble roots. Use the widest zigzags to stitch up and down again. Go back and zigzag over the whole tree again and again until the stitches are built up to your liking.

Change to a straight stitch and begin to stitch small circles at the top to crown the branches. Go from one to another. Cut or poke out the centers of some or all of the circles to give a lacy look to the tree top.

If you've used water-soluble stabilizer, then wash it out on completion of your work.

In the sample, I trimmed the tree from the background to show you the type of appliqué I add to my collages. It has a lacy look you can see through, which adds depth to the embroidery it's placed over. But sometimes I place the untrimmed appliqué over a background fabric and stitch it in place. After trimming it back to the stitches, I freely embroider over it with more satin stitches, with more ridges, building up more and more texture.

If you do a large enough square of threads pulled together with satin stitches, it can be used as a design for your tote bag. Or leave it untrimmed and still in the hoop for a window hanging.

CHAPTER 4

Adding Fabric to Fabric: Appliqué

- **Lesson 9. Methods of applying appliqués**
- **Lesson 10. Appliquéing with feed dogs up**
- **Lesson 11. Appliquéing with feed dogs lowered**

Once you know your machine as I know mine, you won't be satisfied stitching down all your appliqués with satin stitches. This chapter will show you several ways to place an appliqué onto a background successfully and teach a variety of methods for stitching it in place.

You'll make tote bag squares, Carrick-macross lace, and shadow work in these lessons. You will also work samples for your notebook to practice other appliqué methods.

Lesson 9. Methods of applying appliqués

Applying fabric to fabric takes two steps. Both are equally important. The first is to place the appliqué on the background in a way that keeps it in place, without puckering the fabric and with edges held down firmly, to enable you to do a perfect final stitching. The second step is the stitching. In Lessons 10 and 11, we'll try blind hems and blanket stitches, straight stitching, blurring, scribbling and corded edges.

In appliqué, the best results are achieved when the applied and background fabrics have similar properties. For example, if using a cotton background fabric, it is best to use a similar weight appliqué fabric, and one that can be washed like the cotton. If washable, prepare the fabrics by washing and ironing them. They may be easier to work with if they are starched.

Match the grain lines of the appliqué to those of the background fabric. It's usually necessary to use a stabilizer under the fabric to prevent puckers when stitching. There are several methods for the first step.

The first one wastes fabric, but the results are worth it.

Method A

Stretch both fabrics tightly in a hoop. I use a wooden hoop for this step because the fabric can be stretched and held more tightly than in a spring hoop. The fabric for the appliqué should be underneath—on the bed of the machine—with the top-sides of both fabrics down. Draw the design on the wrong side of the base fabric, or place a paper pattern in the hoop, either pinning it there or catching it in the hoop with the fabric.

With the machine set up for free machining, single stitch around the design. Take the fabric out of the hoop, turn it over and cut the applied fabric back to the stitching line. Place the fabric back in the hoop with the appliqué on top this time. Use one of the methods for final stitching discussed in Lessons 10 and 11.

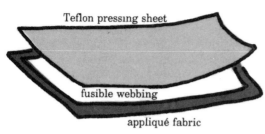

Fig. 4.1 To prepare an appliqué with fusible webbing, first place a piece of the fusible on the back of the appliqué fabric, cover it with the special Teflon sheet, and press in place.

Method B

For the next method, fusible webbing and a Teflon pressing sheet are needed. This will produce a slightly stiffer appliqué than the first method, but if done correctly, it will never produce a pucker.

Cut a piece of fabric and a piece of fusible webbing slightly larger than the appliqué (Fig. 4.1). With the fusible webbing on top of the appliqué fabric, place the Teflon sheet over it and iron until the fusible webbing melts (Fig. 4.2). When it cools, the Teflon can be peeled away. Cut out the appliqué from this piece of fabric and then iron it to the background fabric, using a Telfon sheet on top to protect your iron.

Method C

An alternative to fusible webbing is the appliqué paper backed with "glue." To use this paper, cut a piece of it and fabric approximately the size of the appliqué. Draw the design on the non-adhesive side of the paper, then iron the paper to the back of the fabric. After it adheres and cools, cut around the design and fabric, then peel the paper off the appliqué. The glue will have been transferred from the paper to the fabric. Iron the appliqué to the background.

If doing lettering or an appliqué where direction is important, then remember that this method gives you a flipped or mirror image of the original.

Method D

Plastic sandwich bags can also be used as a fusible—or try cleaners' garment bags. Cut out a piece of plastic the size of the appliqué and place it between the backing fabric and appliqué.

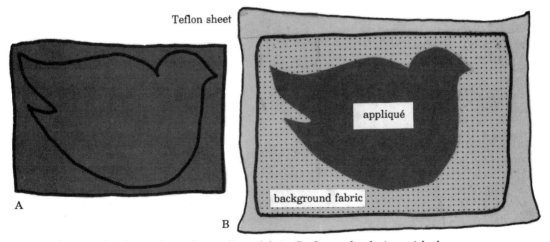

Fig. 4.2 Cut out the design from the appliqué fabric. B. Cover the design with the Teflon sheet again to press in place on the background fabric.

Put brown wrapping paper over and under this "sandwich" so any plastic that is peeking out will be ironed onto the brown paper and not your iron or ironing board. Press it with an iron hot enough to melt the plastic and fuse the fabrics together.

Method E

If you wish to use blind stitch (#3) or blanket stitch (#10) or, on cartridge 4 (#3), dial down to a narrow width and slowly stitch around the edge of an appliqué for step two, the appliqué must be prepared in another way (Fig. 4.3).

First, straight stitch around the appliqué on what will be the fold line. Cut the appliqué from the fabric, leaving a $\frac{1}{4}''$ (6.3mm) seam allowance. Clip the edges and turn under on the stitched line. Trim

off more seam allowance wherever fabric overlaps or creates bulk. Baste with stitches or a glue-stick. Press the edges flat. Baste in place on the background fabric—I find it more accurate when done by hand. There is a wash-away basting thread on the market. If you use this it eliminates the need to pull out the basting later, and if it gets caught in your final stitching—no problem, it washes away. Now you can blind-hem or blanket stitch the appliqué to the foundation.

If the appliqué is to be embroidered, it is sometimes best to do it first to prevent puckers in the background fabric. Embroidered patches can be appliquéd in many ways, the most common being satin stitching around the edge. But another way is to leave the edge almost devoid of stitch-

Fig. 4.3 A. To prepare and apply an appliqué for blind hemming, stitch all around it $\frac{1}{4}''$ (6.3mm) from the edge (top). B. Fold under on the stitching, apply to the background and blind-hem-stitch in place. C. Blanket stitch around the appliqué for another finish.

ing, cut out the appliqué and apply it with the same free stitches as the embroidery, to blend it into the background.

Even if fabric is to be heavily embroidered, embroider first on another piece of fabric, cut it out, and make it an appliqué. Use a glue stick or pin it in place. These appliqués are usually too thick to attach with fusible webbing.

Lesson 10. Appliquéing with feed dogs up

Satin stitches three ways

In addition to keeping your machine in excellent condition, the perfect satin stitch is achieved by matching of fabric, needle, and thread. Always sew a sample, using the same fabric, needle and thread that will be used on the finished piece. Don't watch the needle, but keep your eyes on the line you'll be stitching. Check to see if the fabric is being fed through evenly. Open or close the length of the zigzags. Each machine has its own personality, so you must work this out for yours.

Standard method

Keep a few things in mind when attaching an appliqué with satin stitches: First, the stitch width should not overpower the appliqué. I almost always use a setting no wider than 4, along with the J foot, because the satin stitches fit inside the groove on the underside of the foot.

Stitch width: 4–5
Stitch length: 1—adjust for your machine
Presser foot: special purpose J
Feed dogs: uncovered
Tension: slightly loosened

I prefer to cover the edge of an appliqué in two passes rather than one. Instead of a 1½ length, start with 2 or one between 1½ and 2. At the same time, dial the first pass slightly narrower than the final one. Instead of 4 width, dial down to 3¾ for the first pass.

Use a needle appropriate for the thread. The needle must be large enough to let the thread pass through freely and it must punch a large enough hole in the fabric to prevent the thread from fraying. For example, with rayon embroidery thread I use a #90/14 needle; on cotton embroidery thread, I use a #80/12 needle. On woven materials, I use a pierce-point needle instead of a universal point because I feel it gives me a more perfect edge. (The universal point is slightly rounded, so it deflects off the fibers and slips between them. When satin stitching on closely woven materials, this needle may create an uneven edge.)

Stained-glass method

Stained-glass is a type of satin-stitch appliqué in which your satin stitches are gray to black and extend out from the appliqué to the borders of the design. It is important to remember this, since not every design is appropriate for stained-glass.

Reverse appliqué

Reverse appliqué is the technique of layering from one to many fabrics on top of a background material. A design is straight-stitched through layers, then the fabric is cut away from portions of the design to reveal the fabric beneath. It is finished by satin stitching over the straight stitches. Reverse appliqué can be combined with appliqué from the top as well. To do a perfect reverse appliqué, put both fabrics in a hoop, topsides up, your appliqué fabric underneath. Draw the design on the top fabric or place the pattern on top of the fabrics in the hoop and straight stitch around the design. Remove the paper.

Take the fabrics out of the hoop and cut out the top fabric inside the design area. Put the fabric back in the hoop, slip stabilizer between hoop and machine, and then satin stitch the edges. When finished, you may want to cut away the extra appliqué fabric on the back to eliminate bulk.

This method often affords better control of the appliqué when applying small pieces to a design.

Project
Tote Bag Square (Reverse Appliqué)

This square, shown in the color section, is reverse appliqué. Four layers of fabric are stitched together, following the outline of the design; then layers of the design are cut out, revealing the colors beneath. After that I used #5 pearl cotton to cord the edges of the sections, and also to embellish the design.

Stitch width: 0–7
Stitch length: 0–1
Needle: #80/12
Feed dogs: uncovered
Presser foot: modified J foot
Tension: normal
Fabric suggestions: lightweight cotton, 9″ squares of yellow, red, and green; two 9″ squares of purple
Thread: purple machine embroidery cotton, wash-away basting thread (optional)
Accessories: dressmaker's carbon, empty ballpoint pen, tracing paper and pencil, glue stick, vanishing marker
Stabilizer: ironed-on freezer paper

Transfer the design in Fig. 4.4 onto tracing paper. Use dressmaker's carbon between the design and the yellow fabric, transferring the design to the fabric. Then layer the squares, beginning with green.

Place one square of purple over the green, then red over the purple, and yellow on top. Pin layers together and baste by machine (use wash-away basting thread and stitch a grid of basting stitches) or by hand to keep the layers from shifting when you stitch in the design.

Next, straight stitch on the lines you've drawn and cut out the layers carefully, following the diagram and color code. If any edges pull out from under your stitching, carefully work glue stick under edges to hold in place while satin stitching.

Place purple #5 pearl cotton under and against the inside left edge of the modified J foot to guide the cord when stitching over it—stitch width 3, stitch length $1\frac{1}{2}$. Cover the edges with corded satin stitches. After the first pass, go back over the cord again—stitch width $3\frac{1}{4}$, stitch length $1\frac{1}{4}$ or between this and $1\frac{1}{2}$ (the fabric must feed smoothly).

Next, use the vanishing marker to draw in the remaining lines. After completing the cording, back the square with the remaining purple fabric, then press the freezer paper on the back and finish the square as shown in Chapter 12.

Blind and blanket stitching

A second way to attach appliqués to a background is with the blind stitch (#3) or blanket stitch (#10). Use the blind-stitch foot. Prepare the appliqué according to Method E (see Fig. 4.3) and use monofilament thread on top. Use your machine's #3 blind stitch or #10 blanket stitch with mirror image, stitch width 2, or adjust for your preference. Adjust length as you wish. If you have cartridge 4, then use stitch #3, narrowed and shortened.

Stitch around the appliqué, letting the short stitches fall just outside the appliqué, with the bite of the widest stitch catching the edge. You can set up the machine to give the look you want. Do you

| blue | green | red | yellow |

Fig. 4.4 Reverse appliqué tote bag square.

want a wide bite? Then set the width to a higher number. The length of the stitch determines the closeness of those two stitches that go up and back, holding the appliqué in place. Find the right length by doing a sample. Use this method to attach patch pockets and to couch down heavy threads and cords. Usually monofilament is used on the top because it is almost invisible.

If you change the monofilament to a thread that will contrast with the fabric, the blanket stitch gives the look of buttonholing by hand.

Edge stitching

To apply fabric with a straight stitch on the edge you will place the appliqué on the background as you did for blanket stitching (if you are working with non-wovens like suedes or felt, don't press the edges under). Use the zipper foot. Set the straight stitch at slightly shorter than 4 and stitch width at 0.

Place the zipper foot directly on the edge of the fabric so stitches fall to slightly within the appliqué. Change foot from left to right position, depending on the direction you're sewing. Stitch around the motif.

Project
Tote Bag Square (Edge-Stitch Appliqué)

This tote bag square shown in the color section uses straight stitching on felt.

Stitch width: 0
Stitch length: 4
Needle: #80/12
Feed dogs: uncovered
Presser foot: zipper

Tension: normal
Fabric suggestion: two 9″ (22.9cm) squares of red felt; scraps of green, yellow, navy blue, orange and white dotted fabrics
Thread: clear monofilament, navy blue machine embroidery thread
Accessories: fusible webbing, Teflon pressing sheet, tracing paper, pencil, white chalk pencil
Stabilizer: tear-away

This simple appliqué is also an example of reverse appliqué. The top fabric is cut out to reveal fabrics underneath.

Press fusible webbing behind one piece of red felt and the scraps of dotted cotton fabrics. The other red fabric will be the background onto which you will appliqué. Within that 9″ red square, draw a square $6\frac{3}{4}″$.

Transfer the design in Fig. 4.5 to tracing paper. Cut out the lettering from the red felt; then the dotted fabrics. Cut slightly larger than the openings.

Place the piece of felt lettering over the other red square. Slip the colored cotton pieces under the lettering. Place a Teflon sheet on top and press in place.

With navy blue thread in your machine, straight stitch around the edges of the cutouts. Trim with a sharp embroidery scissors if needed.

Finish the square as described in Chapter 12.

Project
Tote Bag Square (Straight Stitch)

The next sample also uses straight stitches to hold appliqués in place, but is otherwise quite different. I used red, orange, yellow and green fabric on this one and layered several of the designs. The background is yellow (see color section for finished square).

Fig. 4.5 Design for tote bag square, edge-stitch appliqué technique.

Stitch width: 0
Stitch length: normal
Needle: #90/14
Feed dogs: uncovered
Presser foot: general purpose B
Tension: normal
Fabric suggestion: light or medium-weight
   cottons, two 9″ (22.9cm) squares yellow
   for background and for backing; green,
   red, yellow, orange scraps for circles and
   leaves.
Thread: yellow machine embroidery on top;
   sewing thread the same color on bobbin
Accessories: fusible webbing; Teflon press-
   ing sheet; vanishing marker; tracing pa-
   per, pencil
Stabilizer: ironed-on freezer paper

Apply fusible webbing to all fabrics except the two yellow squares, using the Teflon pressing sheet.

Cut leaf shapes from green fabric and cut half a dozen circles of yellow, red, and orange in sizes as shown (Fig. 4.6). You won't use them all, but you will need many as you design this square yourself.

First, place leaf shapes on the yellow square, then arrange and rearrange the circles over them until you are pleased with the arrangement. Then fuse them in place using Method B for fusible webbing.

With the vanishing marker, draw lines from top to bottom every $\frac{1}{2}$″ (12.7mm) across the square. Starting at the top right corner, straight stitch to the bottom on the first line. Turn and stitch back, bottom to top, on the next line. Continue across the square.

Go back and stitch between those lines. You can use the side of your presser foot as a $\frac{1}{4}$″ (6.4mm) measuring guide. If you wish, make one last pass and stitch between the lines again. There are now straight-stitch lines from top to bottom every $\frac{1}{8}$″ (3.2mm).

Instead of row after row of straight stitches to hold appliqués in place, try nar-row satin stitches or use a double needle. Also try couching down metallics and thick cords. Finish the squares as described in Chapter 12.

Cording edges

Corded edges give appliqués and decorative patches a neat, exact finish. Use the modified J foot (see Chapter 1). You may also try the narrow hemmer or unique zipper foot to guide cord.

When finishing patches, sew the corded edges in two passes. Place the patch over typing paper or tear-away stabilizer. You'll need two pieces—one for each pass—and they must be large enough to extend past the edge of the patch. However, if you don't use stabilizer for the second pass, the cord is wrapped by satin stitches without stabilizer being caught in the stitches.

On the first pass, apply the cord, sewing at a narrower stitch width, and with stitch length slightly longer than the final pass.

The final stitching is done with a close satin stitch, the needle stitching down in the fabric on one side of the cord, but stitching off the cord and fabric on the other side. Leave enough cord at the beginning and end to poke to the back and work into the stitches. Use a needle with a large eye to do this by hand. Or, when you reach the end of the first pass, cut the cord to slightly overlap the start. If you can cut it on an angle, the join will not be noticeable when the second pass is completed.

It is not necessary to cover the entire cord if the cord itself is decorative or is a color that adds to the effect you wish to achieve. When I had to appliqué dozens of velveteen crosses to a woolen ecclesiastical garment, I used a velour cord and an open zigzag, and sewed with a thread the color of the velour. When finished, the velour edges looked like an extension of the velveteen.

*Fig. 4.6 Pattern for tote square. Trace petal shapes and circles of several sizes from $\frac{3}{8}$"
to 2" (9.4mm to 5cm) in diameter. Cut out several circles of each size in different
colors. Use the fusible webbing method to attach geometric shapes to the background
fabric, then stitch evenly spaced lines of straight stitching to hold them.*

Lesson 11. Appliquéing with feed dogs lowered

In this lesson, the appliqués are sewn in place freely; sometimes edges are not completely covered.

Set up your machine by covering the feed dogs, using either a hoop or ironed-on freezer paper, and loosening the top tension slightly.

Blurring

What is blurring? Apply a fabric to another by starting to stitch within the appliqué. Then, following the shape of the appliqué, stitch around and around it, extending the stitching out into the background fabric. It's difficult to tell where one begins and the other leaves off. That is called blurring.

Although the sample here uses trans-

Fig. 4.7 Blurring the edges of appliqués.

parent fabrics, blurring can be done with any type of fabric. I chose to combine blurring with sheers and overlays to show you how to create pictures that look like watercolors. Thread color is usually the same as the appliqué, but never limit yourself. Use other colors as well.

When working with transparent fabrics, use pins to hold the appliqués in place. If possible, hold both in a hoop while sewing. Attach one layer at a time, sewing a straight stitch around the appliqué and then cutting back to the stitching. Blur the edges. Then stretch the next transparent fabric in the hoop, stitch and cut away excess, then blur the edges.

To blur edges, find any point inside the appliqué. Stitch round and round, in ever-widening circles, until the edge of the appliqué is reached. But don't stop. Keep stitching past the edge and into the background. Three transparent circles applied in this way, one overlapping the next, the third overlapping the others, makes a good sample (Fig. 4.7). Possibilities will grow from this one idea: try many colors, overlapping them to make other colors; give depth to a picture by overlapping so that the color becomes more intense as the layers are built up, and recedes where only one layer is used.

Project Flower of Sheers and Overlays

Use this floral piece as a pillow top or slip it into your notebook. To do the flower sample (Fig. 4.8), set up the machine.

Stitch width: 0–widest
Stitch length: 0
Needle: #80/12
Feed dogs: covered
Presser foot: darning foot G
Tension: slightly loosened
Fabric suggestion: 10″ (25.4cm) square medium-weight white fabric for the background; ¼ yard (22.9cm) green transparent fabric; ⅛ yard (11.4cm) pink transparent fabric; 12″ (30.5cm) square off-white bridal veiling
Threads: machine embroidery in yellow, green, and pink
Accessories: 7″ (17.8cm) spring hoop
Stabilizer: tear-away

Use the circle and leaf shape to make the patterns. Cut out several dozen 1″ (2.5cm) circles in pink transparent fabric. Also cut the same number of 2″ (5.1cm) long leaf shapes from green transparent fabric. Patterns are provided in Fig. 4.9. You may not use all of these petals and leaves: It will depend upon how much they are overlapped and how large an area you're covering with the design.

Arrange and overlap the leaves in a circle on the background fabric, points toward the center. Plan so they will fit within the hoop, keeping the leaves at least an inch (2.5cm) inside. If the presser foot gets too close to the edge, it will be difficult to sew around the appliqués without hitting the darning foot on the hoop.

Lay down the circles of color for the flower head, starting in the middle of the leaves. New colors pop out for the leaves and petals as you overlap, arrange and rearrange. Leave the center of the flower open. Don't pin down any of these small pieces.

After completing the arrangement of the sheers and overlays, cover with the piece of bridal veil to help hold them all in place. Pin the veiling down in several places near the center of the flower and at the edges of the fabric. Lift this carefully from the table and place it in a hoop. Slip stabilizer under it.

Fig. 4.8 Use bridal veiling to hold small pieces of appliqué fabric in place.

Fig. 4.9 Patterns for the flower design.

71

Start by sewing around the petals of the flower. Use pink thread on the top, green thread on the bobbin. Stitch the petals very freely. Bring the stitching out past them, or inside, or make stitched circles between them. Stitch circles within circles.

Then change the top thread to green. Stitch around the leaves in the same free-flowing way. Go up the centers and down, stitching in veins on some and leaving others without.

Now only the center is left to stitch. Change the top thread to yellow and set stitch width to the widest zigzag, stitch length 0. Anchor your threads in the center of the flower. Stitch in the same spot at least a dozen times to build up a nubby "seed" (see Fig. 3.2). Anchor the threads again. Lift the presser foot and move to another place. Do another seed. There's no need to clip threads until all the seeds are completed. Keep building up the nubs and moving your needle from one place to the next until the flower center is to your liking. Then clip the threads between the zigzag areas.

Change the top thread back to green. Set stitch width back to 0. Sew around the seeds. Go from one to another until all are outlined. When the picture is complete, take it out of the hoop. Most of the stabilizer will drop away; the rest can be pulled off (or left on, since it won't show).

The bridal veil can be left as is. However, I often clip out areas to create color changes.

Scribbling

Scribbling is like darning over appliqués, but you will use both straight and zigzag stitches. It's a good way to lay in big areas of color without having to cover the areas with heavy embroidery.

The appliqué picture in Fig. 4.10 was placed on the outside of a tote bag. Use the patterns in Fig. 4.11 as a guide, enlarging or reducing to fit your purpose.

Stitch width: varies
Stitch length: 0
Needle: #90/14
Feed dogs: covered
Presser foot: darning foot G
Tension: slightly loosened
Fabric suggestion: medium-weight cotton
Thread: machine embroidery on top; sewing

Fig. 4.10 This is part of a design that has been appliquéd to a tote bag, using free-machining to hold the appliqués in place.

Fig. 4.11 Use these patterns to create one element of the design shown in Fig. 4.10.

or darning thread on bobbin
Accessories: glue stick
Stabilizer: ironed-on freezer paper

Apply the appliqués with a dab of glue stick and begin to stitch the edges down freely with either a straight or a zigzag stitch. Sew freely over the entire appliqué first to anchor it before embroidering the designs. Stitch inside and over the edges

of the appliqués. If you can live with raw edges, then don't be too particular about covering them exactly. Here is a good place to blur edges. Add to the design by laying in different colors with the same free machining. Add as much stitching as you wish, but don't cover the entire appliqué, as that would defeat the purpose. Let most of the color show through. It's like sketching with colored pencils.

Stitching Carrickmacross

Carrickmacross is an Irish lace made with appliqués of batiste. Tiny pops, or eyelets, are embroidered in the fine hexagonal net which is used as the ground, and it has a picot edge. If hand done, this type of lace is very fragile, but our machine version is both beautiful and sturdy.

Project
Carrickmacross Doily

Instead of batiste, we'll use organdy. I've used a polyester for the veiling, so my fabric will be the same. It will be white on white, typical of Carrickmacross lace (Fig. 4.12).

Stitch width: 0
Stitch length: 0
Needle: #70/10
Feed dogs: covered
Presser foot: darning foot G
Tension: slightly loosened
Fabric suggestion: white polyester organdy; fine white polyester hexagonal veiling
Thread: white cotton machine embroidery thread
Accessories: 9″ (22.9cm) hoop, large darning needle, water-erasable pen, white opaque marker
Stabilizer: water-soluble

Place water-soluble stabilizer in the hoop. Trace the design in Fig. 4.13, using the white opaque marker. Slip the veiling underneath the organdy and put them both into the hoop over the water-soluble stabilizer.

Set up your machine for free embroidery. Don't anchor stitches—it isn't necessary, as you will be stitching around each motif several times. Begin by stitching around each flower and around each leaf

three times. Stitch twice around the centers of the flowers.

It is easy to plot the course of your needle so that you can go from one flower to the next when you stitch. When you stitch the centers, lift up the presser foot and move from one place to another. Stitch around the edge three times, and around the inside edge twice.

To add pops to the centers of the flowers, stitch three times around each tiny center circle. With the darning needle, poke through the center of each circle. Set your machine to stitch width 2. Zigzag around each circle by letting the needle stitch into the center on one swing and over your three lines of stitching on the other. Rotate the hoop slowly as you stitch the eyelet. You will be almost hand-walking the machine in order to satin stitch closely around the tiny circle.

When finished, take the design out of the hoop and cut out all the areas that are to be free of organdy, but don't cut around the edge of the doily yet. Use sharp, fine-pointed scissors when cutting out the fabric. It helps to lift areas away from the net with the point of a seam ripper and then clip. Also clip unnecessary threads and thread ends.

Should you cut the net, don't panic. Put it back under the needle, sew a few lines of straight stitching over the cut, blending it into the other stitches already there. If the cut is too large, carefully remove the whole section and place another piece of veiling underneath (be sure to arrange the veiling so it matches the direction of the veil in the hoop). Stitch around the damaged area to attach the patch. Cut the veil back to the stitching lines.

Put the work back in the hoop and finish the flower centers by stitching from the inside line up to the center pop, then back down again. Stitch a small blob of thread there by stitching in a circle to build up a tiny pindot. Travel along the inside line to the next spot. Stitch to the center and

Fig. 4.12 Appliquéd lace (Carrickmacross), is made quickly using organdy and fine hexagonal net.

back to the inside line again. Make another dot, then continue on to the next. Continue like this until all the flower centers have been completed.

Now remove the embroidery from the hoop. Cut back on the net only, leaving the organdy and stabilizer. Put the lace back in the hoop. With a water-erasable pen, mark small dots every ⅛″ (3.2mm) along the edge to use as a guide for the picots.

Following the edge, stitch around each dot three times, making small loops on top of each other at each mark.

Again, take the embroidery out of the hoop and cut away the stabilizer and the organdy up to the picots—including the few threads of fabric that remain between each picot. Wash the remaining stabilizer and blue pen marks out of the fabric.

What we've made is a small doily but,

Fig. 4.13 The pattern for appliquéd lace.

if you're like me, you are not big on small doilies. This is a fast technique, so think big. Try it for the edge of a bridal veil or for the bodice and puffed sleeves of the wedding dress itself. Now that's what I call a long-cut, but definitely worth it.

Layering transparent fabrics

Shadow work is my favorite. I love the painterly effects of combining colors and toning down with whites. It's done using sheers and overlays. In the picture made in the following project, the color does not come from a colored cotton fabric layered between organdies; instead, these flowers are created only from transparent fabrics.

Project
Shadow Work
Picture

In this project, I switch from feed dogs up to feed dogs lowered or covered, but most of the stitching is done freely, so I've put it in this lesson. The design in Fig. 4.14 will give you an idea of what can be done with only white, mauve and green organza.

Stitch width: 0–4
Stitch length: 0–1½
Needle: #70/10
Feed dogs: covered, uncovered
Presser foot: J foot, darning foot G
Tension: slightly loosened
Fabric: white, mauve, and green organza
Thread: green machine embroidery
Accessories: spring hoop; water-erasable marker
Stabilizer: water-soluble

Place the white organza over the design in Fig. 4.15 and trace it off with a water-erasable marker. Layer two mauves behind each flower on the white organza and pin them in place. Put this in a hoop.

With the machine set for free machining, without anchoring the threads, straight stitch around the flowers twice. Lift the needle and go to the flower centers. Stitch twice around each center, also: The lines should be next to each other, not on top of each other. Cut back to the stitching around the outside edge, but not too close.

Place the green organza behind the leaf

Fig. 4.14 Layers of transparent fabrics give a painterly effect to shadow work.

areas and stitch in place with two lines of stitching. Cut back to the stitching at the edges.

Set up your machine for normal sewing. Uncover the feed dogs and use the J foot, stitch width 4, stitch length 1½ or a setting that will produce a smooth satin stitch. Sew around the flowers and leaves. Be careful: sew too closely and the stitches will cut the fabric.

From the front of your picture, cut the white organza from one flower, the white and one mauve layer from another. Turn the hoop over. Cut out one layer of mauve from the back on another. Or from the back, cut out both layers of color, leaving only the white organdy and the flower center intact. Can you imagine the combinations and shades of mauve you can create?

Fig. 4.15 Shadow work design.

The large leaf is divided into four sections. In the first section, cut out the top white layer and place a layer of green behind the remaining green layer to darken it. In the second area, cut out the white and leave just green. In the third, place white behind the section to make it three layers. The fourth is left as is, the white in front of the green.

Once you have finished the flowers and leaves, go back to the flower centers and blur them out by stitching spirals from the centers out to the edges. Or start at the edges and travel to the outside of the flowers. Leave some flowers with only the first stitching around the center.

Satin stitches should be sewn through at least two layers of fabric. Ordinarily, we'd add stabilizer, but tear-away could leave specks in the fabric that might show through. To prevent this, use green organza as a backing for the stems. The lines are satin stitched, then the stabilizing organza is cut back to the stitching.

Finish up with straight stitching. Set up again for free machining. Using water-soluble stabilizer behind the fabric, set the machine on stitch width 0, stitch length 0, to sew in the accent lines.

If one of the fabrics has pulled away from the satin stitches, don't give up. Layer a piece of transparent fabric underneath and stitch it on. Then cut away the original one. Or put a piece of organza underneath, use straight stitching or zigzags to sew in some lines, and pretend you wanted it that way. On the flowers, too: If by mistake you cut through two layers instead of one, leave it or layer something behind it. Sometimes blurring out more lines of stitching will attach and hide any mistakes.

Keep the stitching light and airy, with no wide satin stitches. There should be more fabric showing than stitching. When finished, wash out the stabilizer and pen marks.

This type of shadow work is quite fragile and I suggest using it for pictures or window hangings, rather than for clothing.

Project Stitching Three-dimensional Appliqués

One of the prettiest dresses I've ever seen was at a fraternity dance back when we thought we had to wear yards of tulle and gobs of ruffles. This dress was a beautiful white organdy exception. Over the entire skirt were scattered lavender and peach pansy appliqués of organdy. They were attached only at the centers. It was a plain dress except for this scattering of flowers.

Detached appliqués do not have to have a heavy satin stitch edge, and I think you'll agree that straight stitching on fine fabric is easier and more beautiful. After all, that was a long time ago and I've never forgotten that dress.

Stitch width: 0
Stitch length: 0
Needle position: center
Needle: #60/8 or #70/10
Feed dogs: covered
Presser foot: darning foot G or no presser foot, tailor-tacking foot (optional)
Tension: loosened
Fabric suggestion: mauve and green organdy
Thread: machine embroidery thread to match
Accessories: spring hoop; water-erasable marker
Stabilizer: water-soluble type

Place a layer of water-soluble stabilizer between two layers of mauve organdy. Clip this into the spring hoop. Draw the design in Fig. 4.17 on it with a water-erasable marker. You will copy both petal designs.

Fig. 4.16 Three-dimensional appliqué design.

The small sample is done in pieces and combined later (Fig. 4.16).

Stitch three times around the edges with a straight stitch. Lines should be close together but not on top of each other. Use a colored thread that matches or is a shade darker than the fabric. Cut out the petals close to the stitching, but not too close.

The leaves should be worked in the same way on green organdy. Stitch only straight stitches as you follow the pattern. Go into the centers and stitch the veins as well. Cut out the leaves.

Place the flower petals on top of each other—stagger them so the petals underneath are not hidden by the top layer. Place this over the leaves and stitch them together with mauve thread by following the stitching in the center of the petals. You

may go a step further and fringe the center. Using the tailor tacking foot, green thread, stitch width 2 and stitch length almost 0, stitch in several places in the center of the flower. If you don't have a tailor tacking foot, then add several green satin stitch blobs in the center of the flower, stitch width 7. Clip through the centers to fringe them if you wish. Finish by holding the flower under the faucet and rinsing out some, but not all, of the stabilizer. Shape the flower and leaves carefully and let them dry. They will be stiff, as if heavily starched, and will retain their shapes. How can you use these three-dimensional appliqués? Add a band of them to a bodice of Carrickmacross lace. Make an utterly fake corsage or a flowered hat. Add the flower to a cord for a necklace.

Fig. 4.17 Pattern pieces for floral 3-D appliqué.

Helpful hints for appliqué

If an appliqué bubbles, fix it by taking it out of the hoop and nicking the base fabric beneath the appliqué, which will then allow the base to lay flat.

Or slit the back a bit and fill the appliqué area with cotton. This is called trapunto. Hand whip the slit closed. Machine stitch on top of the appliqué to add to the design and hold the batting in place.

Another way to keep appliqué puckers from showing is to hide them by hand or machine embroidering over the appliqué.

When layering net, there is sometimes a moiré look to it that spoils the effect of your picture. To eliminate it, change the direction of one of the layers.

Don't limit yourself to fabric appliqués; thread appliqués are also effective. Work spider webs in another fabric, cut them out, and apply.

Work lace in space inside a small ring. Apply it to a background by free machining all around the inside edge of the ring. Then cut the ring from the lace.

Check out Lesson 6 on beads, baubles, and shishas.

Do pulled and drawn threads with the machine on one fabric and attach them to another background.

CHAPTER **5**

Stitching Across Open Spaces

- Lesson 12. Cutwork and eyelets
- Lesson 13. Free-machined needlelace
- Lesson 14. Battenberg lace
- Lesson 15. Hemstitching
- Lesson 16. Stitching in rings
- Lesson 17. Making Alençon lace

People have been stitching in space for a hundred years; you can, too. However, if you are nervous about doing it, stitching on water-soluble stabilizer usually produces the same effects with sometimes better results. Water-soluble stabilizer is so thin and pliable that placing multiple layers of it in a hoop, along with fabric, is no problem. Another reason I am sold on it is that, once the design is drawn on the stabilizer, it can be stitched exactly, as if stitching on fabric. That isn't possible when actually stitching in space. I use it for cutwork because it holds the cut edges in place while I stitch them and sometimes I use it on both sides of the fabric to give it even more stability.

I use stabilizer when stitching in rings, too. It keeps threads in place until they are anchored. There is no problem with slipping, as often happens when stitching in space. Practice on water-soluble stabilizer, but if your machine is capable of it, graduate to open space and try that. There are occasions for both techniques.

This chapter includes cutwork, stitching in rings, creating needlelace, and stitching both Battenberg and Alençon laces. Hemstitching is included, as well. Be sure to keep all your samples in your notebook. You may not use an idea today or tomorrow, but maybe next year you'll refer back to your notebook and find just what you're looking for to make a special gift, or welcome a new baby. My notebook is especially valuable when I want to find machine settings for a technique I haven't used in weeks. No matter how well you know your machine, you can't remember everything.

Lesson 12. Cutwork and eyelets

Cutwork

Cutwork is the forerunner of all needlemade laces. It was common as early as the sixteenth century. In handmade cutwork, part of the background fabric is cut away and threads are stretched from one side of the open area to the other. Bars of buttonhole stitches are worked over the stretched threads and the cut edges. Cutwork can be done by machine using satin stitches in place of buttonhole stitches.

Project
Cutwork
Needlecase

When I wanted to do a cutwork project on the machine without dedicating my life to a large, time-consuming sailor collar or tablecloth, I found that the needlecase in Fig. 5.1 was exactly the right size. The single design can be used as a repeat pattern and it can be combined with embroidery, appliqué or shadow work.

I traced the pattern (Fig. 5.2) on paper two different times. On one pattern I added lines where I wanted the thread bars, called "brides," to be.

Before you begin this or any project, practice, using the same fabric, needle and threads, stitch settings and stabilizers you will use on your finished piece. For this design, I practiced turning corners and satin stitching curves, as well as filling spaces with thread bars.

Cutwork is not usually backed by anything, but on this needlecase you can see that it is a necessity.

Stitch width: 0–4
Stitch length: 0 to satin stitch
Needle: #80/12
Feed dogs: covered or uncovered
Presser foot: darning foot, open J foot
Tension: slightly loosened
Fabric suggestion: closely woven linen or kettlecloth
Thread: machine embroidery
Accessories: spring hoop; tracing paper, small, sharp embroidery scissors; pencil, water-erasable marker, and permanent white marker
Stabilizer: water-soluble

Place the pattern without the thread bars on the back of the fabric and slip them both into a hoop. The topside of the fabric will be against the machine. Lower or cover the feed dogs and take the presser foot off.

Fig. 5.1 The cutwork design on this needlecase can be used once, or as a repeat pattern.

Straight stitch around the outlines of the design two times with the same thread you'll use for the satin stitching. (Do not stitch the bars at this time.)

Take the fabric out of the hoop and peel off the pattern. Cut out the larger area. Put a piece of stabilizer over the topside and one underneath the fabric, and place all three layers in the hoop. Slip the second pattern under the hoop. With a permanent white marker, trace the bars on the top stabilizer. Put the pattern aside until later.

With stitch width set to 0, freely stitch in the bars. Do the long, middle branching line first. Anchor the thread at the top by sewing in one place a few stitches, make

Fig. 5.2 Cutwork pattern to copy.

a pass from top to bottom and then back again. As you sew from the bottom on that second pass, stitch the branches out and back as well.

Change to stitch width 3. Stitch the first pass from top to bottom, moving the hoop quite quickly (remember the branches). Then, stitch back up from the bottom: This time move your hoop slowly. The stitches will be closer together. Remember, you control this by how fast you move the hoop. The stitches will look like satin stitches in space. Anchor each branch by sewing at 0 width into the fabric just beyond the stay-stitching. Zigzag to the top and anchor the thread.

Stitch the short bars at each side next. Anchor the threads at the top of the first bar, just beyond the two rows of straight stitching. Sew straight stitches across to the other side, anchor the threads again, and come back on the same line. Then begin zigzagging back across these threads with a 3 stitch width. When you reach the other side, stop, turn the width to 0 and follow the stay-stitch line to the next bar position. Sew across, back, and then zigzag as you did the first one. Complete all the brides on each side.

Cut out all three smaller shapes that are left in the design. Try to do this without cutting through the stabilizer on the back, but if you clip it, you can always slide another piece of stabilizer underneath. Put another piece of stabilizer on top and place all layers in the hoop. Using your pattern again behind the hoop, draw the bars on the stabilizer. Proceed with these branched bars as you did with the large cutout.

When you have finished all the bars, change the machine settings. Raise the feed dogs and set the machine on stitch width 4. Use the open J foot. Begin sewing at the point of the heart. Anchor the threads and proceed clockwise. To fill in the curves smoothly, stop with the needle down on the right side, lift the presser-foot lever, pivot the hoop, lower the presser foot, and stitch again. Repeat several times when negotiating curves.

Satin stitch around each cutout. Carefully pull away the stabilizer and rinse out any remaining pieces. Press the embroidery from the back.

Eyelets

I've used eyelets in my embroideries, clumping them together for a center of interest, and one of my teachers uses them to decorate lovely bed linens. If you have Sew Ware cartridge 4, use #19. By using the single pattern button, you will be able to place these where you wish. When finished stitching, poke out centers with awl or large darning needle.

Lesson 13. Free-machined needlelace

The terms *cutwork, lacy spiderwebs,* and *openwork* all describe a machine stitchery technique far removed from darning holes in socks or shredded elbows. But, like darning, they do entail stitching across open spaces.

Stitch width: 0
Stitch length: 0
Needle: #80/12
Feed dogs: covered
Presser foot: darning G or no presser foot
Tension: normal
Fabric suggestions: any weight
Thread: one color, machine embroidery or polyester
Accessories: 6″ (15.2cm) wrapped wooden hoop; water-soluble stabilizer (optional)

Openwork is done in a hoop with the fabric stretched tightly. Place the hoop, fabric side down, on the machine bed. Draw a circle on the fabric: Circles are easier to control than the squares, crescents and paisley shapes you may want to try later.

Start stitching at the edge of the circle by bringing the bobbin thread to the top. Anchor the threads by sewing a few stitches in one spot. Guide the hoop slowly as you stitch around the circle three times (Fig. 5.3A). Take the hoop off the machine and, without removing the fabric from it, cut out the circle close to the stitches. If you have opted to use water-soluble stabilizer, now is the time to slip it into the hoop under your fabric. Replace the hoop and secure the threads once again at the edge of the hole.

Now you will begin to lay in a network of spokelike threads across the space. To do this, begin by stitching across from one side of the hole to the other side. Move the hoop slowly, but run the machine moderately fast to strengthen and put a tighter twist on the spoke. When your needle enters the fabric again, move along the circle to another spot, secure threads, and sew directly across the hole again. Continue in this manner until you have as many spokes as you wish. On the last pass, go up to the center and backstitch right at the center of the wheel to strengthen the web. Starting at that backstitch, fill in the spokes by sewing in ever-widening circles around the center until the "but-

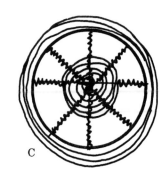

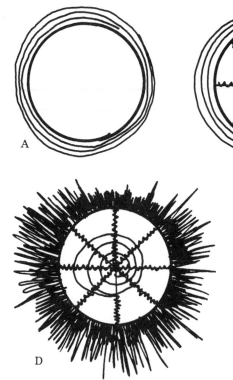

Fig. 5.3 Making needlelace. A. First sew around a circle three times. B. Cut out the center, embroider across the hole, creating spokes. C. Add circles of stitches around the center. D. Stitch radiating lines over the edge, into the fabric.

ton" is the size you wish it to be (Fig. 5.3C). Sew a few stitches into the button to lock the thread in place and again move to the outside to anchor the threads and complete that spoke.

Would you like a lacier filling? Sew one backstitch over each spoke after crossing it as you stitch around the center. This keeps the threads from slipping to the center. Travel around and around in wider circles till you reach the edge of the hole. Also, if using water-soluble stabilizer, the circles of thread stay in one place, rather than traveling to the center even after washing out the stabilizer.

Although there are as many ways to finish off the edges of the spaces as there are ways to fill them with stitches, one of the softest looks is accomplished by straight stitching from the edge of the hole, out past it and back again, moving the hoop back and forth as if stitching sun rays. You can also use the widest zigzag and accomplish the same rays. Or, satin stitch around the edge and combine that with other embroidery. These are only a few ideas; try some of your own.

If you have used stabilizer, place your embroidery under a faucet and wash it out when your work is completed.

Create your own samples by placing a piece of medium-weight cotton in a hoop and drawing several circles on it. Stitch around one circle three times. Cut out the center. Stitch a spider web in the hole and finish it off on the edges. Go to the next circle and stitch both the center and the edges in a different way from your first sample. Then do another and another until you have many needlelace samples for your notebook. Or back them with another fabric as squares for your tote bag.

Lesson 14. Battenberg lace

Battenberg lace was popular in the late 1800s. Straight, machine-made tape was shaped into a design and basted to stiff paper. Then the open spaces were filled with bars and embroidery stitches, which held the tape in shape. After the stitchery was completed, the paper was removed and the Battenberg lace could be used to decorate dresses, curtains or linens.

Project
Small Lace
Motif

This lesson will teach you how to make a small piece of Battenberg (Fig. 5.4). From there, you can go on to bigger projects, but let's see if you like Battenberg lacemaking by machine.

There is a variety of white, off-white, gold, and silver Battenberg tape to choose from. It's available by mail-order (see Sources of Supplies) and from some needlework shops.

Should you create your own design, choose a tape that doesn't overpower the pattern. The one I used is $\frac{1}{4}''$ (6.3mm) wide. On each side of the tape is a thread that is thicker than the others. Pull gently to curve the tape into the shape you want.

Place 2 pieces of water-soluble stabilizer in a 7" spring hoop, then over the design in Fig. 5.5 and trace the outline with a white permanent marking pen. Place this on a flat surface. This design is done with only two pieces of tape so there are only four joins. Measure the length you'll need.

Fig. 5.4 Battenberg is embroidered after narrow tape has been shaped into a design.

Before I begin to shape the tape, I tie an overhand knot in the thick threads at one end. Then at the other end, I pull on the threads and gather up the whole length of tape. I begin working from the knotted end. Shaping the gathered tape goes quickly, no matter which thread I pull, when I begin this way.

Leave enough tape at the beginning to stretch across under the tape that crosses it (Fig. 5.5). Pull up the thread on the tape, pinning in the shape on the stabilizer as you go or using glue stick to temporarily hold it in place. Hide the ends by stretching the tape underneath the tape that crosses it. I find it more satisfactory to baste the design to the stabilizer by hand than by machine, using wash-away bast-

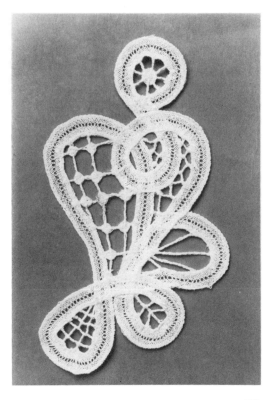

Fig. 5.5 Battenberg pattern.

ing thread, after I've pinned and glued the tape in shape.

When the tape is in place, put the hoop over the pattern again. Draw in the stitching lines with a white opaque marker. Extend them by drawing dots onto the tape with a water-erasable pen. At times the stabilizer may be cut out and these dots can be used for reference.

Set up your machine for free embroidery.

Stitch width: 0–3
Stitch length: 0
Needle: #70/10
Feed dogs: covered
Presser foot: darning foot G or no foot
Tension: normal
Thread: wash-away basting thread; #50 white machine embroidery
Accessories: 7″ (17.8cm) spring hoop; water-erasable pen and white permanent marker; white Battenberg tape; glue stick; dressmaker's pins
Stabilizer: water-soluble, large enough for hoop (2 pieces)

Before you begin, set your machine to stitch width 3, so when you change from straight stitch to zigzag, all you have to do is push the zigzag button, then push the stitch width button. Because you've dialed it to 3, you can easily change back and forth from straight stitch to the correct zigzag width.

Start by straight stitching around both edges of the tape with machine embroidery thread to prevent the tape from curling. When you come to a place that joins tape to tape, stitch across to the other side with a narrow zigzag. At the tape ends, zigzag over the side of the top tape, also enclosing the cut end in zigzag stitches. (Clip back the tape underneath to the zigzag stitches and dot the threads with Fraycheck when all your stitching is completed). After the design is attached, cut out the stabilizer in the openings, one at a time, as you stitch them. Be sure your machine can stitch without fabric under the needle. If it can't, then do not cut out the stabilizer. With your machine set up for free embroidery, stitch one long pass from the point at the bottom of the large area at center left (Fig. 5.6), up to the center top. Stitch back over this thread for a second pass, then back with zigzag stitch width 3. Follow the illustration; stitch long bars on each side of the middle bar. Follow the tape around to stitch in the horizontal

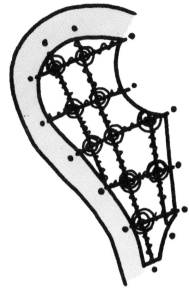

Fig. 5.6 In the large loop at the left, first a grid is stitched, then circles are stitched around the crossed threads, as indicated.

bars. Start at top left and straight stitch across, back and then across with zigzag stitches. To do these zigzags, use a straight stitch (stitch width 0, stitch length 0) and move the hoop back and forth to create a zigzag stitch. When you get to an intersection, stitch in a small circle to make a tiny button. Then move to the next by straight zigzagging, and stitch a button in the intersection. Continue on in this manner until this section is completed.

The same grid design, without the buttons, is done in the bottom left motif (Fig. 5.7).

To do the leaf shape at lower right, first cut out the stabilizer if your machine will stitch across open space. Stitch from the center bottom up to the top and back again. See detail in Fig. 5.8. Zigzag (stitch width 3) back down again. Following the side of the tape with straight stitches, stitch to the first branch and then to the center.

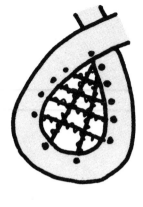

Fig. 5.7 Use the same technique for the small loop at the bottom, but omit the circles of stitches.

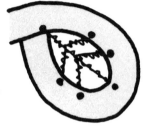

Fig. 5.8 Leaf shapes are filled in with veins.

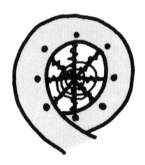

Fig. 5.9 Circles are stitched very closely together in the center of each spider web.

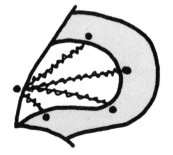

Fig. 5.10 Stitch four brides in a fan shape.

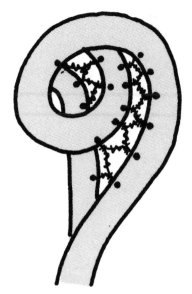

Fig. 5.11 Zigzag over brides to fill in last section of lace.

Take a stitch backward to anchor, then stitch to the other side and back with straight stitches. Zigzag back. Go down to the next branch. Stitch down to the center, anchor, and go up to the other side. Continue in this manner until you finish the last one.

To make the spiderwebs (Fig. 5.9), cut out the stabilizer or, again, leave it in place, then lay in all your threads and zigzag over all of them except for one. Zigzag to the center of this one and begin straight stitching a circle of stitches as you did the buttons. Finish this section by zigzagging out to the tape, finishing the last spoke as you do.

The section above the leaf shape is done simply with three long bars stretching from one side to the curve of the tape (see Fig. 5.10).

Cut out the stabilizer or leave it in the last two areas (see detail in Fig. 5.11). Straight stitch from one side of the tape to the other across one of the areas, and back; then zigzag back at stitch width 3. At the point where the stitches join the fabric, straight stitch into the tape, then leave it again, zigzagging several stitches over both threads to hold them together. Then travel on over the next thread. Stitch down to the tape, anchor, then back over both threads with a few stitches before zigzagging over the next thread to the other side of the tape. Complete both of the areas this way.

After the lace is stitched, wash out the stabilizer and place the Battenberg between layers of toweling to press.

Lesson 15. Hemstitching

Hemstitching is used on garments and table linens whenever a delicate, feminine look is desired. The technique looks complicated and difficult, but it is surprisingly easy to accomplish using both double- and single-winged needles.

Before you begin to stitch the bonnet, practice on two layers of cotton organdy. Set up your machine.

Stitch width: 0 to no wider than the throat plate opening when using a double needle (use double needle button, if available)
Stitch length: varies
Needle: single and double hemstitching needles; double needles
Feed dogs: uncovered
Presser foot: standard J foot, open J foot
Tension: tightened slightly
Fabric: crisp fabric, such as organdy or linen
Thread: cotton machine embroidery

To thread two needles, follow instructions in the basic manual for your machine. Remember to always thread your machine with the presser foot up.

Practice hemstitching by using these stitches: #2, #3, #10, #14, #22. But don't limit yourself to these—try others, also. If you have cartridge 4, use stitches #2, #3, #8, #9. Start with the single-winged needle and use a zigzag. Stitch a row of hemstitching. At the end of the first run, leave the needle in the hole at left, turn and return, poking into the same holes as on the first run.

You can make an all-over design, covering a large area with hemstitches. This is usually worked on the bias, then appliquéd to something else.

Now practice with the double hemstitch needle. Set up your machine in this way:

Stitch width: double needle button
Stitch length: normal
Tension: tightened (auto + 2)
Feed dogs: uncovered
Presser foot: open J foot

Make one pass, ending to the left. Lift the presser foot, turn the fabric and stitch the second pass. The large needle again stitches into the same hole it stitched on the first pass. As it does, the fabric is pulled together, leaving open holes or hemstitches.

Turn your hemstitching into shadow work as well. Cut back the piece of organdy underneath, clipping out both sides of the double fabric on either side of the hemstitches, leaving the hemstitched area with two layers of fabric.

Project
Infant's Bonnet

I've combined hemstitching with built-in stitches and double needles to make the infant's bonnet shown in Fig. 5.12. Also included is a line of ribbon sewing. This

91

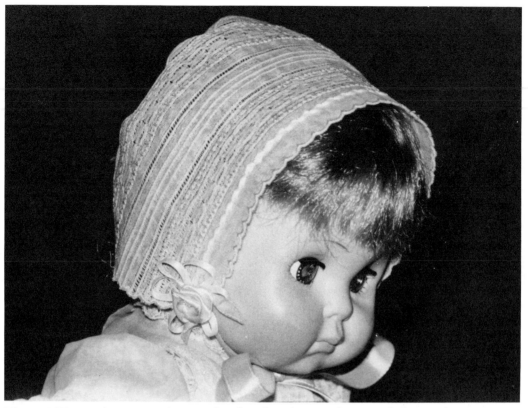

Fig. 5.12 Hemstitching, pintucking, and embroidery decorate the organdy bonnet for an infant or a doll.

can be made in the time it would take you to shop for a baby gift.

Nora Lou Kampe of LaGrange, Illinois, made this bonnet using embroidered eyelet fabric with a scalloped border—a way to make a baby gift in no more than an hour's time. I used her bonnet idea, but took the long-cut and embroidered the bonnet myself; it fits a newborn and you could make one for a christening. A gown can be done in the same hemstitching technique.

The finished bonnet is $13'' \times 5\frac{3}{4}''$ (33.0cm $\times$ 14.6cm). Add to both width and length if you're adapting it for an older baby.

Stitch width: varies
Stitch length: varies
Needle: 1.6mm twin needle; single and double hemstitching needles
Feed dogs: uncovered
Presser foot: standard J foot or open J foot
Tension: normal
Fabric suggestion: white cotton organdy
Thread: light-blue, fine machine-embroidery thread; #5 light-blue pearl cotton; white cordonnet
Other supplies: pearl bead (optional); $\frac{1}{8}''$ (3.2mm) double-faced satin ribbon, approximately 1 yard (91.4cm); $\frac{1}{4}''$ (6.3mm)

double-faced satin ribbon, ½ yard (45.7cm); ½″ (12.7mm) double-faced satin ribbon, approximately 1½ yards (137cm)

Begin with two pieces of organdy, each 18″ × 9″ (45.7cm × 22.9cm). I start with a much larger area than I need because I practice on the margin—running the decorative stitches so they will match when I do a mirror image. If your machine does a mirror image with a push of a button, add the fabric anyway to cut off later for your notebook.

Wash and iron the organdy. Mark the top fabric lengthwise, using a water-erasable marker (Fig. 5.13). Start by marking lines 1″ (2.5cm) apart from the front edge. Use a T-square for accuracy. Draw six lines. Then mark a line ½″ (12.7mm) from the last line, and another ½″ (12.7mm) from that one; 7″ × 13″ (17.8cm × 33.0cm) is marked. Pin the two pieces of fabric together at the top of the lines.

Once you have learned how to hemstitch, the decoration is up to you. The following is only a suggestion: Thread the double-wing needle with light-blue thread. The first line of hemstitches are stitched 1″ (2.5cm) from the front edge. Use stitch #22 or use cartridge 4, stitch #3 or #17. Use the blue line as your guide and stitch on top of it. When you reach the end, turn

and go back, cutting into the same hole you stitched on the first run. Sew slowly. If the needle does not hit exactly in the right place, stop and move the fabric by one or two threads. Continue.

Spread the fabric apart. The pintucking is done between the blue lines on the top piece only.

Change to the 1.6mm double needle. Use the open J foot if you have one, light-blue #5 pearl cotton, feed dogs uncovered, stitch length at standard setting. Place pearl cotton under the fabric and between the double needles. This can be done easily with a dental floss loop (Fig. 3.19). Watch and guide the blue pearl between the needles. It feeds through well and you can see it through the one layer of organdy.

There are three lines of pintucking, so stitch the first line exactly in the middle, between the blue marker lines. Stitch the others on either side of this one.

If you wish, stitch all four groups of pintucks between the blue lines at one time, then go back, change to the hemstitching needle, and continue to hemstitch on the blue lines with the stitches you've chosen. Remember, when you pintuck, work on one layer of fabric, but hemstitch on both layers.

Complete 4½″ (11.4cm) of the bonnet (shaded area on Fig. 5.13) by filling in the

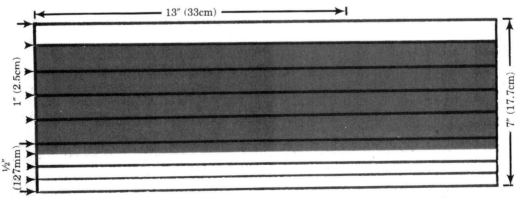

Fig. 5.13 The shaded area of the diagram indicates the portions to be embroidered.

empty spaces between the hemstitched patterns and the pintucks. Use the open effect of the single-wing needle, sewing in a straight line. Remember to come back again, punching holes in the same places where the first ones were.

Should you still want more decoration, use a built-in stitch of your choice. When you have decorated the fabric enough, straight stitch around the edge of the bonnet rectangle. Cut back to the stitching line. Put the piece you've practiced on into your notebook.

Fold the bonnet rectangle in half (Fig. 5.14). The fold will be the top of the bonnet. Pin the fabric together, matching decorative stitches so it is exact. Round off the front corners where the rosettes will be sewn (see Fig. 5.12). Open up and stitch $\frac{1}{8}''$ (3.2mm) in from the edges of the bottom and front.

Change to crescent stitch #15 or satin stitch to stitch the front edge and the sides of the bonnet. Trim edges if you used the crescent stitch. Be careful not to clip into your stitches.

Cord the edge with the modified J foot if you satin stitch the edge. Use #80/11 needle, stitch width 3 or 4, stitch length 1 (or whatever works best for you to cover cord smoothly). Do a sample first.

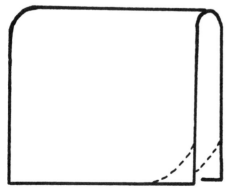

Fig. 5.14 When stitching is completed, fold the rectangle in half and round off the front corners, as shown.

Stitch down on the line $\frac{1}{2}''$ (12.7mm) from the edge (back of bonnet) and stitch another $\frac{1}{2}''$ (12.7mm) from that line. Fold the back under $\frac{1}{2}''$ (12.7mm), then again another $\frac{1}{2}''$ (12.7mm). Stitch across the first fold to make the ribbon casing.

Next, wind the bobbin with $\frac{1}{8}''$ (3.2mm) double-faced satin ribbon. Tape the end onto the bobbin and wind by hand. Bypass the tension spring. Insert the bobbin into the machine and bring the ribbon to the top (see Fig. 3.20). Pull out at least 8" (20.3cm) of ribbon before beginning to sew. Set the machine on basting #6 or a stitch length 7. Experiment first on a sample piece.

Place the bonnet front on the bed of the machine. The ribbon will be stitched with the general purpose B foot from underneath, $\frac{1}{2}''$ (12.7mm) from the front edge. When you finish stitching, pull out 8" (20.3cm) of ribbon and cut off.

Here is an alternative to using ribbon in the bobbin. Leave 8' of ribbon for a bow and begin tying overhand knots every inch until you have enough knotted ribbon to stretch from one rounded corner to the next across the top front of the bonnet. Then, attach each knot by invisibly stitching it to the bonnet by hand.

Cut two $\frac{1}{2}''$ (12.7mm) satin ribbons, each 12" (30.5cm) long, for the bonnet ties and attach by stitching several zigzag stitches in one place at the rounded corners under the $\frac{1}{8}''$ (3.2mm) ribbon.

Make six loops from the 8" (20.3cm) of $\frac{1}{8}''$ (3.2mm) ribbon. Tack them by hand at the center on top of the ribbon ties. Make ribbon roses as shown in Fig. 5.15A, or tiny bows from the $\frac{1}{2}''$ (12.7mm) ribbon and attach these over the loops by hand (Fig. 5.15B). Use double thread. Poke the needle up from the inside of the bonnet, through the ribbon ties, loops, and the center of the flower and a pearl bead. Then poke the needle back through the flower, loops, ribbon tie and bonnet. Do this several times. It's not necessary to go through the

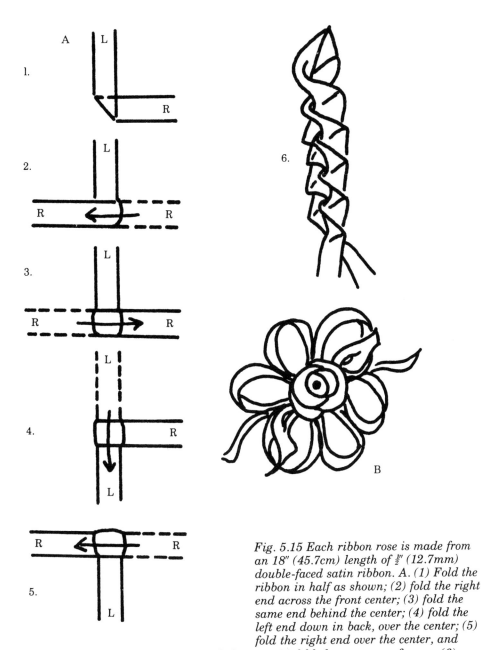

A

1.

L

R

2.

L

R ← R

3.

L

R → R

4.

L

R

L

5.

R ← R

L

6.

B

Fig. 5.15 Each ribbon rose is made from an 18" (45.7cm) length of $\frac{1}{2}$" (12.7mm) double-faced satin ribbon. A. (1) Fold the ribbon in half as shown; (2) fold the right end across the front center; (3) fold the same end behind the center; (4) fold the left end down in back, over the center; (5) fold the right end over the center, and continue folding over the center until there are 30 folds between your fingers; (6) holding the last fold between your thumb and forefinger, release the rest of the ribbon, then pull on the ribbon end under the last fold to create the rose. B. By hand, stitch from the back to the center and back again to keep the rose from unwinding. Leave $\frac{1}{2}$" (12.7mm) ends and cut each on a slant. Hold the loops in place with a small ribbon rose or tie small bows at the centers.

bead each time. Anchor the thread underneath.

Thread 18″ (45.7cm) of $\frac{1}{4}$″ (6.3mm) ribbon through the back casing on the bonnet and pull up to tie into a bow at the back (Fig. 5.16). Cut off at the length you prefer. There you have it—a priceless gift.

Lesson 16. Stitching in rings

Stitching in rings is like making needlelace (Fig. 5.17). Instead of fabric surrounding a space, in this lesson the thread is attached to narrow gold rings about 2½″ (6.4cm) in diameter. See Sources of Supplies for ordering these rings.

Project Christmas Ornaments

A stabilizer isn't always needed when you sew in space, but it will depend upon your machine. I used to make these Christmas ornaments without a stabilizer and it worked beautifully. But with water-soluble stabilizer underneath, you can stitch more intricate designs, and the thread will stay in one place, as if you were stitching on fabric.

Set up your machine.

Stitch width: 0–4
Stitch length: 0
Needle: #80/12
Feed dogs: covered
Presser foot: bare needle
Tension: slightly loosened
Thread: gold metallic on top and bobbin
Accessories: 2½″ (6.4cm) gold ring or narrow metal bracelet; 7″ (17.8cm) spring hoop; permanent white marker
Stabilizer: water-soluble

Fig. 5.16 Pull on each end of the back ribbon and tie into a bow to shape the crown of the bonnet.

Double the stabilizer and put it into the hoop. Place the gold ring in the center. Draw a design in the ring.

Dip the needle down at the side of the ring and bring the bobbin thread to the top. Hold the threads to one side. Anchor the ring by hand-walking the needle from the outside to the inside of it. Stitch from one side to the other several times. Hold onto the ring and stitch across to the other side. The chain of stitches will be tighter if you sew fast but move the hoop slowly. Anchor the thread on the other side by sewing over and back on the ring as you did at first.

Work back across and anchor on the other side. Keep doing this until you have laid in the spokes of the design. Remember,

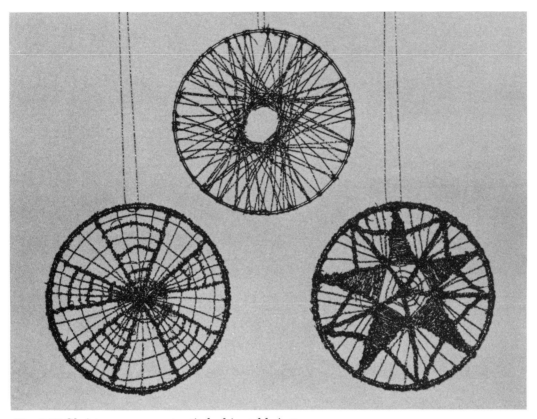

Fig. 5.17 Christmas ornaments stitched in gold rings.

with water-soluble stabilizer you can change direction when stitching in open spaces. After the last anchoring stitches, go back into the ring and finish the piece. It can be symmetrical or not. I feel that the lighter the look, the better. Stitching it too thickly will be a detraction, but you may want to zigzag over threads, as in cutwork, to add variety to the design.

Anchor the last stitches and take the ring out of the hoop. Cut back the stabilizer, then dissolve it by holding the ring under running water. Hang it from your Christmas tree with a cord.

Lesson 17. Making Alençon lace

Alençon lace took its name from the French town. The lace was developed there and was so expensive it was rarely seen, except in shops with a wealthy clientele, where it was sold as yardage and used as trimming for lingerie, dresses, and household items.

On the fine, mesh net background is a heavy design, so closely woven it is almost clothlike. Characteristic of Alençon lace

97

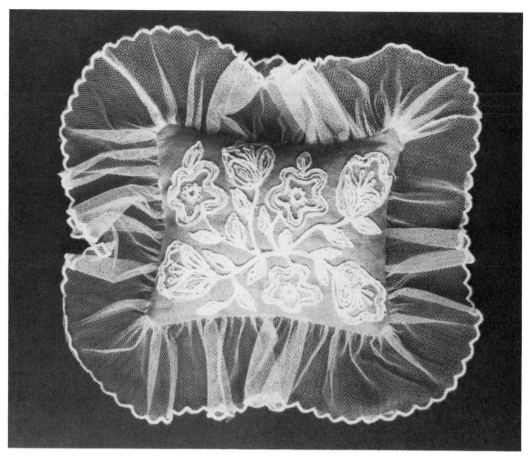

Fig. 5.18 Alençon lace pincushion.

is the heavy thread that outlines the design.

Project Alençon Pincushion

Our Alençon is made on a single layer of bridal veiling. The design is freely embroidered by machine, then outlined with pearl cotton or cordonnet (Fig. 5.18).

Stitch width: 0
Stitch length: 0
Needle: #80/12
Feed dogs: covered and uncovered
Presser feet: darning foot G and special purpose J or open J feet
Tension: slightly loosened
Fabric suggestion: bridal veil, 36″ × 5″ (91.4cm × 12.7cm); light blue linen, 4½″ × 11″ (11.4cm × 28.0cm)
Thread: #100 or #120 fine white sewing thread; #8 pearl cotton or cordonnet on bobbin to match

Accessories: 7″ (17.8cm) spring hoop; permanent white marker; 2 cups of sawdust
Stabilizer: tear-away and water-soluble

Prepare a sample of your stitching to be sure it looks like you want it to. I like a slight bubbly look to the pearl cotton, but you may want a tighter or even looser stitch. If so, tighten or loosen the top tension.

Put the water-soluble stabilizer in the hoop. Place it over the design in Fig. 5.19 and copy it with the permanent marker. Then place the veiling over the stabilizer in the hoop.

Thread with fine thread in the top and bobbin. Bring the bobbin thread to the top and hold both threads to one side. After stitching a few stitches, clip these ends off.

I don't anchor the threads as they will be sewn in anyway.

Begin by filling in your design with rows of freely stitched lines that follow the pattern in Fig. 5.19. Sew a line next to the outline, then another within that and another, and so on until you have filled it in. If some of the lines overlap, don't despair, as this will happen. Just try to keep from building up heavy stitching lines.

Go from one side of the design to the other, filling in flowers as well as leaves. If the vine threatens to become too heavily stitched with the numerous passes you'll make, stop, clip the thread on top and begin again where you wish to continue. There's no need to bring up the bobbin thread again, as long as it is still connected to the fabric.

Fig. 5.19 Lace pincushion design.

If there are any long threads to be brought to the back, do so when finished stitching. If you wish, dot with Fray-Check on the back and clip close to the work. Actually, a project such as this will not receive the wear a collar will and you can forego the Fray-Check, as it is not necessary when the lace is backed with another fabric.

Change the bobbin to the one containing pearl cotton. Take the veiling out of the hoop and turn it over. The topside of the lace will be underneath. Double check the tensions by sewing on another piece of veiling in another hoop. The pearl cotton should lay flat underneath without pulling; yet it should not be so loose it looks loopy.

Dip the needle into the veil and bring the pearl to the top. Hold it to one side as you begin: Don't anchor it. Outline the design. It is very important to keep from going over lines too many times. You want it to be thick, but not ugly.

When you complete outlining, cut off the pearl cotton, bringing any long ends to the back. Work those under a few stitches on back by hand and clip them off. Put your lace, still in the hoop, under the faucet to wash out the stabilizer.

Measure the top of the pincushion. The finished size will be 4″ × 5″ (10.2cm × 12.7cm) so add ½″ (12.7mm) to each measurement; 4½″ × 5½″ (11.4cm × 14.0cm). Cut two pieces of blue linen this size.

But first, a helpful hint: When I sew two pieces of fabric together, as I am doing with the blue linen, I cut out only one, the top piece, to the size I want. I leave the second piece several inches larger for a reason: It's easier to stitch the two pieces together and have them fit beautifully if I use the larger piece underneath the one that is cut exactly to size.

This hint is especially helpful when the fabric has lace or cording at the edges or is a bulky fabric. By the way, I back all my tote bag squares this way, too, then I trim off the excess fabric after I've straight stitched around it (joining the top and backing). To finish, I satin-stitch the edge. But back to the pincushion. Stitch the lace to the top piece. Seam allowance is ¼″ (6.3mm).

Cut a piece of veiling 45″ (114.3cm) long (2½ times the perimeter of the pincushion), and 5″ (12.7cm) wide. Cut a piece of tear-away stabilizer the same length and 2″ (5.1cm) wide. Pin the cut edges of the veiling together to hold it in place. Slip tear-away under the fold. Set your machine to the scallop stitch (refer to your manual).

Turn feed dogs up. With the right edge of the J foot placed just within the edge of the fold, stitch width 7, length at 1 or whatever would give you an attractive crescent (#15), stitch down the length of the veiling and cut back to the stitching.

To gather the ruffle, use zigzag stitches over cordonnet. Zigzag the length of the cut edges (stitch length 2, stitch width 3). Use the cord to gather the ruffle.

Join the two ends of the ruffle by placing one end over the other about ½″ (12.7mm). Using a 3 stitch width, and 1 length, satin stitch down the width of the piece of veiling. Cut back to the line of stitching on both sides.

Gather the ruffle, placing the seam at a corner. Corners should be heavily gathered to make sure they lay beautifully when completed. Distribute the ruffles around the edge of the pincushion. Remember that the embroidered edge will be toward the *center* of the pincushion. Stitch in place. It's not necessary to remove the cordonnet.

The last step is to sew the back of the pincushion to the lace. Place right sides together, and work all the net ruffles inside as you pin around the edge.

Sew within the stitching line on front. Trim and clip corners diagonally. Leave a large enough opening so you can turn the pincushion to the outside. When turned, fill it very tightly with sawdust. Stitch the opening shut by hand.

I've made appliqués on bridal veil the same way as I made Alençon lace. The only difference is that I filled in the design more heavily with the lines of free-machined straight stitches. With pearl cotton I also stitched around the outlines, as well as inside the appliqué flowers and leaves. In other words, the design was thicker and heavier, although net could still be seen in areas inside the flowers. When completed, I took the appliqué out of the hoop and placed it on the satin background I'd chosen. With my machine set on a narrow zigzag (stitch width 1) I freely attached the lace to the fabric—inside and at the edge of the design.

Once attached, I cut off all the veiling around the motif, added seed pearls, and it went to a wedding.

Do you like making lace? Try other variations by using built-in stitches, satin-stitch star flowers, or bands of intertwined cordonnet at the edges.

CHAPTER 6

Drawing Threads Out of Your Fabric

■ **Lesson 18. Needleweaving**

To create an area of free, lacy openwork called needleweaving, first draw threads out of a fabric, then stitch over the remaining threads. On this long-cut, I used exactly the same color thread on the top and bobbin as that of the dress; I'm constantly being asked how it was stitched. The solution to the mystery follows.

Lesson 18. Needleweaving

Because needleweaving is worked in a straight line, I chose to decorate the sleeves of a summer dress (Fig. 6.1). I knew this dress would be washed many times, so I chose a polyester sewing thread for durability. I matched it perfectly, both spool and bobbin, with the fabric.

First do a small sample of needleweaving for your notebook. The openwork is 1″ (2.5cm) wide. Pull out a horizontal thread at the top and the bottom where the openwork will be. Straight stitch across those lines using a thread color slightly lighter than the color you'll use for embroidery. Then pull out the horizontal or weft threads in that space.

Project
Openwork
on Sleeves

You will machine stitch over the vertical or warp threads, drawing them together as you zigzag (Fig. 6.2).

Stitch width: 0–5
Stitch length: 0–1
Needle: #80/12
Feed dogs: Covered, uncovered
Presser foot: open J foot, darning G, or no presser foot
Tension: normal
Fabric suggestion: loosely woven
Thread: Metrosene polyester
Stabilizer: tear-away, or construction paper to match thread; water-soluble (optional)

Take off the regular presser foot and use a bare needle or darning foot. Try working without a hoop on this project. The stitching goes fast and a hoop would only slow you down.

You may stitch with water-soluble stabilizer behind your work, but that is optional and depends upon whether you're comfortable stitching across open space or not. Prepare your machine for embroidery by covering the feed dogs. Be sure the presser bar is down before you start to stitch. Dip the needle down and bring the bobbin thread to the top. Anchor the

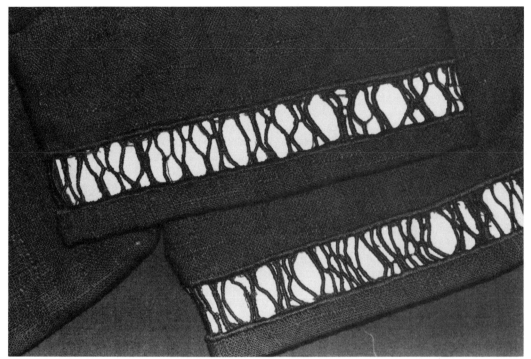

Fig. 6.1 Needleweaving decorates the sleeves on a summer dress.

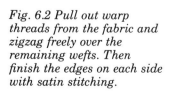

Fig. 6.2 Pull out warp threads from the fabric and zigzag freely over the remaining wefts. Then finish the edges on each side with satin stitching.

threads. Set the machine on stitch width 5 and normal tension.

Using both hands, grasp the top and bottom of the fabric between your fingers, stretching it slightly as you stitch. Keep the fabric as close as you can to the needleplate, and keep tension on the warp threads.

Begin to move from just below the stitched line at the bottom to just over the stitched line on top. Move the fabric slowly, but sew at a comfortable speed, catching several warp threads together as you zigzag to the top.

When you reach the top, move sideways to the next several warp threads and begin stitching those together. About halfway down, move the fabric to the side and catch a few stitches into the previous group of zigzagged threads. Then move back and continue to the bottom of the threads. Finish all the warp threads in the same manner, satin stitching up and down, while at the same time catching threads from the previous run in one or two places. This adds interest and strength to your openwork and is an integral part of your needleweaving.

After finishing, remove water-soluble stabilizer.

Next, draw two parallel lines, 1″ (2.5 cm.) apart on your construction paper or tear-away stabilizer. Place the stitching on the construction paper or tear-away stabilizer and adjust the embroidery so it lies flat between the two lines drawn on the stabilizer. Spray with water to enable you to pull the piece back into shape. Press.

Set up your machine for straight stitching with feed dogs uncovered and the open embroidery foot on. Sew a line of straight stitches across the top and bottom on the same guidelines you stitched at the beginning. You'll see them clearly as they are a lighter color. This will hold the needlelace in place and stabilize it for the final stitching.

Set the machine to a 5 width zigzag, feed dogs still uncovered, stitch length 1 (or whatever will result in a perfect satin stitch). Loosen tension slightly and satin stitch over those lines, covering the edges in two passes—the first narrower and more open than the second. This takes longer, but the results are more professional-looking. The stitching will fall just to one side of the fabric and will catch the fabric on the other side to neatly finish the edge of the needlelace. Tear off the stabilizer and steam press the embroidery carefully.

If the stabilizer can still be seen behind the stitches, it may be possible to remove it by dampening it, then using a tweezers to remove it. Or use this trick: if you can find a permanent marker the same color as the thread, dab in the color where necessary.

Try needleweaving across the yoke or pocket of a blouse, or down the middle of sleeves, or combine two rows of this with lacy spiderweb circles scattered between.

If you don't like the see-through look, or if you want to add another color, back the open area with another fabric.

You are more than halfway through the book. Do you know your Singer?

CHAPTER 7

Layering Fabrics: Quilting

I've always taken time to make handmade gifts for special people. But if I make a crib quilt, for example, I'd like to know that the baby won't be twice as long as the quilt by the time the gift is presented. If I'm sewing clothes, I'm realistic: I want the garment to be in style when the recipient opens the box.

So, although I love hand quilting and hand sewing, they often take too long. Machine quilting, on the other hand, is speedy and sturdy. You can use heavy fabrics like corduroy, as well as thick batts, and you will have no trouble stitching them together. If machine quilting is done properly, it can be as fine as handwork.

In this chapter I've included quilting with the feed dogs covered and uncovered, trapunto, and Italian cording.

Remember several things when doing any type of quilting. The first is to pre-shrink all fabrics. I usually use cotton polyester blends for my quilts so they stay new-looking for a long time. Sheets are excellent backing materials. They come in a myriad of colors and prints, can be of excellent quality, and they won't have to be pieced. When I make a quilt, I use a sheet that is larger than the top.

I usually quilt with a polyester sewing thread. Most brands come in a wealth of colors. Should I want to emphasize the stitching line, I will double the thread. But when I sew on a patterned material or a fabric that changes color throughout, I choose a monofilament. I may or may not use monofilament on the bobbin, depending upon the samples I do first.

Using safety pins instead of hand basting is my favorite method of holding the fabrics and batt together before I quilt. I don't use dressmaker's pins because many of them fall out before the quilt is completed—and those that don't usually stab me.

Lesson 19. Quilting with feed dogs uncovered

Instead of a regular presser foot, I use an even-feed foot when I sew lines of straight quilting stitches. It minimizes puckering on the backing fabric, as the top and bottom fabrics are fed through at the same speed with no slipping.

Before I had one of those helpful attachments, I grasped the quilt in both hands and kept it taut as it fed through the machine. As I progressed, I stopped and looked underneath to be sure I had a smooth lining. I must admit I became an expert at sewing without puckers. It may take a little longer, but the lack of a walking foot should not deter you from starting your first quilt experiment.

Can you imagine how fast you could make a quilt using striped fabric or a striped sheet for the top? Use the stripes as quilting lines. If you use stripes for garments, keep in mind that the more rows of quilting, the smaller the piece becomes. I either quilt the fabric first and then cut out the pattern, or I cut my pattern larger than necessary, do the quilting and then lay the pattern back on it when finished. I recut the pattern where necessary.

If you piece a quilt and decide to machine quilt it by using stitch-in-a-ditch, you may prefer using the zipper foot. Stitch-in-a-ditch is done on top of the quilt by stitching in the seam lines (the ditches). With this presser foot, it is easy to stitch exactly in the ditch because you have the openness of the zipper foot for clear visibility.

Project
Tote Bag Square (Appliqué and Quilting)

This quilted sample, shown in the color section, can be used as a square for the tote bag in Chapter 12.

Stitch width: 0–7
Stitch length: 0–normal
Feed dogs: uncovered
Presser foot: special purpose J or open J foot
Needle: 70/10
Tension: normal
Thread: red cotton machine embroidery
Fabric: four scraps of yellow, red, purple, green (see pattern for size); two 9″ (22.9cm)

blue squares; 10″ (25.4cm) square of fleece
Accessories: water-erasable marker; white marking pencil; light-colored dressmaker's carbon and empty ballpoint pen; fusible webbing; ruler, Teflon pressing sheet; tracing paper and pencil
Stabilizer: heavy tear-away

Using the Teflon sheet, iron fusible webbing onto each of the fabrics except for the two blue squares.

Trace the design in Fig. 7.1 twice and write the name of the color in each section. Cut apart one of the tracings. Place the pattern pieces on the correct colors except for the blue and draw around them with a water-erasable marker or white marking pencil.

Then transfer the design from the other tracing to one of the blue squares to use as the backing and guide when you assemble the colored pieces. To do this, use a light-colored dressmaker's carbon and empty ballpoint pen.

Have you noticed how butting pieces of appliqué next to each other usually leaves gaping areas, no matter how careful you are? To help prevent this, be extremely careful when you cut them out. Also, by using blue fabric as a base, there is no need to cut out blue pieces. That means you'll have only one edge to cover on several of the passes. Covering edges with wide satin stitches is also insurance.

After you place the fabric pieces together on the blue background, press in place. Use red machine embroidery thread to attach your appliqués as follows: First back the blue square with stabilizer and then satin stitch the long curved line (stitch width 6, stitch length 1½). Continue by satin stitching the straight lines. Then go back over the stitching lines with stitch width 7, stitch length 1¼. Sew at a moderate speed and always turn with the needle in the fabric.

When you have finished satin stitching

blue   green   purple   red   yellow

Fig. 7.1 Quilted tote bag square.

the fabric in place, back the square with fleece, and under that use stabilizer if you wish. Go back and straight stitch down each side of the satin stitches. This gives the satin stitches a clean finish and quilts the square at the same time.

Finish the square as described in Chapter 12.

Lesson 20. Quilting with feed dogs covered

As you can tell from the lesson title, this will be free-machine quilting. The machine setting will not control the length of the stitches; you will. If you move the fabric fast, the stitches will be longer than if you move it slowly. Not working in a hoop, you must use a darning foot to prevent skipped stitches. And no hoop means you must hold the fabric taut while stitching.

Stitch width: 0
Stitch length: 0
Needle: #90/14
Feed dogs: covered
Presser foot: darning foot G
Tension: slightly loosened (auto − 1)
Fabric suggestion: medium-weight cotton; fleece or quilt batting
Thread: machine embroidery
Accessories: water-erasable marker

One of the easiest ways to learn free quilting and to practice control at the same time is to quilt around the motifs of a printed fabric as shown in Fig. 7.2. Even the underside looks terrific: you may like the looks of the lining better than the printed side. If so, it makes for stunning reversible jacket.

When quilting any fabrics with feed dogs covered, don't place the stitching lines too closely together, unless you want to emphasize the area that *isn't* stitched. Closely stitched, it will be too stiff and you'll lose the contrast of light and dark shadowing that makes this type of machining so effective.

Fig. 7.2 Cotton print, batting and velveteen are quilted together by stitching the butterfly design.

Lesson 21. Trapunto

In trapunto, two pieces of fabric are stitched together, following a design. Then the quilter selects the areas of the design to be stuffed with fiberfill. Usually trapunto is done from underneath the fabrics.

Layer two pieces of material together—one plain muslin, the other a printed fabric. Place both fabrics in a hoop. Freely stitch in the design, using monofilament or machine embroidery thread the same color as the fabric.

Make small slits in the backing fabric behind the parts of the design you wish to quilt. Add fiberfill, poking it in with a tool that is not sharply pointed. Whip stitch the slits closed by hand.

You can trapunto from the top by appliquéing on top of a base fabric. Slip filling inside the appliqué before you've attached it all the way around. You may want more stitching over the appliqué to hold the stuffing firmly and to add to the design.

Lesson 22. Italian cording

Italian cording is often mistaken for trapunto. The difference is that the area to be stuffed in Italian cording will be the space between two stitching lines. Instead of using fiberfill, thread a cord of appropriate size through the double lines of stitching.

It's also possible to create the look of Italian cording in one pass of the machine, on one layer of fabric when stitching with a double needle. Use the open J foot. Tighten the tension slightly (auto +2 or your preference) to raise the fabric between the stitching lines, giving the pintuck the look of corded quilting.

Project
Tote Bag Square
(Italian Cording)

This square (Fig. 7.3) was done using a single needle. I found a design like this in a book picturing old Moorish tiles. I used it on an ecclesiastical stole, choosing part of the design that resembled a cross, then modifying it for my purposes. If you stand the square on one of its corners, the cross is recognizable.

Stitch width: 0
Stitch length: 4
Needle: #80/12 sharp
Feed dogs: uncovered
Presser foot: open J foot
Tension: normal
Fabric suggestions: lightweight cotton for top; stiffer cotton for backing
Thread: shiny rayon or machine embroidery cotton
Cord: appropriate-size acrylic yarn or cable cord
Accessories: hand-sewing needle; large-eyed hand-sewing tapestry needle to thread cord through the design; water-erasable marker

Draw your design on the fabric with a water-erasable marker, indicating where the lines will cross and which ones cross over, which under.

When you are stitching the lines, don't anchor threads when the lines cross. Instead, pull several inches of thread out of the needle. Hold the thread to one side.

Fig. 7.3 Italian cording tote bag square.

110

Skip over the intersection; then begin stitching again. When finished, go back and clip the threads in the middle. Thread up a sewing needle and poke all the top threads through to the back and work them in. Finish up by working the cord through the design by hand.

It's difficult to turn corners with cording and make those corners look sharp. Poke the needle out of the back fabric at a corner, and then back in again in the same place, leaving a small loop of the cord out in back.

When working with a double needle, turn corners in three steps. Stitch to the corner. Stop. Needles should be grazing the fabric. Lift the presser foot. Half-turn the fabric. Lower the presser foot and turn the wheel by hand to make one stitch. Raise the needles and again bring the needle points down to barely touch the top of the fabric. Lift the presser foot again and complete the turn. Lower the presser foot and continue stitching.

Directions for finishing the square are in Chapter 12.

Look for inspirations for Italian cording in books on Celtic designs or bargello borders.

CHAPTER 8

Adding Interesting Seams to Your Fabric

- ■ **Lesson 23. French handsewing by machine**
- ■ **Lesson 24. Seaming with feed dogs uncovered and covered**

In previous chapters, the emphasis was on decorative stitchery. In Chapters 8 and 9, the focus is on sewing. The chapters are so closely related that at times they even overlap. Included in Chapters 8 and 9 are many of the sewing long-cuts I mentioned in the Preface and Chapter 1. But now, instead of decorating a garment by em-

broidering or appliquéing on it, you'll learn to make the garment unique by changing the seams, hems and edges.

Let's face it: seams are not always interesting. Most of them are hidden and it's not necessary that they do anything but hold two pieces of fabric together. On the other hand, seams can be the focal point of your creation. This chapter includes seams for the finest lace to the heaviest canvas—seams purely practical and those that combine decoration with practicality. Stitch up samples of all of them for your notebook. You'll discover that knowing your Singer is a joy.

The project in this chapter is a wedding handkerchief (Fig. 8.1). After learning how to accomplish French handsewing on the machine, work this project. It can also be used as a pillow top.

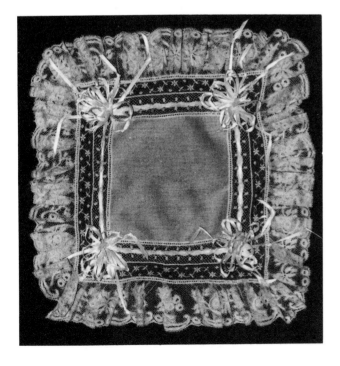

Fig. 8.1 Wedding handkerchief, made using machine techniques for French handsewing.

Lesson 23. French handsewing by machine

When I first heard about the type of clothing construction called French handsewing, I thought it was something new—until Marcia Strickland, a friend from Birmingham, Alabama, showed me her daughters' dresses. They were made of laces, with pintucks and embroidery, entredeux and hemstitching, and looked like our family's christening gown. I knew French handsewing; I just hadn't been acquainted with the term. We'd always called it "sewing by hand" and I had agonized over it years ago, when I was sure I'd be struck blind by the tiny stitches before I made it through junior high school. It was hard for me to believe that I could accomplish the perfection of Marcia's clothing on my sewing machine (called "French handsewing by machine," "French machine sewing" or "heirloom sewing").

Then, my friend, Carol Ahles, of Houston, Texas, taught me several new techniques to make French machine sewing easier. Beginners, especially, are in luck, as Carol's methods simplify the attachment of laces to entredeux; entredeux to fabric. I like her methods because they often eliminate rolling and whipping edges, as well as streamlining other heirloom techniques. When applicable, I'll include both methods. Your choice may depend on your machine and on what presser feet you own.

It's possible to find lace and tucked blouses, skirts and dresses in any department store today. Because this feminine look is expensive in ready-to-wear, if you learn the following hand-sewing techniques by machine and sew them yourself, you will save money and have a lot of fun besides.

First, I had to learn basics before I could stitch collars or dresses. Marcia taught me

that if I apply fabric to lace, one of the rules of French handsewing is that I must always have entredeux between.

Entredeux literally means "between two." It is purchased by the yard in fabric shops. The fabric on either side of the ladderlike strip down the center is usually trimmed off before it is attached. I also learned that the holes in entredeux are never evenly spaced, no matter how expensive it is. Irregular holes are a part of "handmade" attractiveness.

I've discovered that stitch 3 on cartridge 4 can create entredeux. Use a single hemstitch needle to sew on a double layer of cotton organdy. Stitch down the length needed for all the entredeux in your project. At the end, turn fabric and stitch back in the same holes on one side. This pulls the threads together and tiny holes are formed in the center—much like the look of entredeux. Tighten tension until you get the look you want (Fig. 8.2).

Use a straight stitch setting when you attach the entredeux face-to-face with the fabric (Fig. 8.3). Fold back seam allowance. Finish by stitching a fine zigzag (stitch width $1\frac{1}{2}$, stitch length 2) on top of the seam from the top.

Marcia suggested size 100 pure cotton thread and #70 needle for sewing. She uses an extra-fine thread because the batiste fabric used is extremely lightweight, and stitches are visible when attaching lace and entredeux or stitching pintucks. And she suggests using cotton thread for heirlooms because it will last a long time.

I always choose a top quality cotton/polyester for fabric (and thread), as it doesn't wrinkle like pure cotton. For machine sewing I used J. P. Coats Dual Duty Plus—extra fine thread like Carol uses.

I learned so much from Marcia and Carol

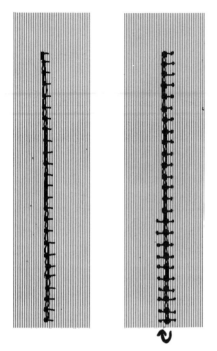

Fig. 8.2 Make entredeux using cartridge #4, stitch #3.

Fig 8.3 Attach entredeux to fabric using this method (see also Fig. 8.9).

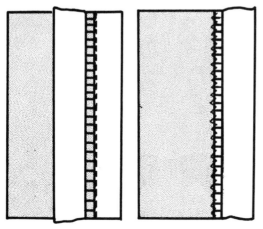

that I filled a notebook with samples, ideas, and shortcuts. When you stitch up samples for your own notebook, if a technique can be done several ways, do them all and then decide which works best for you. The following techniques are all you need to learn for French machine sewing.

Sewing French seams

French seams are used on lightweight, transparent fabrics to finish the seams beautifully, disguising raw edges. They are also found on smocked garments as a fine finish.

The seams are accomplished in two different operations (Fig. 8.4). Begin with fabric pieces, wrong sides facing. Stitch the seam, using a #70/10 needle and fine sewing thread. Open and press seam to one side. Cut back the seam allowance evenly, to $\frac{1}{8}''$ (3.2mm). Turn the fabric back over the raw edges, press again (the seam will be at the edge), pin, and stitch again, enclosing the $\frac{1}{8}''$ (3.2mm) seam allowance.

Stitching rolled and whipped edges

To roll and whip, I can use two different feet. Which works best for you? With the general purpose foot B, set the tension on auto +1, stitch width 4, stitch length 3. Place the fabric under the foot (Fig. 8.5A) and holding the edge of the fabric, pull it toward you a slight bit to place tension on the fabric. Stitch.

To use the modified J foot, first tighten the tension (Fig. 8.5B) slightly. Place the edge of the fabric at the right side of the opening with stitch width 4, stitch length 3, the zigzag stitches off one edge, then into the fabric on the other side, which rolls and whips the edge.

Both of these methods take practice, but there are occasions when you need to roll and whip in French machine sewing.

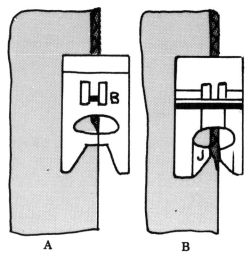

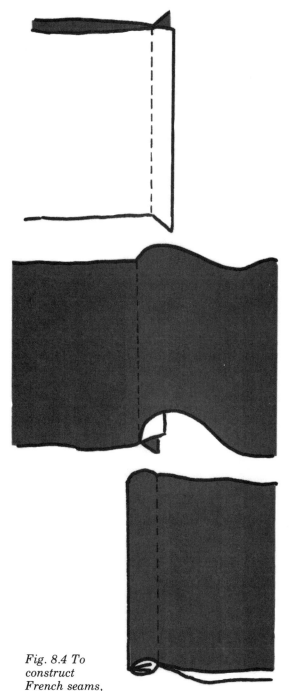

Fig. 8.5 A. Rolled and whipped edges using the general purpose foot B. B. Using the modified J foot to roll and whip edges.

Gathering rolled and whipped edges

Before you roll and whip, stitch (stitch length 2) ⅛″ (3.2mm) inside the edge of the fabric. Instead of anchoring your threads, leave several inches of thread at the beginning and end of the stitching. Starting at the top again, overcast the edge as you did before rolling and whipping the gathering stitches (Fig. 8.6A). The straight stitching must not be caught in these zigzags.

The left, inside edge of the modified J foot is placed directly above the gathering stitches. Use stitch length 3, stitch width 3.

Hold the thread ends at the beginning of your line of straight stitching to keep them from slipping through as you gather. Pull on the top thread at the other end of the line of straight stitches and evenly distribute the ruffling (Fig. 8.6B).

Applying insertion

Insertion is lace with two straight sides. It is easily applied by machine (Fig. 8.7).

Fig. 8.4 To construct French seams, place fabrics wrong sides together, stitch the seam, trim to ⅛″ (3.2mm), then fold the fabric back over the seam allowance and stitch down outside the allowance.

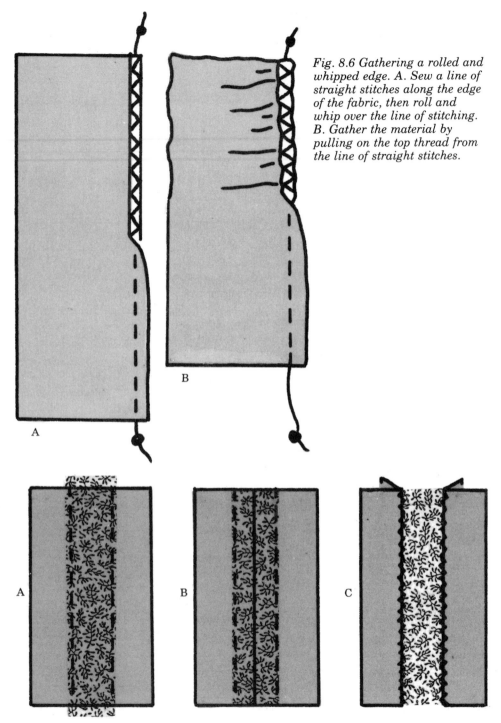

Fig. 8.6 Gathering a rolled and whipped edge. A. Sew a line of straight stitches along the edge of the fabric, then roll and whip over the line of stitching. B. Gather the material by pulling on the top thread from the line of straight stitches.

Fig. 8.7 A. Sew lace insert to fabric by straight stitching down each side of the lace. B. Cut through the fabric behind the lace from top to bottom. C. Turn back the seam allowances on both sides and zigzag down the edges of the insertion. Trim the seam allowances back to the stitching.

Draw two lines the width of the lace on the fabric. Pin the lace inside the lines. Machine straight stitch down both sides of the lace to hold it in place. Cut straight down the fabric behind the lace, allowing seam allowance on fabric. Fold the seam allowances back and press.

Then zigzag over the edges of the lace and the straight stitching to attach the lace and finish the edges simultaneously. Cut the seam allowances back to the stitching.

Apply scalloped lace as an insertion by placing it on the fabric and basting it down both sides. Cut down the fabric behind. Zigzag closely over the edge, following the scallop. Cut away the fabric underneath. This method can also be used for straight-edge insertion, but the join will not be as strong as folding back the seam allowance and stitching over the doubled fabric.

Joining scalloped lace

Find the most heavily patterned place in the design to join scalloped lace. Overlap two identical patterns, and stitch a fine zigzag (stitch width 2, stitch length normal), with feed dogs uncovered. Follow the edge of the design as shown in Fig. 8.8. Trim back to the line of stitching.

Using entredeux

Entredeux is used between fabric and lace. Only the ladderlike strip of stitching down the center of the entredeux is attached.

Stitch width: 2 or adjust
Stitch length: 3 or adjust
Needle: #70/10
Feed dogs: uncovered
Presser foot: general purpose foot B
Tension: normal
Fabric suggestions: batiste
Thread: #100 cotton or J. P. Coats Dual
  Duty Plus—extra fine

Do not trim entredeux or fabric. Place edge of entredeux on edge of fabric, right sides together. Straight stitch at side (in ditch) of entredeux, as close to the entredeux as possible. Trim edges to $\frac{1}{8}''$ (3.2mm) (Fig. 8.9A).

Zigzag stitch, with one of the needle swings going off the edge of the fabric on

Fig. 8.8 Join two pieces of lace together by overlapping the design at each end, zigzagging the "seam," then cutting back the surplus lace to the stitches.

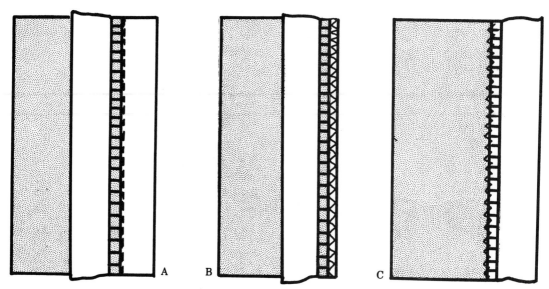

Fig. 8.9 To apply entredeux to fabric, place it on the fabric, right sides together. A. Straight stitch at the side of the entredeux. B. Trim seam allowance, then zigzag over it. C. Open and zigzag on top to hold the roll in place.

one side and next to the entredeux on the other side. Hand walk the machine for the first few stitches and adjust width and length. The seam allowance will roll slightly.

Open out the fabrics and stitch from the top at the edge of the entredeux to keep the roll in place (Fig. 8.9C). One stitch will go into a hole of the entredeux, the side into the fabric. Don't let the stitches take too large a bite into the fabric. It isn't necessary to stitch in every hole of the entredeux because it won't show, but don't stitch any holes closed.

Gathering lace edging

There are several threads at the edges of lace. Use a pin to find the one that gathers the lace and then pull up the thread. Hold onto both ends of this thread, or you might pull it all the way through when gathering the lace. Evenly space the gathers.

Attaching straight-edged lace to rolled and whipped edges

Place the topside of the lace against the topside of the fabric (Fig. 8.10) Be sure the edges are even. Use a zigzag at a setting of stitch width 2 and length 3. The needle should stitch within the edges of lace and fabric on the left, and stitch off of them on the right swing. Flatten out and press.

Attaching entredeux to lace insertion

Stitch width: 3, or adjust
Stitch length: 3, or adjust
Presser foot: special purpose foot J or open J foot

Trim fabric from one side of the entredeux. With topsides up, place the trimmed edge of the entredeux up next to the edge of the lace.

Zigzag the edges together so the needle

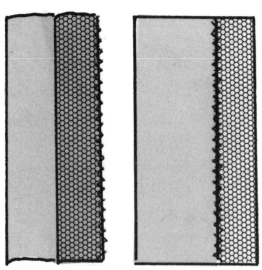

Fig. 8.10 Place insertion on top of a rolled and whipped edge; zigzag to attach. Press open.

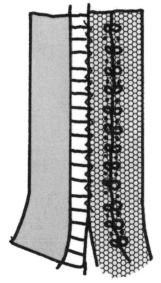

Fig. 8.11 To attach entredeux to lace insertion, place edges next to each other and zigzag together.

barely catches the lace and goes into each hole of the entredeux (Fig. 8.11). Start by using a 3 stitch width and 3 stitch length, but make adjustments in these figures if you find they are needed.

Sewing lace to lace

Stitch width: 3 or adjust
Stitch length: 4 or adjust
Presser foot: open J foot

Butt the edges of the two laces. Use general purpose foot A, stitch width 3, stitch length 4. Sew the length of the lace.

Fagoting

There are times when we need different detailing on a bodice, sleeve or skirt. It may not be called for in the pattern, but it's a way to make that garment our own, so we choose to take a long-cut and add a creative touch of our choosing to the original pattern.

Fagoting is one way to change a seam or add one. With your machine, you need only a tailor tacking foot, since it's like making fringe.

Stitch width: 3
Stitch length: 1
Presser foot: tailor tacking

Make a sample first. Set up your machine by loosening the top tension slightly (auto − 1). Place two pieces of fabric together, with right sides facing. Stitch along the seam line. When the line is completed, pull the seam open to reveal the stitches. Change to the special purpose foot J and put stabilizer underneath your work. Choose a decorative stitch or even straight stitch to sew each side of the fabric close to the fold.

Go even further with fagoting and bundle the stitches: Sew down the center of the openwork over four stitches with a free-machine straight stitch, back up, and go forward again, stitching past the first bundle and four more stitches (Fig. 8.12). Back

119

Fig. 8.12 Fagoting and bundling stitches for an open seam.

up over those four stitches, then stitch forward and over four more stitches. Continue like this until you finish bundling all the stitches.

If your machine has a triple straight stitch, the backward-forward motion will bundle the middle section automatically. On the 6268, use stitch #9, fagoting, but use stitch width 0, which results in a triple straight stitch. Use the stitch length you prefer.

Another way to fagot a seam is to fold under at least a $\frac{1}{2}''$ (12.7mm) on one side of each piece of fabric.

Baste fabrics to a piece of water-soluble stabilizer (if possible) or regular tear-away (but remember that removing the paper later may be difficult). Leave an $\frac{1}{8}''$ (3.2mm) open space between the folds. Use #9 stitch and stitch down this opening. Again, stitch

down on both sides of the opening. Then carefully remove the stabilizer.

Use fagoting above the hem of a skirt or around a sleeve or square collar.

Project
Wedding Handkerchief

Many of the techniques you have learned for French machine sewing will be used to make the handkerchief (see Fig. 8.1). You will need: 5″ (12.7m) square of fine batiste; $\frac{1}{2}''$ (12.7mm) lace insertion; 1″ (2.5cm) beading; entredeux; lace edging; $\frac{1}{8}''$ (3.2mm) double-face satin ribbon, about 6 yards (5.5m); a ruler and water-erasable marker.

How to figure exact amounts of lace and entredeux is included in the directions below; the width of your lace will determine the length you will need. Use a #70/10 needle and #100 sewing thread.

For the center of this handkerchief (Fig. 8.13), I rolled and whipped a 5″ (12.7cm) square of batiste. Entredeux was added to the edges; do one side of entredeux at a time, cut and overlap the openings of the entredeux at the corners.

Stitch the beading (the lace with holes for threaded ribbon) and lace strip together before attaching them to the entredeux. Together, the strip of lace is $1\frac{1}{2}''$ (3.8cm) wide.

Estimate how much lace you'll need for your wedding handkerchief by first measuring around the center square of batiste and entredeux; the example is approximately 20″ (50.8cm).

Double the width measurement of the strip of lace you've made when you stitched the beading to the lace insertion:

$$1\frac{1}{2}'' \times 2 = 3'' \ (3.8\text{cm} \times 2 = 7.6\text{cm}).$$

120

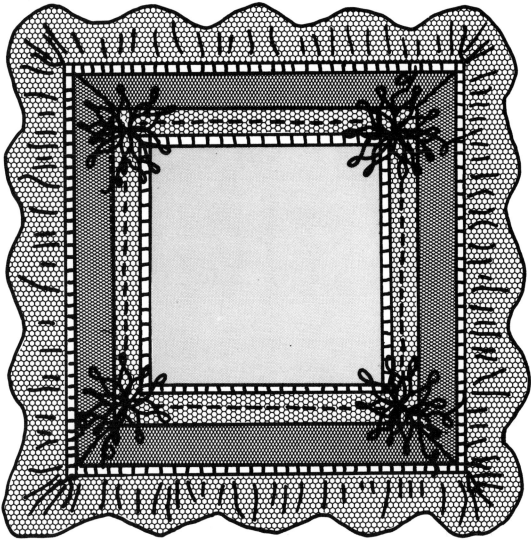

Fig. 8.13 Wedding handkerchief pattern (see also Fig. 8.1).

Multiply 3″ × 4 = 12″ (7.6cm × 4 = 30.5cm) to arrive at the number of inches (cm) needed for the corner miters.

Add the distance around the center square (20″ or 50.8cm) to the corners miters (12″ or 30.5cm). Exact measurement of the lace needed is 32″ (81.3cm). Add 2″ (5.1cm) more for safety.

Leave 2″ (5.1cm) of lace at the corner before you begin attaching lace to the entredeux (Fig. 8.14). Trim the entredeux. Place the edge of the lace strip next to the entredeux so the edges touch (see Fig. 8.14A). Stitch along the first side, ending with needle down at the corner, extending the lace $1\frac{1}{2}$″ (3.8cm) beyond the corner (this

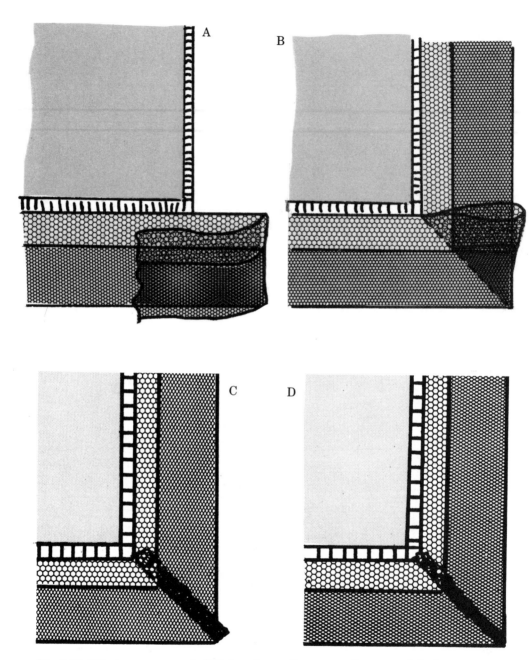

Fig. 8.14 Mitering a corner. A. Stitch as far as the corner, then extend the lace past it the width of the lace. B. Fold the lace back on itself, pin, and fold again, placing the lace next to the entredeux to continue stitching. C. Go back to each corner and straight stitch diagonally, then clip open and zigzag down the middle of the seam. D. Cut back on both sides to stitching.

is the width measurement of the strip of lace I used). Raise the presser foot. Fold the lace back on itself by the same measurement, $1\frac{1}{2}''$ (3.8cm) or the width of your lace. Pin the lace together at the corner and then fold the lace so it will lie at the edge of the entredeux on the next side you will stitch (Fig. 8.14B). Turn your work to continue stitching, and put the presser foot down. Hand-walk the first stitch to be sure it catches the lace. Continue stitching slowly to the next corner. Attach lace to the other sides as you did the first.

After the strip of lace has been attached, go back to each corner and fold the lace diagonally to miter it. Check carefully that the corners will lie flat. Pin each one. Mark with a ruler and water-erasable pen where the line of stitching will be. Sew down the line with a straight stitch on the marked line (Fig. 8.14C). Clip to open the lace so it can be pressed open. From the top, use a narrow zigzag over the seam. Trim back both sides to stitching (Fig. 8.14C).

Attach entredeux to the edge of the lace, overlapping the holes of each piece at the corners, as done previously.

Measure around the outside edge. Double this for the gathered lace measurement. Sew the ends of the lace together by overlapping and at the same time matching the designs top and bottom. Sew a narrow zigzag along the design and cut back to the line. Place this seam in a corner.

Gather the lace edging by pulling the correct thread and attaching it to the entredeux. Pin the gathered lace to the entredeux first to adjust the gathers. Keep the corners of the lace ruffle quite full. Next, stitch the lace to the entredeux. This can be done in two ways: (1) Place entredeux on top of the gathered lace, topsides together. Line up the edges and proceed as if attaching the entredeux to rolled and whipped edges; or (2) Place gathered lace next to the entredeux, topsides up, and zigzag stitch as you did in "Attaching Entredeux to Lace Insertion."

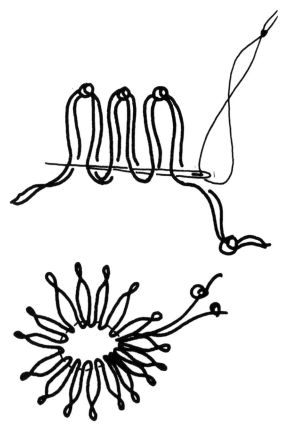

Fig. 8.15 To make a rosette, tie overhand knots in the ribbon every $2\frac{1}{2}''$ (6.4cm). Fold the ribbon into loops with knots at the tops. Sew through each loop, then pull into a rosette.

Thread $\frac{1}{8}''$ (3.2mm) double-faced satin ribbon through each of the four sides. Leave 3" (7.6cm) tails at each end. Tie overhand knots at the ends. Stitch the tails in place by hand to keep the ribbon in place.

Make rosettes for each corner (Fig. 8.15). First tie an overhand knot every $2\frac{1}{2}''$ (6.4cm) along a length of ribbon until you have 16 knots. Leave long ends. Use a double-threaded needle. Make loops on the needle by arranging the ribbon with knots at the top (Fig. 8.15). Sew back through all of the loops again. Pull up and attach the rosettes to the corners of the handkerchief. Tie knots at the ends of the ribbons.

Lesson 24. Seaming with feed dogs uncovered and covered

Sewing a flat-felled seam

To make an even flat-felled seam easily and quickly without a special presser foot, use my method.

This method does not produce a bulky seam, and there are no raw seam edges. The only drawback with a flat-felled seam is that it cannot be used on intricate curves. Rather, use these heavy duty seams on the straight.

First, overlap (wrong side to right side) ⅛″ from the edge. Stitch together the two pieces of fabric that are to be joined (Fig. 8.16A). Trim to stitching.

Then fold back a bit beyond raw edge on under fabric (Fig. 8.16B). Stitch ½″ (12.7mm) from the fold (Fig. 8.16C). Open out, fold seam toward side, and stitch again at edge (Fig. 8.16D).

Sewing a fake lapped seam

Use your B or J foot. With right sides together, stitch down the ⅝″ seam. Open and press the seam allowance to the left (Fig. 8.17).

For the second pass, stitch ⅛″ (3.2mm) from the seam line. Then sew down ¼″ (6.4mm) to ⅜″ (9.5mm) from that for a fake-felled seam.

It's also possible to use the widest double needle (4mm) and stitch down both sides at one time.

Stitching over thread on knits

No more stretched-out seams on knits and jerseys when you use this method.

Stitch width: 2½–3
Stitch length: 2
Needle: #80/12
Feed dogs: uncovered
Presser foot: modified J foot
Tension: normal
Thread: polyester sewing

With a separate spool of thread, place polyester under the presser foot from front

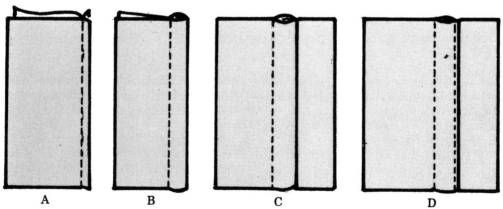

| A | B | C | D |

Fig. 8.16 Constructing a lapped hem. A. Place two pieces of fabric together and stitch together ⅛″ (3.2mm) from edge. B. Fold back, wrong sides together, and press. C. Stitch ½″ (12.7mm) from fold. D. Open out, fold seam toward side, and stitch at fold to complete seam.

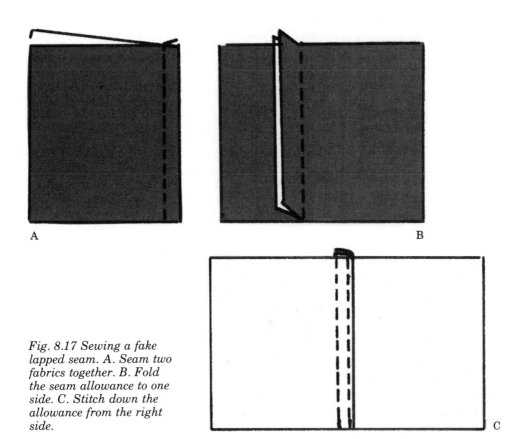

A

B

Fig. 8.17 Sewing a fake
lapped seam. A. Seam two
fabrics together. B. Fold
the seam allowance to one
side. C. Stitch down the
allowance from the right
side.

C

to back and zigzag stitch over the thread,
pulling on it gently as you stitch.

Imitating hand-piecing
on quilts

Here is a seam shown to me by a quilter.
After stitching two quilt pieces together,
run a narrow zigzag (stitch width $2\frac{1}{2}$) over
this line of straight stitches, stitch length
normal (Fig. 8.18). When the seam is
pressed open, it gives the impression of
perfect hand piecing. Why not skip the

Fig. 8.18 To create the look of
hand piecing, zigzag over a
seam of straight stitches. Then
press the seam open.

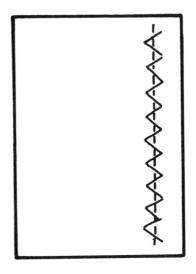

first step of straight stitching? Because the two passes will make the quilt seams sturdier, and the line of straight stitching is an excellent guideline for the zigzagging.

Joining veiling with a scallop stitch

What kind of a seam can be used on veiling? In Lesson 17, a straight seam is stitched on Alençon lace, using a close zigzag stitch. A more decorative seam is stitched with the crescent #15 or ribbon #16 stitch. Overlap the edges, stitch, then cut back excess material on each side to the embroidery.

Using built-in stitches

Don't overlook the built-in honeycomb stitch #22 on your machine. It is sewn from the top of the fabric and used for sewing ribbing onto sweatshirts or for top decoration.

Built-in stitches can be sewn between two pieces of fabric to create an open, interesting seam (Fig. 8.19). Stitch #9 is one of the most versatile stitches. Not only is it used to sew fabrics together, but I also use it on quilt tops to stitch the layers together; when embroidering flowers, the stitch becomes stems or vines.

I also used the #18 vine stitch for the butted seams on a Bermuda bag I made from Ultrasuede scraps. Using a commercial kit, I cut the scraps into strips—enough to cover the pattern. I used the Teflon presser foot and polyester thread to stitch the strips together. You can substitute a plain zigzag also. I like the multi-stitch

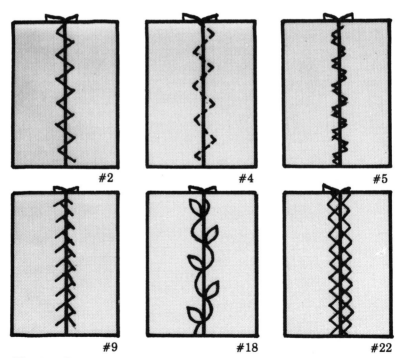

#2 #4 #5

#9 #18 #22

Fig. 8.19 Decorate and stitch a seam with these stitches: zigzag #2; multi-stitch zigzag #4; M stitch #5; fagotting #9; vine #18; honeycomb #22.

126

zigzag as well. It locks the stitches in the fabric as it sews from side to side so there's a built-in stability to the seam. When the stitching was completed, I placed the pattern over the Ultrasuede and cut off fabric projecting beyond the edges. After that, I was able to finish the bag according to the kit directions.

The vine stitch is beautiful, but "busy." That's why I don't use it when stitching intersecting lines unless I can cover the intersection with a bow or button (when quilting).

Don't overlook stitches such as the "M" stitch (#5) which can be combined with a mirror image of itself, then placed in memory to create a symmetrical stitch. Use these to decorate or stitch two pieces of fabric together with an open seam. Prepare two pieces of fabric by folding each edge over $\frac{5}{8}''$ (15.9mm), then placing the folds about $\frac{1}{8}''$ (3.2mm) apart on top of a stabilizer. Practice with this setting: stitch #5, stitch width 4, stitch length 4, enter, mirror image, stitch width 4, stitch length 4, enter, memory.

To sew stretch fabrics together, use the "M" stitch (#5). This will stitch the fabrics together and finish the edges in one step (Fig. 8.20). Another stitch to use to seam

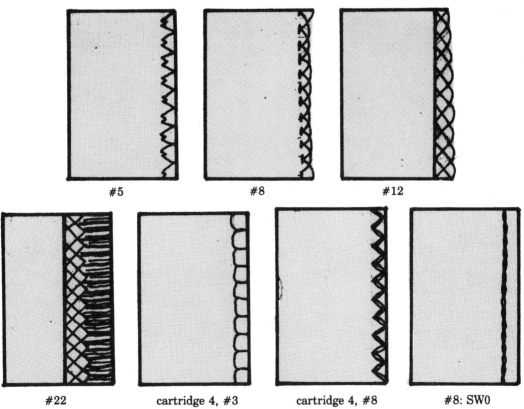

Fig. 8.20 Use these seams for stretch fabrics: M stitch #5; overedge #8; overlock #12; honeycomb #22 on ribbing; cartridge #4, picot stitch #3. Use these stitches to seam heavy-duty fabric: cartridge #4, rickrack #8; triple straight-stitch #8 (stitch width 0).

and edge at the same time is overedge (#8) and overlock (#12).

On cartridge 4, use picot (#3) on very fine knits, overlock (#9) and triple zigzag (rick rack stitch) (#8) for an extremely strong seam. Also, use stitch #8 with stitch length changed to "0" for a triple straight stitch, another useful, heavy-duty seam.

Creating seams with feed dogs covered

If you use a similar seam with fabric instead of Ultrasuede, fold under seam allowances at least ⅝" (15.9mm) and press. Move the two pieces of fabric about ⅛" (3.2mm) apart, topsides down. If the fabric is washable, you may want to slip water-soluble stabilizer under it and baste the fabric ⅛" apart. Use thick cord in the bobbin. Lower the feed dogs and use the darning foot. Sew freely from one side of the fabric to the other, making loops as you enter and leave it (Fig. 8.21). When you finish, turn it over and stitch down along the folds again. Then cut back underneath to the stitching.

These techniques only scratch the surface of interesting seams for your fabric. New seams are introduced every time a new utility or decorative stitch is incorporated into a machine. They are welcome, of course, but in the meantime there is no lack of beautiful and practical work you can do.

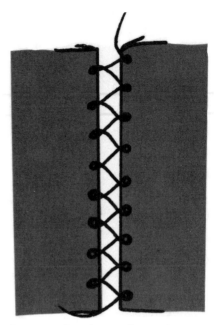

Fig. 8.21 Stitching a decorative seam using free machining.

CHAPTER **9**

Adding Hems and Edges

I remember when "good clothes" didn't mean "clean jeans." There were puffed sleeves, sweetheart necklines—always braided, piped, or embroidered in some way. We wanted to dress like movie stars. Dresses were molded to them and then decorated creatively. Designers always took many long-cuts.

The more you know about your machine, the more inventive you can become; no more boring clothes! You may not think you'll ever use all the decorative hems and edgings in this chapter, but make samples for your notebook anyway. You may be surprised.

With the range of fabrics and styles now available, and the variety of effects we want to achieve, choosing the appropriate hem or edge is not always easy. Before sewing a hem or decorative edge on anything, ask yourself these questions: What type of fabric? What type of garment? Who is the garment for? Will it be worn forever? How decorative is it to be?

I have my favorite ways to hem and finish edges. I've also learned hems and edges I will never do again. What makes the difference? Appearance, of course, and ease of stitching. I think I have tried every imaginable variation, and those that follow are the ones I prefer because they are useful and good-looking.

Stitch samples of each and put the results in your notebook for reference. Include your own favorites as well. Write the machine settings on each one, along with comments such as what fabrics work well, where you would use them, whether they were long-cuts with happy endings or more trouble than they were worth.

Lesson 25. Turning hems once

I used to cringe at the thought of hems turned only once—all those raw edges! But I have changed my way of thinking.

Using double needles on knits

My favorite hem for T-shirts and other casual knits is turned once and stitched in place with a double needle. The two stitching lines share one bobbin thread, giving the stitches the stretch they need.

Stitch width: 0
Stitch length: 4
Needle: double, at least 2mm
Tension: normal
Fabric: knit
Presser foot: special purpose J foot
Thread: polyester
Stabilizer: tear-away

It is simple to fold up the hem and sew with a double needle from the topside of the fabric. When finished, trim the fabric back to the stitching underneath.

The multistitched zigzag #4 can be used for variation. Push down the double needle button so the zigzag will clear the needle plate opening. You may want to use the even-feed foot attachment.

Hemming with a double needle on sheers

Use a double needle for sheer fabrics, too. When a narrow hem would be neither suitable nor attractive, fold up a 4″ (10.2cm) hem on lightweight fabrics. Pin, then baste in place and sew across. Lightweight garments hang better with the weight of a deep hem and it's also more attractive when the hem of the underskirt isn't visible underneath.

Of course you can add more rows of stitching, evenly spaced from the first. Cut back to the top of the stitching.

Hemming with built-in stitches on front

The next hem for delicate fabrics is much the same, but uses a single needle and the built-in crescent #15 stitch.

Fig. 9.1 Use light flannel between hem and skirt, then quilt the hem with lines of straight stitching.

Stitch width: 5
Stitch length: 2
Presser foot: special purpose J foot

Fold up 4″ (10.2cm) for hem and baste, using stitch #6, 1″ (2.5cm) from top of edge. Place fabric front side up, with left side of presser foot against basting line. Stitch, then trim underneath back to crescent stitches.

To hem heavy, canvas-type fabrics with a triple straight or zigzag stitch, use fagoting stitch #9, stitch width 0, stitch length 7, or if you have cartridge 4, use stitch #8 for a reinforced straight stitch (stitch width 0, stitch length 7).

A triple zigzag or rickrack stitch is found on cartridge 4, stitch #8. Set up the machine for a triple zigzag or straight stitch.

Stitch width: varies
Stitch length: varies
Needle: #110/18 jeans
Presser foot: general purpose B

This is an extremely strong stitch. Use it for anything from deck furniture canvas to jeans.

Refer back to the stitch samples you did in Chapter 2. You may prefer other decorative built-in stitches to those mentioned here. Experiment with different fabrics and built-in stitches, keeping all your samples in your notebook.

Quilting a hem

Another single-fold hem can be done on heavy materials such as wool or velve-teen. Use the even-feed foot. Allow about 8″ (20.3cm) for the hem of the skirt. Put light batting, such as flannel sheeting, inside and pin in place. Sew four or five rows of straight stitches (I like at least a stitch length 5), one line at a time, to quilt the hem (Fig. 9.1). Space the lines of stitching as you wish. Try quilting a long Christmas skirt using metallic thread.

Other variations? Use two threads with a topstitching needle. Or turn the skirt inside out and put pearl cotton on the bobbin to contrast with the skirt. The topside will be against the bed of the machine. Stitch rows, then cut back to the last line of stitching. This can be done around sleeve bands or down jacket facings as well.

Lesson 26. Blind hemming

I remember when most of the hems I put in garments were blind hems worked by hand. Times have changed, but that doesn't mean I've given up blind hems. The only difference is that I do them more quickly now—by machine.

To begin the hem, decide first if you can live with a raw edge. If you can, then leave it as it is, but if you hate that unfinished edge, then attach a lace edging over it or stitch around the edge with the multi-stitch zigzag #4 before you proceed.

Turn up the hem 1½″ to 2″ (3.8cm to 5.1cm) and pin very closely around it, about an inch from the top. If the fabric slips, the hem will be a mess, so don't try to save time by not pinning a lot.

Or use Tami Durand's method. Baste (stitch #6) the hem and skirt together, by machine, ¼″ (6.4mm) from the edge of the turned-up hem. There will definitely be no slipping. Fold back and proceed as you do with the pinned hem. When finished, pull out the basting.

Set your machine up. An alternative to setting width and length is to push the double needle button if your machine has one.

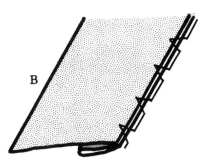

Fig. 9.2 Blind hemming. A. Fold over the hem, then fold the skirt back, letting ⅛″ (3.2mm) show beyond the edge; stitch on the edge of the fabric. B. Or fold the garment back even with the edge, and stitch off the fabric, the left swing stitching the fold.

Stitch width: 2 or varies
Stitch length: normal
Feed dogs: uncovered
Presser foot: blind stitch K
Built-in stitch: blind stitch (#3)
Tension: loosened, auto − 1
Thread: sewing
Accessories: dressmakers' pins

Fold the garment back on itself, leaving $\frac{1}{8}''$ (3.2mm) of hem at the edge to stitch on (Fig. 9.2A). Put the fold of the fabric against the left side of the extension. Adjust the screw at the side of the foot, if you wish, to allow you to stitch on the edge of the fabric and let the needle catch about 2 threads of the fold. Check the settings on scrap fabric first to determine the correct stitch width and length. Thick fabrics will require different settings than lightweight fabrics.

I made a fine batiste bishop dress with yards of blind hemming, but the stitching pulled too tightly. Despite the fine thread, loosened tension, and a #60/8 needle, I didn't like the looks of it. The answer? I sewed from off the fabric. I folded the fabric back so the fold met the edge exactly. Then I stitched outside the fabric and the left bite held it together with no pulling (Fig. 9.2B). I've tried it on other weights of fabric as well, and it works beautifully.

Still hesitant about stitching in space? Then place water-soluble stabilizer under your stitching.

Lesson 27. Sewing narrow hems

Next to hemstitching needles, the most unused accessory is the narrow hemming presser foot. I think I know why: few stitchers ever take time to practice with it. It's a great time saver, but I had to learn to use it, too. Now after yards of hem samples, I can't do without it.

Set up your machine. Before you begin to hem a garment, cut back the seam allowances that have to be sewn over. Then learn to start the fabric. I hated starting a hem because of those first problem inches until I tried Gail Brown's method, which follows.

Straight stitching

You'll need lightweight cotton to hem and a 3″ (7.6cm) square of tear-away stabilizer.

Overlap the piece of tear-away stabilizer with the fabric about $\frac{1}{4}''$ (6.3mm) and sew them together. Start rolling the stabilizer into the scroll of the hemming foot. By the time the fabric is introduced into

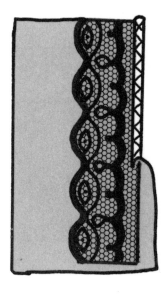

Fig. 9.3 Lace is attached with a finished edge in one step.

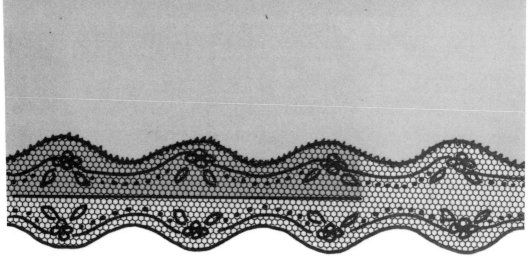

Fig. 9.4 Attach scalloped lace to fabric by overlapping it, zigzagging along the scalloped edge, then cutting the fabric back to the stitching line.

the hemmer, the hem is being sewn down starting on the first thread of the fabric.

Guide the fabric by holding it taut and lifting it slightly as it rolls through the foot. The edge of the fabric must be vertical. As long as you pay attention, guiding and holding the fabric correctly, the machine does the rest.

Sewing on lace

This method is simple and it does save time.

Stitch width: 5
Stitch length: 3
Tension: auto +1
Presser foot: modified J foot
Fabric: lightweight cotton, lace edging
Thread: fine sewing thread to match

Place the lace on top of the fabric, topsides together, the edge of the lace $\frac{1}{8}''$ (6.3mm) from the edge of the fabric.

Use the modified J foot and place the lace edge directly under the foot—the fabric should *not* be caught under the other side of the presser foot, because the needle must stitch within the edge of the lace on the left swing, and off the fabric on the right swing. Use a zigzag setting of stitch width 5, stitch length 3. As you sew, the fabric will roll and be whipped over the heading of the lace (Fig. 9.3).

Open out and fold seam allowance toward the fabric. Zigzag from the topside, down the roll. This zigzag must be so tiny it is unnoticable. Use stitch width $1\frac{1}{2}$, stitch length 3.

See other methods of sewing lace to fabric in Lesson 25, "French handsewing."

Attaching scalloped lace

Apply scalloped lace to fabric, topsides up, by overlapping it to make a hem (Fig. 9.4). Let the fabric extend well past the curve on top of the lace. Baste lace to fabric. Zigzag along the edge, following the scallop. Cut back the fabric underneath to the stitching line.

Stitching shell edging

This is a good hem and edging for lingerie (Fig. 9.5). Or use it to decorate ribbon and tucks.

Set up your machine.

Stitch width: widest (7)
Stitch length: longest (7)
Feed dogs: uncovered
Presser foot: general purpose B
Built-in stitch: overedge #8
Tension: auto +2

133

Fig. 9.5 A shell edge on tricot, stitched with the overedge.

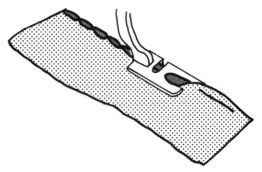

Fig. 9.6 Roll and shell edges are used for decorative hems on lingerie fabrics.

Roll and shell hemming

The narrow hemmer not only makes a narrow, straight-stitch hem, but it also rolls and shells as shown in Fig. 9.6, if the machine is set on zigzag. Usually it's the finish of choice when hemming tricot, as it decorates and hems in one operation. It's impossible to turn square corners on these hems, so round off any corners before you begin to stitch. Because tricot rolls to one side, hem with the right side up. If you will stitch over a seam while hemming, first cut back the seam allowances you'll cross so the fabric will feed in without a problem. As the fabric is rolled into the foot, it will curl and be sewn into a narrow, puffy scallop.

Stitch width: 7
Stitch length: 7
Feed dogs: uncovered
Presser foot: narrow hemmer
Built-in stitch: #2
Tension: normal

It's important to keep the fabric straight ahead of the presser foot and raise it a bit to keep it feeding easily. The needle goes into the fabric at the left, then off the edge of the fabric at the right.

If you are going to cross a seam when hemming, then cut back the seam allowances that will be sewn over to reduce bulk.

The foot rests on the fabric for this one; you do not feed fabric into the foot. Fold the fabric under ½″ (12.7mm) and place the folded edge to the right. Stitch, letting the right swing of the needle sew over the edge, creating the shell pattern. At the end, cut back to the stitching underneath.

134

Lesson 28. Using bias tape

I must admit, I equate bias tape with the edges of Grandma's apron, but now that I can apply it so easily, I'm finding new ways to use it. I especially like it for toddlers' sunsuits and dresses.

This is the only method I use; what I like best about it is that the tape is sewn on almost invisibly. You don't need a bias binder accessory.

Stitch width: 0
Stitch length: normal
Feed dogs: uncovered
Presser foot: special purpose J (for visibility)
Needle: #80/12
Thread: monofilament
Fabric: lightweight cotton, double-fold bias tape
Accessories: glue stick, pins

Look at the bias tape: One side is wider than the other. The wide side will be on the back of your work. Open the bias tape and place the narrow side on top, the cut edge of the tape along the cut edge of the fabric. If there is a $\frac{5}{8}''$ (15.9mm) seam, cut it back to fit the width of the bias. Pin in place. Stitch along the crease.

Fold the tape over the edge. I sometimes dab the underside with glue stick between tape and fabric. Pin if you wish, or baste by hand.

Press the bias and check that the underside of the bias extends slightly beyond the seam line on the topside.

From the topside, stitch in the ditch of the seam. Adjust the fabric under the presser foot to enable you to sew exactly in the ditch. The stitching catches the edge of the bias underneath.

Lesson 29. Zigzagging a narrow edge

This is only one of several methods to produce a strong, finished hem or edge of tiny, tight zigzag stitches. Use it to finish ruffles, napkins and scarves.

Stitch width: 3
Stitch length: 1½
Presser foot: special purpose J
Built-in stitch: #7 right needle zigzag

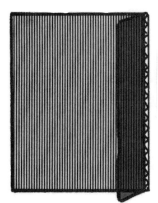
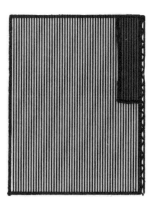

Fig. 9.7 From the top of the fabric, sew a narrow, close zigzag down the folded edge (left). Cut back the fabric underneath to the stitching line.

135

Fold the fabric under about ½″ (12.7mm) and find a place on the J foot to use as a guide as you sew. Then watch that spot as you zigzag. Do a sample first. Stitch on the fabric with the left swing of the needle, the right swing stitching just off the right side of it (Fig. 9.7). After stitching is completed, cut the fabric back to the stitched edge, as partially done below.

Lesson 30. Covering wire for shaped edges

In a bridal shop I saw yard goods that included nylon filament at the edges of chiffon and organdy ruffles. It was an attractive finish for the ruffles that can be applied to skirt and sleeve hems or across the drop-shoulders of wedding gowns and formal wear.

A case displayed dozens of headpieces using the same nylon filament to keep bows perky and ribbons from wilting. You are invited to create your own, combining fil-

ament and sheer fabrics, beads and silk flowers.

I could also see many Halloween costume possibilities here. Use the filament at the bottom edge of a long, filmy skirt or, if you want to make an angel costume, use heavy gauge filament for floppy wings.

Nylon filament is available by the yard at stores that sell bridal lace and fabrics. But I found that it is much easier to buy 25-pound-test fishing line in a sporting goods store. Cheaper, too. I've used both and I don't think there's a difference. There are different weights to fishing lines, which means they come in different thicknesses.

For super-thick costume fabric, you can use weed-trimmer line. It comes in a 50-foot length and the diameter to use is .05mm.

Stitch width: 5 or adjust
Stitch length: 4 or adjust
Presser foot: open J foot

I placed the filament about ⅛″ (3.2mm) from the edge of the fabric (the needle should stitch off the edge of the material on the right swing). As you sew, the edge of the fabric will roll over and enclose the line (Fig. 9.8).

Milliner's wire or florist's wire is available already covered with thread. Both of these can be stitched into the edge of fabric in the same way as nylon filament. They both come in different gauges. Unlike the nylon edge, the wire can be bent into shapes. Buy milliner's wire at bridal shops and florist's wire at craft shops. Make flower petals and leaves using wire.

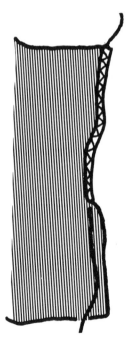

Fig. 9.8 Rolling fabric over nylon filament or wire creates a rigid, finished edge.

Lesson 31. Cording edges

Covering cords

Covered cord produces one of the finest, prettiest edges to use on table linens, on scarves, collars, wherever you want a delicate but very strong edge.

Stitch width: 2½ or adjust
Stitch length: 2 or adjust
Presser foot: modified J foot
Thread: machine-embroidery or sewing thread; #5 pearl cotton

Fold the fabric under about ½" (12.7mm) and press. Place the cord at the side of the fold and against the left inside edge of the presser foot (Fig. 9.9). Cut back to the stitching underneath when it's completed.

If you use this method to finish the edge of a collar, you won't need to turn the collar. Instead, sew with wrong sides of upper and under collar together to eliminate the bulk of a turned-in seam allowance.

First, straight stitch around the collar at the stitching line. Do not cut off seam allowance yet.

Zigzag cord to the collar edge (your stitching line) with a long stitch length. This is for holding the cord in place only.

Now cut back seam allowance to cord. Trim close, but don't cut any stitches.

Next, zigzag back over the cord smoothly with a satin stitch to cover the cord and anchor the stitching firmly on the collar.

Use a stabilizer underneath if your machine balks when stitching in space.

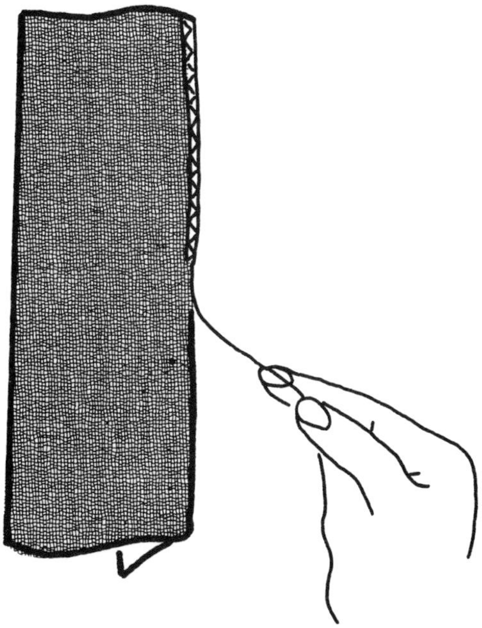

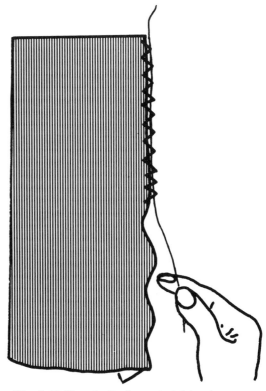

Fig. 9.9 Zigzagging over cord produces a strong corded edge.

Fig. 9.10 Keep knits from stretching by stitching in an elastic thread.

To make a delicate edging for a bridal veil, cord the edge.

Stitch width: 3
Stitch length: 5 (not too tight)
Presser foot: modified J or narrow hemmer
Thread: fine sewing thread to match veil; #8 pearl cotton to match veil

Without folding the veiling, place it so the edge extends past the presser foot on the right. Sew over the pearl. Cut back to the pearl for a fine finished edge.

Reshaping knits with elastic

Elastic can be used to keep stretchy edges in shape, or to reshape them.

Stitch width: 4 or adjust for fabric
Stitch length: 5 or your preference
Presser foot: modified J

Again, guide elastic at inside of foot. The fabric fold is underneath the foot. Keep the elastic at the edge of the knit and sew down the fold (Fig. 9.10).

Lesson 32. Making thread fringe

How many machine owners use a tailor-tacking foot for tailor tacking? I can't find one. Most of the time the tailor tacking foot is used for fringing, fagoting, or for sewing on buttons.

To make thread fringe, you'll need one piece of fabric, folded over at least 1″ (2.5cm) at the edge where you want the fringe to be sewn. Press the fold-line, then open up the fabric so you can stitch on that pressed line (Fig. 9.11A).

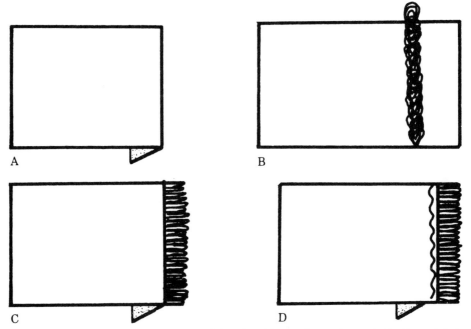

Fig. 9.11 Making thread fringe. A. Fold under fabric edge 1″ (2.5cm). B. Open fabric and use closely stitched tailor tacking along the crease. C. Fold fabric edge under again and smooth down fringe. D. Stitch close to fold to hold fringe in place.

Stitch width: to clear center bar
Stitch length: satin-stitch
Presser foot: tailor tack, special purpose J
Tension: loosened
Stabilizer: tear-away

Stitch on a single thickness of fabric—no stabilizer is needed for this. Be sure the stitches are as close together as you can make them and still have the fabric move easily under the presser foot (Fig. 9.11B).

When stitching is completed, refold on the line and smooth the fringe in place. Press, change foot to "J" and choose a decorative stitch or use a straight stitch to hold the fringe in place. Remember the mirror image button. If you find a stitch, but it is facing the wrong way, turn it around. Slip stabilizer under your work and use the "J" foot as you stitch. I may place a strip of paper over the fringe as I stitch so the threads can't possibly get tangled up in the presser foot. Cut back underneath to your stitching if you wish.

Lesson 33. Piping edges

Miniature piping is especially pretty and colorful on the edges of children's clothing. Use a #3 or #5 pearl cotton and a piece of bias fabric twice the width of the seam allowance. I may not use bias fabric at all. It seems to make little difference, and though held sacrilegious, you can save fabric by cutting on the straight, so try it for yourself. Or cover the pearl with purchased bias tape. Use the zipper foot. Place shank on left of foot and foot against piping. Straight stitch. Use this cording technique, with whatever size cord you wish, when making slipcovers, pillows, etc.

Lesson 34. Topstitching

There is nothing richer-looking on a coat or suit than an even line of topstitching.

When you need a narrowly spaced double line, use a double needle. For topstitching a heavy fabric, I use a topstitching needle with two sewing threads, eliminating the fraying of buttonhole twist. Sew the second line of stitching in the same direction as the first.

When topstitching on lapels, the roll line indicates where the top threads will go to the underside. For this reason, if you use two threads on top, you must use two threads on the bobbin as well. Wind the bobbin with two threads at one time instead of using only one. Then treat the threads as if they were one.

Instead of anchoring threads, leave a long enough thread at the beginning and the end to work in later invisibly by hand.

If you have a machine that will triple straight stitch, experiment (see Chapter 8). Use orange thread and stitch on denim to create the look of commercial topstitching on jeans.

How can you keep topstitching straight? You have several choices. Use the seam guide on the bed of the machine or use tape along the edge of the fabric, and sew next to it.

The straight-stitch foot, along with the straight-stitch throat plate, sews an amazingly precise line of straight stitching. Use it in combination with the seam guide or tape.

Or use the blind stitch foot, keeping the

139

fold or fabric edge next to the inside edge of the extension on the foot. This enables you to keep the fabric straight, $\frac{1}{8}''$ (3.2mm) from the edge if the machine is set up: built-in stitch #7, stitch width, 7, push mirror image button. Amazing! With stitch #7, mirror image, stitch width 7, you get a straight stitch! On any other built-in stitch you get a wide zigzag.

If you place general purpose B foot on top of the fabric—edge flush with fabric edge, stitch #7, stitch width 7, straight top stitch will be $\frac{3}{16}''$ (4.8mm) from edge.

If using lightweight material, set the machine for 10–12 stitches per inch (normal setting). If using medium-weight fabric, a longer stitch looks better. Stitch samples on scraps of the same material to see what stitch length setting you prefer.

I think there is hope for more decorative dressing. Have you noticed how Joan Crawford's clothes don't look so funny anymore?

CHAPTER **10**

Machine Tricks: Adding Threads to Threads

- **Lesson 35. Making cord**
- **Lesson 36. Making tassels**

For nine chapters, we've used fabric and thread for sewing and embroidering. I'll bet you know your sewing machine pretty well by now, but there's more: In this chapter, we'll make monk's cord; then use the cord for practical purposes, such as belt loops and hangers for pendants. We'll also make cords for decoration, bunching them together into tassels.

Lesson 35. Making cord

Twisting monk's cord

Monk's cord is made from several strands of thread or yarn held together and twisted to make a thick cord. The cord may be used in many ways—as a finish around pillows, as a handle for handbags, and as thick fringe in tassels.

When I make monk's cord, I usually ask the help of my friend, Marilyn Tisol. It's easier working with two people, but I'll explain how to twist cord solo as well.

To speed up our job, we use Marilyn's hand drill, with a bent nail substituted for a drill bit. We loop the cord (we like using #3 or #5 pearl cotton) over the hooked nail, then I hold the two ends together (or one end and the ball of pearl) and walk to the opposite side of the room, where I tie the ends of the cord together (and cut off the ball of cotton if necessary) (Fig. 10.1A).

Usually I place a pencil in the loop at the end and keep tension on the cord as

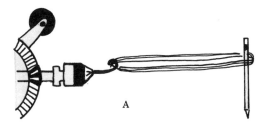

A

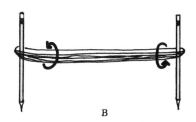

B

Fig. 10.1 Making monk's cord. A. Using a hand drill and a bent nail to twist the cord. B. Twisting cord with two pencils.

Marilyn cranks the drill until the cord is tight enough to twist back on itself.

No hand drill? Then place a pencil through each loop and you and your partner start turning or twisting the pencils in opposite directions until the cord is tight enough to twist back on itself.

If you don't have a partner, tie one end of your cord (you can still double it) to a door knob or place it under the presser foot of your machine. Twist the cord with a pencil or by hand drill.

No matter which method you use, work your pencil out of the loop and, still holding it tightly, find the middle of the cord with your other hand. This is not easy when you work with too long a cord, but there are tricks like walking the cord around a chair before joining the two loops under the sewing machine presser foot, or tying them together on the door knob. Keeping tension on the cord as you walk, bring both ends together and very carefully let the

cord twist to make a monk's cord. Work down the twists with both hands to keep the cord smooth. At this point you will see that it is more successful if you work with a partner.

When the cord is twisted as tightly as it will go, tie an overhand knot to hold the ends together until you actually use it.

I use this cord to make thick fringe for tassels, sometimes slipping washers, bells, beads or a spacer to the middle of the cord after I have twisted it and before I double it and make the final twists (Figs. 10.2 and 10.3).

These quick cords can be used for belt loops, button loops, ties for clothing. Or twist up a batch to tie small packages.

Fig. 10.2 Machine-made monk's cord is used to make this tassel.

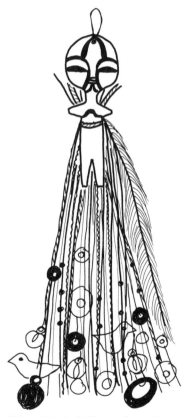

Fig. 10.3 A doll tassel made with monk's cord.

Stitching belt and button loops

Belt loop cords can be made by pulling out the bobbin and top threads and folding them over to make about six strands. Use a stitch width 5 and water-soluble stabilizer underneath if you prefer to stitch with it. Set your machine for free machining, with feed dogs covered. Use the darning foot G or no presser foot at all. Hold the threads tightly, front and back, as you stitch. You will feed the threads under the needle and determine the stitch lengths. These tiny cords work well for corded buttonholes.

You can also zigzag over thicker cords and hold them together. If you add a contrasting thread color, you can make interesting tassels (see the next lesson).

Lesson 36. Making tassels

I'm drawn to tassels. I sketch them when I see them in museums or books, and I have a notebook full of ideas cut from magazines. I've labored over a few myself, using hand embroidery, even tiny macramé knots. Sometimes they look like fetish dolls—another weakness—and so I play them that way.

How can my sewing machine help me make tassels? First of all, I make monk's cord as described in Lesson 35. I combine those with other cords, sometimes stringing beads or bells on them (Figs. 10.4 and 10.5).

I can also use the open J foot to make colorful cord. Holding several pearl cotton cords together, I place them in the groove on the bottom of the presser foot and zigzag stitch over the pearl with a contrasting color. I choose a stitch width 5 to enclose the cords, and a normal stitch length to let some of the cord show through.

Project
Tassel Collar

Several ways to make tassels by machine involve using water-soluble stabilizer. The first method is for a collar of stitched cords to wrap around the main tassel cords.

Stitch width: 5
Stitch length: 1
Needle: #80/12
Presser foot: J foot
Feed dogs: uncovered
Tension: normal
Cord: 16 yards (14.5m) rayon cord (available at fabric shops) for the collar; #5 pearl cotton to match cord; many yards of string, thread or yarn for main part of tassel (the more yarn used, the plumper and more attractive the tassel), cut into 16″ (40.6cm) lengths
Thread: rayon embroidery to match rayon cord
Accessories: water-soluble stabilizer

First fold the 16″ (40.6cm) lengths of yarn in half to find their centers. Use one yarn piece to tie the lengths together there. Knot tightly. Then tie an overhand knot with the ends of that cord to make a hanger for the tassel.

Cut six dozen 8″ (20.3cm) lengths of purchased rayon cord. Place a piece of water-soluble stabilizer on the bed of the machine and lay these cords next to each other across the stabilizer (in horizontal rows as you are looking at them). Starting $\frac{1}{2}$″ (12.7mm) in from the right side, place a strand of #5 pearl cotton perpendicular to and crossing all the cords (Fig. 10.6). Satin stitch over the pearl cotton and the rayon cords. Sew down several more rows

143

Fig. 10.4 Monk's cord is used for the tassels at left *and* center. *A collar, stitched by machine, was used for the one at* right.

of pearl, lining up each pearl cord next to the one stitched before it. When completed, cut off the $\frac{1}{2}''$ (12.7mm) rayon threads protruding from the top of the collar. Zigzag over the edge, which will give the top a smooth finish.

Wrap the collar, inside-out, $1\frac{1}{2}''$ (3.8cm) down from the fold of the tassel cords. Pin the collar tightly around the cords. Remove it from the tassel and machine stitch the ends of the collar together. Cut back to the stitching line and zigzag over the edge. Turn right side out, then pull the yarn tassel cords from the bottom through the collar to complete it. The collar should fit snugly.

Fig. 10.5 More tassels stitched by machine.

Project
Covered Wire
Tassel

Cover 18″ (45.7cm) of milliner's wire with stitches for the next tassel (Fig. 10.7).

Stitch width: 5
Stitch length: 1
Needle: #80/12
Feed dogs: uncovered
Presser foot: modified J
Tension: normal
Thread: rayon embroidery

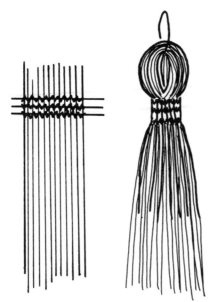

Fig. 10.6 Make a collar for the tassel by placing cords next to each other, then zigzagging over cords laid at right angles across them.

Fig. 10.7 Cover milliner's wire with stitches and twist the wire around cords to make a tassel.

146

Accessories: tweezers
Stabilizer: water-soluble (optional), cut into long strips 1″ wide

Set up your machine and place water-soluble stabilizer under the wire if you wish. Sew over the wire. If the wire doesn't feed well, then use a longer length stitch and go over it twice. The milliner's wire is covered with thread and this keeps the rayon stitches from slipping.

Make 45 thick cords for the tassel by zigzagging over two 12″ (30.5cm) strands of #5 pearl cotton for each one. *Hint:* Stitch two 15-yard-long (13.7m long) cords together and cut them into 12″ (30.5cm) pieces.

To use the wire for the tassel, first fold the 12″ (30.5cm) long cords in half. Slip an end of the wire through the fold, extending it past the cord 2″ (5.1cm). Bend the wire back 1″ (2.5cm) at the end and twist it around itself to make a loop for hanging (the loop will enclose the cords).

With the other end of the wire, wrap the tassel around and around till you reach halfway down the length of it. Hold the end of the wire with the tweezers. Wrap it around the point of the tweezers to make a decorative coil at the end (Fig. 10.7).

Project
Doll Tassel

The fertility doll tassel is a combination of several dozen 10″ (25.4cm) cords, including linen, jute and monk's cords (see Fig. 10.3) all tied to a small African doll. I placed the bundle of cords on the bed of the machine, letting it extend 1″ (2.5cm) to the right of the presser foot and flattening it with my fingers to allow me to stitch over the cords. The machine was set up for free-machining, with feed dogs covered and darning foot G in place. Using the widest zigzag, I stitched forward and back across the cords. When I finished, I spread glue from a glue stick across the stitching on one side of the bundle and placed this at the back of the doll, wrapping and tying it in place with a linen cord.

To decorate the tassel, I slipped a long feather under the linen wrapping cord, and strung some of the tassel cords with beads, brass bells and metal washers. Overhand knots held the objects in place at different heights on the cords. There's a hole in the top of the doll, so I added a loop of cord there to hang the tassel.

Project
Making
Two Tassel Tops
by Machine

For the following tassels shown in Fig. 10.8C and 10.9, the tops are made on the sewing machine. Put a 7″ (17.8cm) square of felt in a 5″ (12.7cm) spring hoop. Draw half a circle and embroider this using decorative, built-in machine stitches. Take it out of the hoop and cut out the half-circle (Fig. 10.8A). Cut out a wedge from the side of the half-circle (Fig. 10.8B). Fold the larger piece in half, topsides together. Straight stitch the cut edges. Turn to the right side.

Cut six tassel cords, each 18″ (45.7cm) in length, from rayon cord or monk's cord. Find the center and tie them together at the middle with a cord 8″ (20.3cm) long. Thread that cord through a large-eyed needle and push it up from inside through the top of the cone. Tie a knot at the end and hang the tassel.

The second tassel is also made of felt, with a machine-stitched top (Fig. 10.9).

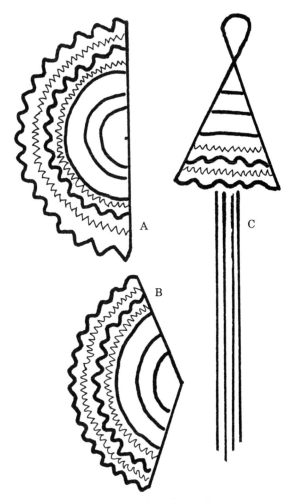

Fig. 10.8 Making a machined tassel. A. Embroider a half-circle of felt. B. Cut a wedge from it, and sew up the sides to form a cone. C. The cone becomes the top of the tassel.

Stitch width: 5
Stitch length: varies
Needle: #90/14 topstitch
Feed dogs: uncovered
Presser foot: overedge; open J foot
Tension: loosened
Fabric suggestion: 9″ (22.9cm) square of felt

Fig. 10.9 A tassel made of satin
stitches on felt.

The finished size of the tassel top is
2″ × 2″ (5.1cm × 5.1cm). I worked with a
9″ (22.9cm) piece of felt so it would fit in
the 7″ (17.8cm) spring hoop. This allows
enough room for the presser foot without
hitting the edge of the hoop, as you will
stitch both sides of the tassel top—2″ ×
4″ (5.1cm × 10.2cm) area—at once.

Trace the pattern from Fig. 10.9. Cut
around the tracing and lay this on the felt.
Draw around the pattern with a marker
(it won't show when tassel is completed).

Begin by carefully stretching the felt in
the hoop. Use the overedge foot for this
top or use corded (#5 pearl cotton) satin
stitches with the modified J foot. Place the
cord at the left inside edge of the presser
foot and through the groove at the back
(see Fig. 3.19). Starting on the right side,
place one line of close, smooth satin stitches.
Add another row next to the first, and continue, changing colors as you wish. Now
sew between the satin stitches, using a
contrasting color and a triple straight stitch
if your machine has one built in or use
fagoting stitch #9 with stitch width 0. You
can also use double thread in a topstitching needle, with a straight stitch.

Cut out the stitched design; then cut it
in half. Place wrong sides together.

Cut about five dozen lengths of pearl
cotton, each 12″ (30.5cm) long. Fold them
in half. Place the folds inside the felt pieces
along the straight edge. Pin the felt together or use a dot of glue stick to hold
everything in place as you stitch. Zigzag
across the straight edge of the felt to keep
the pearl cotton in place. Zigzag around
the curve as well. Then go back with a
satin stitch and stitch around it again with
stitch width at 5, stitch length 1. Add bells
to each side and a hanger at the top.

Try decoratively stitching ½″ (12.7mm)
ribbon for tassels. Using a repeat of your
favorite stitch or combinations of stitches
in memory, stitch down the center of grosgrain or taffeta ribbons. A flimsier ribbon
needs a stabilizer, which is hard to re-

(tassel top will be completely covered with
stitches)
Thread: rayon machine embroidery—I chose
red, yellow and blue; #8 red pearl cotton;
#5 blue pearl cotton (optional)
Accessories: 7″ (17.8cm) spring hoop, small
bells, glue stick, fine-point marker
Stabilizer: tear-away

move. If the ribbon is washable, then use water-soluble stabilizer. Substitute ribbon for monk's cord when making tassels.

Use alphabet cartridges to stitch names or greetings on the ribbon and use the tassels on gifts or Christmas ornaments.

I agree, making tassels is a nutty thing to do (but it's fun). Use them to decorate your tote bag, for key chains, zipper pulls, decorations on clothing, curtain tiebacks. I confess that I hang them all over my sewing room.

CHAPTER **11**

Monograms and Decorative Motifs

- **Lesson 37. Decorating your clothing and accessories**
- **Lesson 38. Decorating your environment**

An easy way to add a personal long-cut is to decorate your clothing and home by adding Singer decorative stitches to garments and gifts: initials, monograms, messages, motifs.

In this chapter, we'll monogram and decorate with 6268 Sew Ware, but I haven't forgotten those of you who own other Singer models. When Sew Ware is indicated on a project, I'll also explain alternate methods to stitch in initials, ciphers and monograms. Built-in decorative stitches can be used, or use free-machine embroidery.

Lesson 37. Decorating your clothing and accessories

Monogramming, the practice of placing one's initials in a design, began during the Middle Ages. Knights in full armor looked too much alike, so over their battle dress they wore particular colors or symbols on their tunics to identify themselves. Churches, as well as noble families, also adopted signs and symbols for identification. Merchants, as a rule, did not have the authority to use crests, so they used simple initials arranged into a monogram or cipher.

Personal marks were put on everything from bedclothes to banners. Usually these marks were elaborate crests or coats-of-arms. It became the style to incorporate into them not only initials, but illustrations to identify the family or business—the Queen of England, for example, uses a crown over her monogram. Those of us who love our sewing machines might in-

corporate thimbles and thread or a sewing machine into a design for ourselves.

Crests and coats-of-arms are still used today, and monograms, as we know them, are direct descendants of this practice. It's an interesting challenge and fun to elaborate on a monogram, incorporating it into a coat-of-arms or logo for your family. Start with the initial of your surname, then add other initials and symbols for your profession, hobby, interests, a medal you won and so on. You don't have to be an artist: use pictures and symbols from books you have, or visit the library for inspiration. The design is personal, so anything goes. Arrange and rearrange your initials and symbols, overlapping them, eliminating what doesn't fit well. Be aware of proportion, spacing of letters, and unity, as well as optical illusions sometimes caused by serifs or the openness of letters.

Once you are satisfied with your choices, plan colors; then find threads for your design and embroider your family coat-of-arms for framing. If you own the Ultra Unlimited 6268, you can plan your design around the initials found on the cartridges. Combine these with free-machine embroidery. Or, if your design is large enough, use appliqué in combination with Sew Ware or free-machining.

Monograms, ciphers, calligrams

I use these terms in this chapter: initial, monogram, cipher, and calligram. Monograms and ciphers are made up of two or more initials combined into a design. In a monogram, a stroke from one letter is usually part of another (Fig. 11.1). A cipher (I used one on the beach towel in Fig. 11.21) is a term not used very often. It is also a

Fig. 11.2 Letters are intertwined, or placed one on top of another, in a cipher.

Fig. 11.1 A monogram is made up of two or more initials; usually a stroke from one letter is part of another.

Fig. 11.3 Calligrams are designs using whole words or names.

151

combination of initials, but the initials are intertwined into a design, or one letter is placed in front of another (Fig. 11.2). For the sake of simplicity, and because there are examples where monograms and ciphers overlap, we'll call them both monograms.

One other term used in the study of lettering is "calligram." I included a calligram in Chapter 4 when I designed the "Singer" edge-stitch appliqué. A calligram is a design made up of an entire word or name (Fig. 11.3). Readability takes a back seat to design.

When planning monogramming projects, it's important to know the correct ar-

Fig. 11.4 A. If the initial for the surname is last, as in Katherine Ann Jensen, all initials in a monogram are one size. B. The surname initial is used in the center if the center initial is larger than those on each side. C. Monogram for a bride using her maiden name, e.g., Jacquelin Lou Hanson. D. Another acceptable monogram for a bride is using her first and last initial on either side of the groom's surname, e.g., Jacquelin Hanson Dodson. E. The most popular monogram today uses the bride and groom's first initials on either side of his surname, e.g., Jacquelin and Charles Dodson.

rangement of letters in a monogram, as well as the correct placement on linens and clothing.

Actually there are no fixed rules for the arrangement of letters in a monogram. However, if the letters are all one size, they are usually arranged in the order in which they are read (Fig. 11.4A). But if the center letter of a three-initial monogram is larger than those on either side of it, then the surname should be the prominent one (Fig. 11.4B).

A holdover from when a woman had an extensive trousseau to take into marriage, linens purchased before a wedding usually are embroidered with the bride's initials, using her maiden name (Fig. 11.4C). But again, there is no hard and fast rule. A bride may use the initials of her first name and maiden name on either side of the initial of her groom's surname (Fig. 11.4D). Or, she may use her first initial, their surname initial, then his first initial (Fig. 11.4E). If using only one initial, use his.

It's important that the monogram be in proportion to what is being embroidered. It shouldn't be lost on a tablecloth or towel, but neither should it overpower the linen nor be too obvious. Singer Sew Ware includes several monogram sizes for block and script initials. Refer to the cartridge manuals for methods to apply the letters in diamond, block, and diagonal arrangements.

With Sew Ware cartridges, the monograms are stitched in perfectly without your having to guide the fabric. Also, the computer correctly arranges the block initials according to the accepted rules of monogramming.

Monogramming clothing

Styles of monograms and placement preferences change periodically, so you can refer to the following to monogram on cuffs, if that's the style for the season, or the collar, if that is the style. I recently read

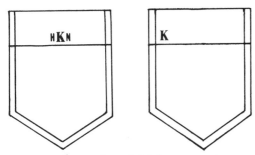

Fig. 11.5 Center three initials on a pocket a fraction above the line of stitches. Place one or two initials at the lefthand side of a pocket.

in a Chicago newspaper that it's more acceptable today to monogram a shirt on the left side (as you wear it) hidden under the suit coat, but I'll include the placement of all the alternatives and then it's up to you. When planning your monograms, left pocket, cuff and collar are preferred. All of the following suggestions refer to adult clothing. If monogramming for children, the placement is the same, but reduce the measurements, if necessary, to fit the garment.

If using three initials on a pocket, center the initials above the stitching of the turnover (Fig. 11.5). If using two initials or only one, move them over to the lefthand side of the pocket (Fig. 11.5).

I like initials on cuffs no matter what is "in." First fold the cuff in half vertically and mark the center. Open up the cuff, with the button to the left as you sew it. Place the first letter near the bottom of the cuff, to the right of the center mark and 2½″ (6.4cm) from the buttonhole (Fig. 11.6). If you are sewing two letters, the right side of the second initial will fall 1¾″ (5.7cm) from the buttonhole. A third initial and the space between the last initial and the buttonhole is 1½″ (5.1cm).

For sweaters, place a monogram in the center front, 3″ (7.6cm) below the ribbing of a crew neck or turtle neck (Fig. 11.7A). If the ribbing on the turtle neck is to be

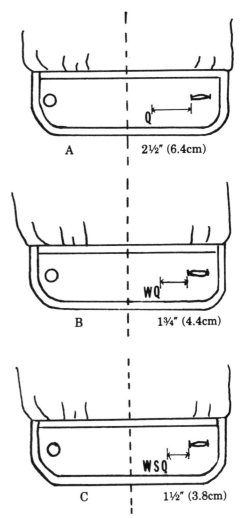

Fig. 11.6 A. To place one monogram on a cuff, measure back 2½″ (6.4cm) from the left side of the buttonhole as shown. The initial is placed a fraction from the topstitching. B. To place two monograms on a cuff, measure back 1¾″ (4.4cm) from the lefthand side of the buttonhole. C. To place three monograms on a cuff, measure back 1½″ (3.8cm) from the lefthand side of the buttonhole.

153

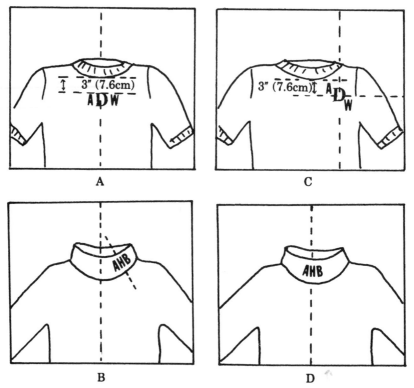

A   C

B   D

Fig. 11.7 A. Place a monogram in the center, 3" (7.6cm) from the ribbing of a crew neck or turtleneck sweater. B. Place a monogram halfway between the center and side seam on the collar of a turtleneck sweater. C. To place a monogram diagonally on any sweater, measure 3" (7.6cm) down from center front at the ribbing and draw across to meet another line drawn from the side neck edge. The center of the monogram will fall where the two lines meet. D. Place a monogram in the center of the turtleneck collar.

embroidered, stitch the initial centered halfway between the side seam and center (Fig. 11.7B).

If monogramming off-center and diagonally on a crew neck, first mark two lines: one down the center of the sweater, another parallel line from the right side of the ribbing (as you look at the sweater). Mark another line three inches down from the center ribbing (follow the line) and perpendicular to it. Draw the line across

to the right of center, intersecting the other perpendicular line (Fig. 11.7C). The middle (large) initial will be centered at the intersection of the two lines. The other two initials will be placed on a diagonal above and below the middle letter (Fig. 11.7C).

Ladies' tailored blouses can also be monogrammed on the cuff, as on a man's shirt, but consider adding a monogram to the front, on a line across from the third button (Fig. 11.8).

154

Fig. 11.8 On a woman's tailored blouse, the monogram is placed across from the third button.

A short-sleeved sport shirt can be embroidered with straight initials centered above the sleeve hem (Fig. 11.9). On the body of the sport shirt, use a diagonal monogram on a line drawn from the second button. The midpoint is on this line (Fig. 11.9).

Fig. 11.9 A monogram on a short-sleeved sport shirt can be placed across from second button, or the initials can be centered above the sleeve hem.

Project
Monogrammed Scarves

For scarves similar to mine (Fig. 11.10) use the large (#6) diamond-shaped monogram on the cartridge. My scarves were made from loosely woven fabrics that fringe easily, approximately 20″ (50.8cm) square. Dish towels or large napkins work beautifully. Today they're found in an array of colors, checks and plaids. Be sure you wash, dry in a dryer, and iron the fabric. Then cut the dish towel, if you use one, into a square; mine was $21\frac{1}{2}$″ (66cm) square after washing, drying and ironing. Next, use the pattern in Fig. 11.11 to cut the neck opening. Stitch around that opening $\frac{1}{8}$″ (3.2mm) from the edge, turn it twice and stitch again.

Cut off the selvages from the square or open the narrow hems on the two sides, then measure the fringe, if it has fringe, and make a mark on the other sides the length of the fringe you'll make (usually $\frac{1}{2}$″ (12.7mm)). Pull a thread at the mark as a guide for fringing. Straight stitch all four sides where the threads have been pulled out, using a thread color that blends with the scarf. Fringe up to the stitching.

The scarf is complete as is, but we'll make it more personal by monogramming the front corner with the diamond-shaped monogram. I measured 2″ (5cm) up from the sides and marked the lines with a vanishing marker. Using the two lines as a guide, I used the diamond template to find the center point for the monogram (Fig. 11.13). I backed the monogram area with tear-away stabilizer and placed the scarf in the embroidery unit, the point directly in front of me. With cotton machine embroidery thread on the machine, I stitched the monogram in once, then again to cover and slightly raise the letters from the fabric.

155

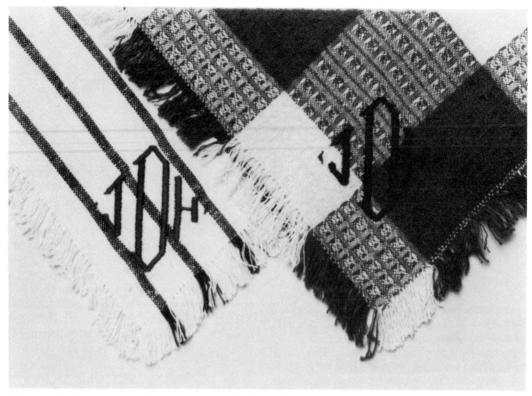

Fig. 11.10 Monogrammed scarves, using the Sew Ware Cartridge.

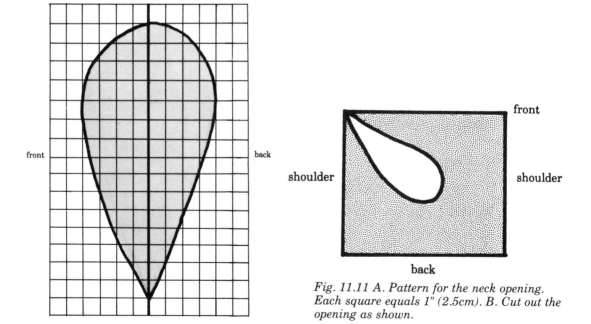

front

back

front

shoulder

shoulder

back

Fig. 11.11 A. Pattern for the neck opening. Each square equals 1" (2.5cm). B. Cut out the opening as shown.

Fig. 11.12 The scarf is worn tied at the side.

Project
Stitched Paper Earrings

A new dress and no earrings to match? Have a minute? Well, a little more than a minute—but this is so much fun, you'll make earrings in every possible color once

you begin, and you won't notice the time. See color section for several finished pairs.

Stitch width: varies
Stitch length: varies
Feed dogs: uncovered
Needle: #80/12
Presser foot: special purpose J
Tension: normal
Thread: metallics, machine embroidery cottons or rayons
Accessories: rotary cutter, paper cutter (optional), scissors for cutting paper, earring backs, thick craft glue, Super Glue, watercolor markers, clear acrylic spray, water-based varnish (optional)

Start with heavy, textured watercolor paper from an art supply store. Estimate how large you want your earrings, then cut out a piece of paper large enough for two earrings. See Figs. 11.14 and 11.15 for several of my ideas. Use these as patterns, or come up with your own designs.

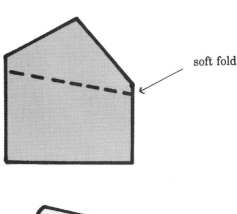

soft fold

Fig. 11.13 Measure 2″ (5cm) from each side of the corner to find the template placement. Mark the center point.

2″ (5cm)

Fig. 11.14 One of my favorite earring designs, easy to make.

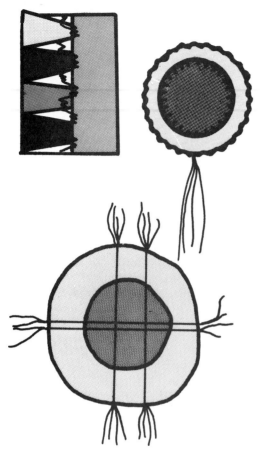

Fig. 11.15 More paper earring designs in
several sizes and shapes.

Paint the front of the paper with a colored
marker. I use water-based markers because they are more transparent than permanent colors and I can still take advantage of the texture of the paper. When dry,
spray the painted side with clear acrylic
sealer and put it aside until the sealer is
dry. (I usually do many of these at one
time; while one is drying, I am painting
or stitching another.)

After the clear acrylic dries, I cut out
the shape I want using a rotary cutter or
paper cutter if possible for clean edges. If
the earrings are round, then I use sharp
paper scissors.

The next step is stitching a sample to
find the stitches I want to use, the stitch
width and length, needle size and thread.
Long straight stitches are better than short
to prevent tearing the paper and I never
use needles larger than #80/12—otherwise, the holes are visible and unattrac-
tive. I used star flowers (see Ch. 2) on one
pair to attach scraps of red paper and at
the same time hold the curve of the blue
paper base in place (Fig. 11.14). Practice
other decorative stitches, changing lengths
and widths until you find the right combinations. Use the mirror image button or
combine several stitches in memory. Use
your imagination! I like leaving thread
ends dangling at the beginning and end.
It's often the answer to what to do with
the ends, rather than trying to hide them.
But I've also discovered that, if I don't want
them to dangle, once my layers of finish
are sprayed or painted on the earrings, the
threads can be clipped back and they don't
tear out.

Add the earring backs next. I buy them
at craft stores and glue them to the paper
with Super Glue. The type of glue that
comes in two tubes and has to be mixed
works best.

To finish the earring, go back and add
more layers of spray acrylic sealer (I add
at least three). I also seal the backs of the
earrings, but keep the sealer off the metal
findings. I sometimes use water-based
varnish over the sealer. It is thin, easy to
apply, and extremely durable. (If used directly over the paint, the color will run
because the paints are water-based.) Mod
Podge or Liquitex Acrylic Matte Medium
are alternatives, too.

To vary the earrings, stitch down different colored pieces of the same heavy
papers over the base (use a thin layer of
thick craft glue to hold them together while
stitching, if necessary). Try flicking paint
off the brush onto the paper to create a

spatter painting. Paint with temperas, acrylics, or permanent markers instead of water-color markers. Cut the paper into different earring shapes: bend down the corner of a free-form earring and stitch, fold long strips of paper into streaks of lightning and stitch to hold the folds together, then hang from ear wires. Is this enough to inspire you? I'm having so much fun, I hope I never finish experimenting.

Project
Stitched
Necklace

Another quickie project is the necklace I made of threads and tiny Guatemalan worry dolls, which I purchased at a craft store (Fig. 11.16). See the color section also.

Stitch width: 7
Stitch length: 0
Tension: normal
Needle: #90/14
Feed dogs: covered
Presser foot: none
Thread: teal blue, red, bright yellow, fuchsia, and purple rayon machine embroidery; 36" (91.4cm)-long strands of multicolored threads or three hanks of pearl cotton
Accessories: several packages of worry dolls, buttons or beads
Stabilizer: water-soluble (optional)

Pearl cotton comes in hanks, which you can open into large loops and stitch into a necklace. For more color, combine two or more of these hanks into one necklace, satin stitching together alternate hanks (Fig. 11.17).

If the cords you've chosen are not in a circle, or hank, to begin with, first measure the length of the necklace you want to make, and add 4" (10.2cm) more for the join. My necklace is 32" + 4" (81.3cm +

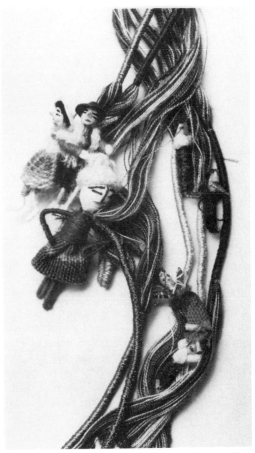

Fig. 11.16 Necklace made from satin stitching over threads and adding worry dolls.

10.2cm) of many dozens of threads laid side by side.

Stitch over water-soluble stabilizer if necessary with your machine. Set up your machine for free-machining and take off the presser foot. Place your left hand behind the needle, right hand at the front with pearl cotton cords taut between them (don't try to stitch over more than can be handled easily). The satin stitch must enclose the threads to give a smooth finish. Use the widest zigzag and satin stitch for about 2" (5.1cm) or 3" (7.6cm) and back

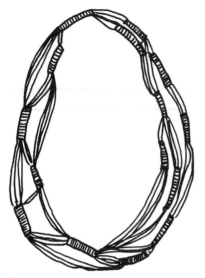

Fig. 11.17 Satin stitch over pearl cotton to hold the necklace together.

it from the needle and bobbin to the next place I want to stitch and so on. Then I have few starts and stops to Fray-check and it adds color to my necklace. Change to another color and go on stitching threads together. Continue holding cords together and satin stitching over them until the necklace is completed to your satisfaction.

Satin stitch over the join (Fig. 11.18), if you have one, and cut back the threads at both ends as shown. You may want to join it a few threads at a time so it looks more like the rest of the necklace.

Add worry dolls, stitching them by hand to the tops of the satin stitches. I found a few larger dolls at a museum shop and added those as well (Fig. 11.19). Other possibilities would be to string beads on the cords before satin stitching them or add decorative buttons instead of the dolls.

again to cover the cords. You control the length of the stitches—keep them close together so you don't see any pearl cotton between them. Stitch several areas of satin stitches with the same color. I stitch one area, then without cutting the thread, pull

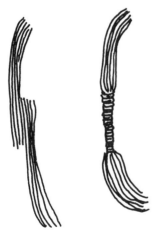

Fig. 11.18 A. Lay cords side by side and satin stitch over them to join. B. Cut back to the satin stitches.

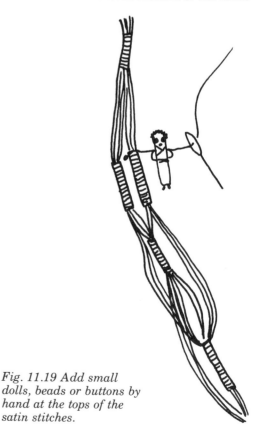

Fig. 11.19 Add small dolls, beads or buttons by hand at the tops of the satin stitches.

Lesson 38. Decorating your environment

Monogramming table linens

When embroidering linens with a single initial, it is larger and more ornate than when two or more initials are used. My suggestions for monogram placements are only suggestions; in truth, there are no hard and fast rules. Placement depends on your preferences. When one initial is embroidered on a tablecloth (preferred today over two initials), the initial is placed to the left of the hostess, 2" (5.1cm) from the edge of the table (Fig. 11.20A). If you embroider four single monograms, place one on each side of the center of the table, halfway between the centerpiece and plates (Fig. 11.20B).

For small napkins, the base of the letter will be diagonal to one corner (Fig. 11.21A). Three letters can be positioned along the right edge (Fig. 11.21B). For a very large napkin, first fold it as it will be folded at the table. Then use a vanishing marker to mark the outline of the monogram in the *center* of the napkin to assure yourself it is in the correct place before you embroider (Fig. 11.21C).

To make festive napkins, combine the initial with a design from one of the cartridges (cartridge 8 includes decorative symbols) or place the monogram within a circle of decorative stitches. Use the single-stitch button and a decorative stitch to embellish on all four sides.

Monogramming bed linens

Sheets and pillowcases are often personalized with monograms placed in the middle of the top sheet, 1" (2.5cm) from the hem when the sheet is folded back (Fig. 11.22A). Or, turn the sheet back at the top and place the monogram in the center,

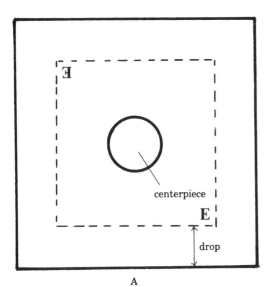

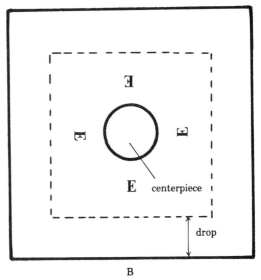

A
B

Fig. 11.20 A. When monogramming a tablecloth, a single initial is placed 2" (5cm) from the edge of the table (indicated by dashed line); two initials are placed diagonally from each other, each 2" (5cm) from the edge. B. Place four single monograms, one on each side of the centerpiece, halfway between the centerpiece and the edge of the table.

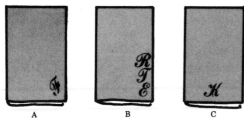

Fig. 11.21 A. Single monograms on napkins are placed with the base of the letter at the corner. B. Or place three initials along the right edge. C. For large napkins, you may choose to place the initial or monogram in the center.

halfway between fold and edge (Fig. 11.22B). Whichever way you choose, the monogram is readable from the foot of the bed.

Pillowcases are monogrammed in the center, 2½" (7.5cm) above the hem stitching line (Fig. 11.23).

Monogramming bath linens

Bath towels, hand towels and washcloths with borders are stitched differently from those with no border. For any of those with borders, place the monogram in the center, ½" (12.7mm) from the border

(Fig. 11.24). If there's no border, then stitch the monogram in the center, 2" (5cm) from the bottom of the edge of the bath towel and 1½" (3.8cm) from the bottom edge of the hand towel and washcloth (Fig. 11.25).

Project Monogrammed Beach Towel

Jan Saunders of Columbus, Ohio, makes these huge beach towels for gifts (Fig. 11.26). When she told me about them, I knew I'd have to make one for our son, Steve. Several things make his towel unique: The length is predicated on Steve's height; a zippered pocket, stitched underneath the towel, is perfect for keys and sun screen; and the towel is monogrammed. The monogram (here is an example of a cipher) makes it his alone and a good project for this chapter. Also, instead of stitching a plain hem on each end of the terry velour, I've used pearl cotton to decorate the stitching line.

When I purchased the fabric, I esti-

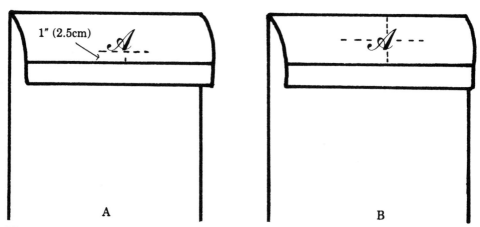

Fig. 11.22 A. Monograms on sheets may be placed 1" (2.5cm) from the hem. B. Or the monogram is placed halfway between the edge of the sheet and the fold.

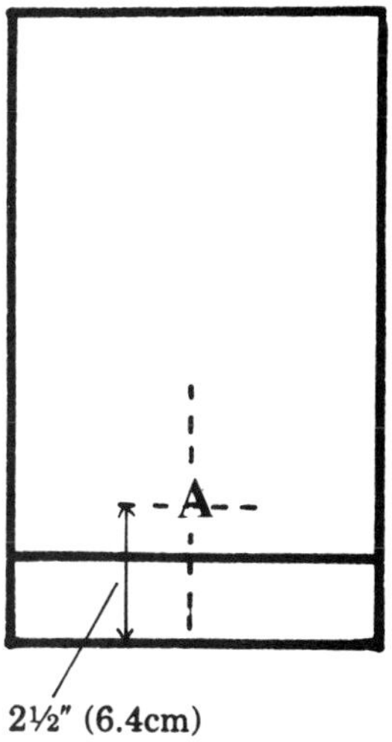

Fig. 11.23 Pillowcases are monogrammed at the center above the hem line, the center of the monogram 2½″ (6.4cm) from the hem stitching line.

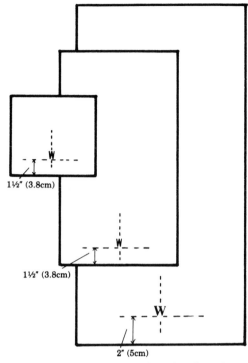

Fig. 11.25 Bath linens without borders. A bath towel is monogrammed 2″ (5cm) from the bottom edge, while hand towels and washcloths are monogrammed 1½″ (3.8cm) from the bottom edge.

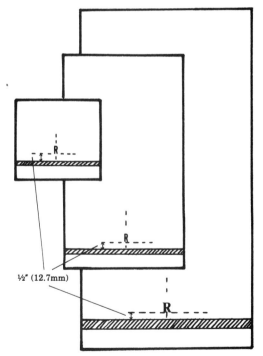

Fig. 11.24 Bath linens with borders. Bath and hand towels, as well as washcloths with borders, are monogrammed in the centers, ½″ (12.7mm) from the borders.

mated the yardage I'd need. Steve is about 6 feet (1.8m) tall, so I started with 2 yards (1.8m). I knew I needed 4″ (10.2cm) for the hems, and I arbitrarily allowed another 8″ (20.3cm) for shrinkage and for evening the ends after washing. The pocket is 5″ (12.7cm) wide (and I added 1″ (2.5cm) more for seam allowances). I added these numbers together and found I needed a piece of fabric 2½ yards (2.3m) long (Fig. 11.27).

After washing and drying the velour, I used a T-square and rotary cutter to even the ends. Then I cut off 6″ (15.2cm) for the pocket.

Stitch width: normal
Stitch length: normal
Thread: blue sewing thread to match towel,

163

Fig. 11.26 Monogrammed beach towel.

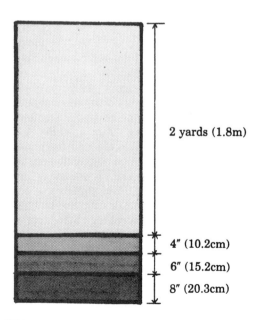

2 yards (1.8m)

4″ (10.2cm)

6″ (15.2cm)

8″ (20.3cm)

white and red machine embroidery cotton, #5 red pearl cotton
Presser foot: Special purpose J, zipper foot E
Fabric: 2½ yards (2.3m) blue terry velour
Needle: #80/12
Accessories: Script Monogram Sew Ware #8 and embroidery unit; 7″ (17.8cm) blue zipper; sliver of soap for marking
Stabilizer: water-soluble and tear-away

First, I hemmed both ends of the towel by stitching a line of straight stitches across the ends 2″ (5.1cm) from each cut edge (I used the seam guide to help keep a straight stitching line). I folded the hem up once on the stitching lines, pressed, pinned, then basted, using the basting stitch on my machine (#6) and thread the same color as the towel. (You can also baste using the longest length straight stitch.) Change to multi-stitch zigzag (#4) with stitch length and width at the normal setting. Leave blue thread on the spool, but fill a bobbin with red pearl cotton (wind by hand). Slip it into the bobbin case, but don't place it in the tension spring. Bring the bobbin thread to the top by dipping the needle down and bringing the thread up, using the hand wheel, or slip the bobbin thread through the loop at the back of the bobbin case and then seat the bobbin (see Fig. 3.20). Turn the towel over, placing the topside down. Stitch across again on the basting stitches. Add other rows of stitching if you wish; use combinations of colors by changing the bobbin color for each row.

Before I stitched Steve's monogram, I practiced combining his initials several ways. It's true that not all initials will fit together as well as his did. To find out if your initials will work as a combination, stitch each separately on stiff cotton organdy. Change sizes (you have three

Fig. 11.27 This is how I estimated the yardage.

choices) and stitch each one. Place one on top of the other, then arrange and rearrange. By using organdy, you'll be able to see through the fabric. I've enjoyed combining initials into designs—at times moving one initial off center slightly to one side or another, up or down. When I found the combination for Steve's monogram that was pleasing to me, I stitched it at center front above the red border.

To begin, I folded the fabric in half lengthwise to find the center, which I marked by pressing the fabric. Then I marked the pressing line with a sliver of soap. I measured 3″ (7.6cm) above the pearl cotton and made a line perpendicular to the first (Fig. 11.28). The towel is huge so I broke the rules of monogramming and placed the monogram further from the border than is usually done. I placed the

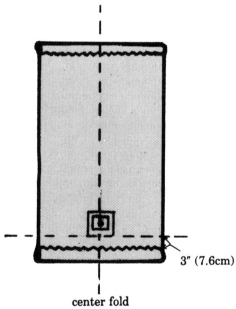

center fold

Fig. 11.28 To begin stitching the monogram, measure 3″ (7.6cm) from the line of pearl cotton. Place the bottom edge of the template on that spot and mark through the hole in the template.

hole in the plastic template far enough above the center crossed lines to leave a 3″ (7.6cm) space from the monogram to the red stitching (Fig. 11.28).

Then I cut a piece of tear-away large enough to fit inside the square of the embroidery unit, where I placed it before centering the towel (I left the tear-away out of the hoop). But before I snapped the hoop in place over the velour, I covered the velour inside the hoop with a piece of water-soluble stabilizer. Water-soluble stabilizer over napped fabric helps make a smooth-looking monogram.

I chose both the medium and large-sized script initials for Steve's monogram and stitched one over the other, each in a different colored thread (see Fig. 11.26). Using white cotton machine embroidery thread, I monogrammed S first, medium size, on the towel—going around the letters twice.

When completed, with the machine at a complete stop, I cut off the thread and changed the top thread to bright red without moving the fabric in the hoop. I changed to large size D, and stitched it over the first. Then I took the towel out of the embroidery unit, and removed the stabilizers.

Without Sew Ware, the monograms can be stitched by using free-machine embroidery or by appliquéing monograms to the towel (Ch. 4). To monogram freely, first draw your monogram on water-soluble stabilizer with a white opaque marker and place this over the towel. Put them both into a hoop. Slip tear-away stabilizer underneath before you begin stitching.

Use at least stitch width 4. Stitch length is set on 0 because the machine is set for free machining—feed dogs covered, darning foot in place. When monogramming freely, practice makes perfect, and it is best to practice on the same fabric. Keep the fabric in front of you, top of the monogram at the top of the hoop in front of you, and never rotate the fabric. Move it

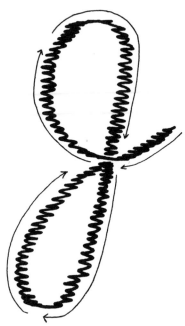

Fig. 11.29 In freely stitched monograms, the satin-stitched up-and-down strokes of the letters are the width of the satin stitch. The cross-strokes are parallel to each other.

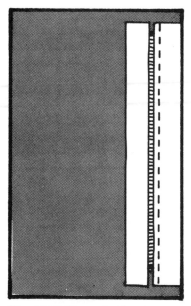

Fig. 11.31 To apply the zipper, stitch it on one edge of the pocket piece.

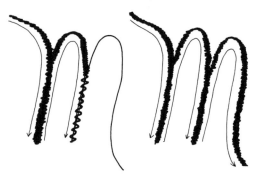

Fig. 11.30 When crossing or stitching on top of other stitching, move the hoop quickly through the first pass, but slowly on the second pass.

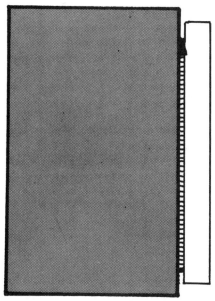

Fig. 11.32 Open and press flat.

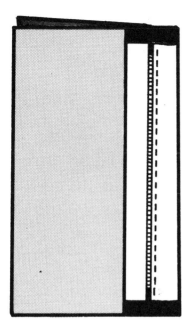

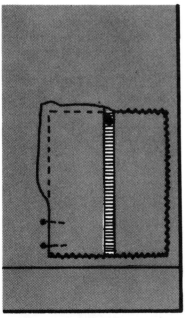

Fig. 11.34 Pin the pocket in place, then stitch in place along the folded edge.

Fig. 11.33 Stitch the other side of the zipper to the other side of the pocket.

up and back, left and right, but don't turn it. This is a simple method. The width of the monogram will be thick on down-strokes, thin on cross strokes, because all the stitches are parallel to each other (Fig. 11.29). You learned control between machine speed and how fast to move the hoop in Chapter 2.

Monogramming is a test of control. If crossing or stitching on top of other stitching (i.e., T, M, N) stitch quickly through the first stroke, then slowly stitch the second pass to cover smoothly (Fig. 11.30).

To finish up the bath towel, put a zipper in the pocket and then attach it to the underside of the towel. Use the 6″ (15.2cm) wide piece of terry cloth you've put aside. Cut two pieces, each 6″ × 8″ (15.2cm × 20.3cm). Sew the 7″ (17.8cm) zipper down the 8″ (20.3cm) side of one piece by first centering it on the fabric, the topside of the zipper on the front of the fabric, matching edges. With the zipper foot on, stitch next to the teeth on the zipper (Fig. 11.31). Open up as shown in Fig. 11.32, and place the zipper on top of the other piece of fabric along the 8″ (20.3cm) side and even with the attached piece. Pin, then stitch in place to attach the zipper into the pocket front (Fig. 11.33). Stitch around the pocket, $\frac{1}{2}$″ (12.7cm) from the edges. Fold under on the stitching line. Place the pocket underneath the towel at a corner on the same end as the monogram, close to the top of the hem and at the edge of the towel. Pin, then zigzag stitch in place along the folded edge (Fig. 11.34).

Project
Lap Robe

This lap robe project (Fig. 11.35) can be done with the Sew Ware monogramming cartridges or you can appliqué the letters and number as I've done. This blanket was made as a joke for my husband's red sports car, using the car's logo, but it ended up being a great idea. It's a rule in our family that each car must carry an Army blanket in case of a blizzard, accident, or both. The kids and I didn't think a drab green Army blanket would do for Dad's new car. Our solution: 2 yards (1.8m) of fake fur fabric lined with red plaid and decorated with an appliqué of the car's logo.

If choosing a monogram cartridge instead of an appliquéd logo, you'll need only one 9″ (22.9cm) square of fabric (to attach to the blanket). Use the largest letters on the monogram cartridge, a style of your choice—diamond, square or diagonal in script or block—and stitch the monogram to the fabric square, then appliqué the square to the blanket.

Stitch width: 0–normal
Stitch length: normal
Tension: normal
Needle: #80/12
Presser foot: general purpose B, special purpose J, even-feed foot M (optional)
Thread: black sewing thread, red machine embroidery thread

Fig. 11.35 Add an appliquéd logo to a lap robe.

Fabric suggestions: 2 yards (1.8m) charcoal-gray fake fur; 2 yards (1.8m) red plaid blend; two 9″ (22.9cm) squares (black and red) medium-weight fabric (match your own car colors for fur and fabric)
Accessories: tracing paper and pencil, dressmaker's carbon and empty ballpoint pen, fusible webbing, long quilting pins
Stabilizer: ironed-on freezer paper

After you wash and dry the fabric, even the ends of the fur with a T-square and rotary cutter, then cut off 7″ (17.8cm) on one end to use as a top binding. Copy the logo directly from the car or use a picture in the car's manual. Enlarge the design on a copy machine, if necessary. (This is my favorite and the only method I use to enlarge or reduce designs. No more graph paper and tedious hours of work trying to duplicate a picture. You can find copiers with this capability in libraries, print shops—even our local hardware store has one.)

Back the red appliqué fabric with fusible webbing, then draw the logo or monogram on top of the fabric. If using Wonder Under, draw the design on the paper backing, but remember to flip over the design before you do so, or your letters will be backwards on the appliqué. Cut out the appliqué and arrange it on the other 9″ (22.9cm) square. Press in place. Iron freezer paper to the back of the square and apply the appliqué with red machine embroidery thread and stitch width 3 satin stitches. Change to black sewing thread. Stitch a line around the inside of the square $\frac{1}{2}″$ (12.7mm) from the edge. Fold, then press on this line and pin to the top of the fur fabric, 4″ (10.2cm) from the edge and 3″ (7.6cm) from the righthand side. Baste in place; then use the blanket stitch (#10) to attach the square to the corner (Fig. 11.36).

Pin the fur fabric and lining, right sides together (lining on top), and place the edge of the presser foot on the edge of the fabric. Helpful hint: follow one of the darker or

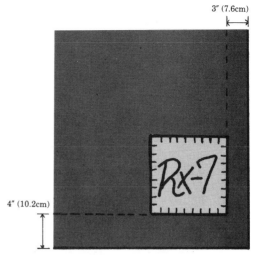

Fig. 11.36 Appliqué the car's logo to the lap robe at one corner, 3″ (7.6cm) from the right edge, 4″ (10.2cm) from the bottom.

lighter threads in the plaid to also help keep the stitching straight. Stitch around three sides, leaving the top open; then stitch around again, this time using the zigzag stitch at normal settings. By using this method of constructing a "bag"—not leaving part of an edge open for turning, as most patterns instruct—the edges are more even. Stitching on fur is a shifty experience, so use the even-feed foot M if you have one. If you don't, then use the general purpose foot B. If you choose an extremely dense fur as I did, you may want to baste the fur and lining together by hand to keep it from sliding before you machine-stitch.

After you turn the blanket to the right side, stitch the top closed $\frac{1}{2}″$ (12.7mm) from the edge. Zigzag across the edge to flatten it and make it easier to attach the binding.

Place the fur binding piece, right sides together, on the front of the blanket and stitch in place with a $\frac{1}{2}″$ (12.7mm) seam (Fig. 11.37). Fold the binding in half the long way, right sides inside, and fold up a $\frac{1}{2}″$ (12.7mm) seam allowance at the edge

169

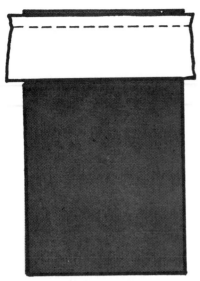

Fig. 11.37 Stitch the binding in place at the top of the blanket.

Fig. 11.38 Fold the binding in half the long way, then fold up ½″ (12.7mm) seam allowance; pin and stitch.

(Fig. 11.38). Pin both ends. Stitch down from the top fold to the bottom fold at each end, then turn to the right side and stitch the hem in place by hand or by machine (Fig. 11.39).

Make fur lap robes in fake mink with "designer" linings for chilly nights in front of the TV, or to wrap up a baby in pastel fur with soft flannel lining, or send one to college in dark blue or red fur with a denim lining.

Jan gave me another quick blanket idea. She bought a wool Navy blanket at an Army-Navy store, bound it with gold felt (school colors) and used the edge-stitch appliqué method to apply a large felt crest with a fraternity monogram to the blanket. The blanket is big enough for two at a football game.

Fig. 11.39 Turn the binding to the right side and stitch the opening in place.

170

Project
Quilted Menagerie Picture

On the next project, shown in the color section, I divided an 8″ × 10″ (20.3cm × 25.4cm) piece of fabric into six squares, two across and three down. In each square I placed one animal from the Sew Ware menagerie cartridge, then quilted the picture by backing it with fleece and stitching over yellow grosgrain ribbon, which I'd basted to the grid lines.

Stitch width: 0–4
Stitch length: 0–3
Needle: #70/10 and #90/14
Presser foot: modified J
Cartridge: Sew Ware cartridge #3
Feed dogs: uncovered
Tension: normal

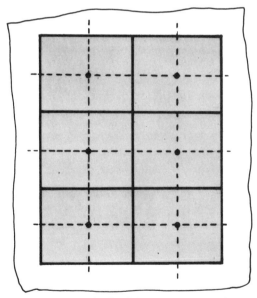

Fig. 11.40 Divide the fabric into six sections, then find the center of each section. Mark for use with Sew Ware templates when embroidering the menagerie.

Fabric: light colored, 12″ × 14″ (30.5cm × 35.6cm) tightly-woven linen-like fabric; 10″ × 12″ (25.4cm × 30.5cm) fleece
Thread: cotton machine embroidery in yellow, green, blue, pink, peach, rust
Accessories: embroidery unit; water-erasable marker; T-square; press-on mounting board, frame and mat; 1 yard (.9m) of $\frac{1}{8}$″ (3.2mm) yellow grosgrain ribbon
Stabilizer: tear-away

To begin, I used the T-square and water-soluble marker to draw a grid on the 8″ × 10″ (20.3cm × 25.4cm) fabric. Each square is 4″ × 3$\frac{1}{3}$″ (10.2cm × 8.2cm). Then I found the center of each section by folding it in half horizontally *and* vertically, then marking the point with a dot from the water-erasable marker (Fig. 11.40).

I placed the animals facing toward the center of the picture when there was a choice, so when you look at it your eye will stay within the frame. Colors were not chosen for realism, but rather to be decorative. I'd chosen the blue frame and yellow mat first, so I began with those colors and built on them.

As I stitched in each color, I remembered to wait until the machine stopped (middle of design) before I carefully cut the thread and then rethreaded the next color without moving the embroidery.

When the menagerie was complete, the embroidery unit was removed and the machine was returned to normal sewing with the special purpose J foot, yellow thread, and #70/11 needle. Fleece was pinned to the back of the picture. Then I basted two pieces of grosgrain ribbon in place on the horizontal grid lines. I attached the ribbon with a narrowed decorative stitch (cartridge #4, blanket stitch #3). Use a zigzag or blind stitch if you prefer. When both ribbons were stitched in place, I added the long vertical ribbon and stitched that as I did the others.

I took the glass out of the frame before I slipped in the mat and my quilted picture. I never put stitchery behind glass since you cannot appreciate its textures that way. Of course, you can eliminate the batting and then use glass if you wish.

Without the Sew Ware cartridges, use coloring books for design inspiration and either appliqué or use free-machining to decorate each square.

Messages and greetings

Another embroidery idea uses alphabet cartridges and words of greeting or names for name tags (Fig. 11.41). What I think is fun about the Singer alphabets is that I can greet people in other languages. In one framed embroidery I used the Danish Christmas greeting: "Glaedelig Jul" (the

"a" and "e" are combined on the upper line of the alphabet cartridge) and then I combined it with the holly on Holiday cartridge #5. Using red (thread) and white (fabric), the national colors, then adding green, makes this a perfect color combination for Christmas. However, if you're Swedish, use blue and gold for "God Jul"; Spanish? Use vibrant variegated threads for "Feliz Navidad." Any of the cartridges can be combined with free machine embroidery. For example, add the Danish folded heart found so often on Danish Christmas trees, the Swedish straw goat, or piñata for the Spanish greeting. Visit the library for design ideas.

These little pictures are simple and fast using the cartridges; if you wish, you can use your own creativity to make them one of a kind. To center lettering correctly, first stitch a sample on the same fabric you'll use on the final piece. Cut a strip of paper and place it under the lettering. Mark the beginning and end of the lettering on the paper and cut off the paper that extends beyond those marks. Fold the paper in half to find the center (Fig. 11.42). Place the fold on the center mark on the fabric you'll be embroidering. Then, with a vanishing or water-soluble marker, place a dot where the lettering begins. One caution: many letters don't actually *begin* at the far left of the letter! Be sure you watch

Fig. 11.41 Use Sew Ware cartridges and decorative stitches to stitch framed messages and small pictures.

Fig. 11.42 To find the center of a word, first stitch the word. Place a piece of paper under the word and mark the beginning and the end of the lettering on the paper; cut off the paper that extends beyond those marks. Fold the paper in half to find the center.

for this when stitching the sample, then place the fabric under the needle in the right place inside the mark you've drawn on your "good" piece.

When stitching letters around a curve, first stitch them on a sample, then cut the sample apart and slash between the letters (Fig. 11.43A). Arrange the letters around the curve and mark (Fig. 11.43B). Take the sample off and begin stitching, one letter at a time. Stop between letters to rotate the fabric slightly to keep the letters on the curve.

To make the welcome sign (see Fig. 11.41), I first placed the purchased frame over my linen fabric and drew around the inside of it with a vanishing marker. This was my stitching guide. Then I used decorative stitches around the inside of this guide and I used the Sew Ware script alphabet #7, centering "Welcome" in the middle of the embroidered piece.

One other helpful hint regarding these or any embroidered pictures: buy your frame first. Most embroiderers create a picture and then look for a frame. Don't! Choose your frame before you begin, so you can use one that's standard size or— as with the welcome sign—so you can fit your design into the frame's interesting shape. It's easier and much cheaper than having a frame made. All of the embroideries in this book were done frame first. On the menagerie picture I wanted a colorful mat, so I chose both frame and mat in the colors I wanted, then geared the

Fig. 11.43 A. When stitching letters around a curve, first stitch them on a sample, then cut the sample apart and slash between the letters. B. Arrange the letters around the curve and mark your good fabric.

animal sizes as well as the colors to fit the frame and mat.

I was pleasantly surprised by the choice of frames I found in craft shops and by mail order (see Sources of Supply). I found small ones backed by pins for wearing, and magnets for the refrigerator. I found heart shapes, house shapes, drapery-ring-sized frames to hang on a Christmas tree or to use as pendants, frames with curved tops, crossed corners, and the colors range from country to sophisticated.

When I found tiny circle and heart-shaped frames that can accommodate one flower motif on the Sew Ware floral cartridge #6, I spent an afternoon with my twin 5-year-old granddaughters, making about a dozen of these in different colors and putting them together for Christmas gifts for aunts and great-grandmother.

We discovered that you can put a heavy weight on the foot pedal (e.g., the sewing table leg or an iron or a big book) and let the machine stitch by itself until it's through.

The girls were mesmerized by the machine embroidering all by itself and never got bored. I had them listen and watch so they could tell me when the machine beeped, stopped, and what thread colors we needed next. They pushed the buttons and felt that they did it all themselves. It's an idea you can try—to introduce your youngsters to the magic of sewing.

After we had the colors put together (I admit I used the power of suggestion), we first chose a design that would fit in the frame. (In the back of the manuals for each cartridge you'll find the exact size of each motif.) Samples were stitched to see if we liked the color choices, and then a large piece of fabric, backed by iron-on tear-away stabilizer (big enough to stitch on a dozen designs), was slipped into the hoop. We stitched leaves, then flowers, then learned that after the flowers were stitched (the machine doesn't come to a stop after the petals), we could stop the machine ourselves and add another color for the flower centers.

Both girls took turns standing in front of my chair—they're not tall enough to sit, sew, and see what's happening—and stepped down on the foot pedal. I explained that they didn't have to hold onto the fabric, but they liked keeping their fingers lightly on the hoop and they know enough not to move them off. When the machine stopped and the thread had to be changed, they took their foot off the pedal while I did so, then stood on the pedal again after I'd threaded the needle. I helped them snip threads and cut out each design to fit the tiny frames. I had as much fun as they did.

I belong to two textile guilds that require members to make nametags using the medium in which we work and then wear the tag at every meeting. I used a combination of the Sew Ware Alphabet cartridge #1 and the decorative stitches to make myself a new nametag and framed it in an attractive 2″ × 3″ (5.1cm × 7.6cm) frame I found in a catalog (see Sources of Supplies). Pins for backing them are also available.

All of these things are quick gifts that can be added to the ribbon on a gift, or can be the gift itself. And remember, if you don't have cartridges, you do have the skill to decorate with free-machine embroidery.

Project
Victorian
Christmas
Stocking

This sensuous stocking, shown in the color section, is a Christmas favorite. The first ones I made were created in desperation when I'd run out of ideas for Christmas gifts for three special friends. We make gifts for each other every Christmas and I needed inspiration. I found it in boxes of old lace, beads, ribbons, braids and buttons I'd been given and collected over the years.

The stocking is 24″ (61cm) long, fully lined, and covered with sumptuous embellishments. No craft ribbons allowed, only double-faced satin, taffetas or exquisite velvets and velveteens. I want an heirloom quality to my stockings. These stockings are never the same twice. I've used the traditional red and green, but now I try to match the stockings to friends' favorite colors.

Stitch width: 0–widest
Stitch length: 0–normal
Needle: #90/14
Presser foot: special purpose J, open and modified J are optional
Feed dogs: covered and uncovered
Tension: normal
Fabric: scraps of velveteen in pastel green, pink, antique white; ¾ yard (68.6cm) green lining (silky type); ½ yard (45.7cm) muslin; ¾ yard (68.6cm) antique white velveteen
Decor: ribbons in three widths, at least 2 yards (1.8m) each for bows; add 12″ (30.5cm) more for each ribbon rose; variety of fine ribbons for stocking front in various sizes (see color photo); laces, beads, buttons
Thread: rayon machine-embroidery threads in pink, green, off-white; off-white sewing thread; 1 yard (.9m) heavy gold cord
Accessories: monogramming, decorative stitch and alphabet cartridges; embroidery unit
Stabilizer: tear-away

Enlarge the pattern in Fig. 11.44 and transfer to the muslin. Cut out one stocking front. On this you'll build your "crazy-quilt" stocking. Next, cut out a stocking back from the velveteen. You'll have fabric left over for other stockings. (I discovered a velveteen called Matinee that has

174

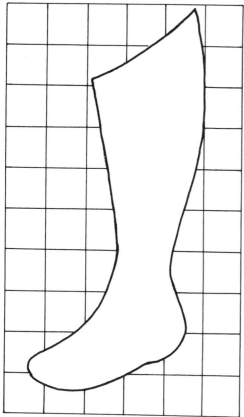

Fig. 11.44 Pattern for stocking. Each square equals 4" (10.2cm).

Fig. 11.45 Crazy-quilt application of ribbons and fabric.

nap, but no direction. When using that, you can buy less fabric because you can place the pattern anywhere on the fabric.) From the green lining fabric, cut a stocking front and back.

I may sketch the stocking first on paper, but usually I design right on the muslin backing (Fig. 11.45). The planning takes the longest, but it is also the most fun. I've sketched hundreds of ideas from books on clothing and costume. Books on military uniforms contain a wealth of ideas for braids, buttons and pleats. Victorian couture gives me ideas for passementerie. But no matter how carefully I plan a stocking,

it never ends up exactly the way I had worked it out. These stockings evolve.

First, overlap the fabric scraps on the muslin, rather than butt them together, when placing one piece next to another. This enables you to decorate, cover or fold under only one raw edge at a time. Cover edges with lace or ribbon or fold under

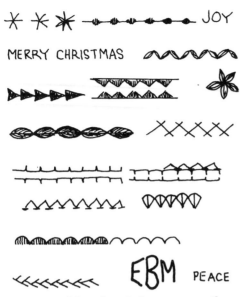

Fig. 11.46 Ideas for stitches to use on the stocking.

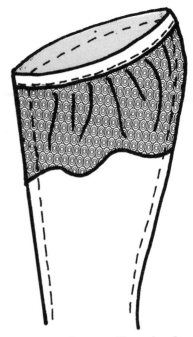

Fig. 11.47 Baste ruffle under the top line of staystitching.

fabric edges and embroider them with decorative stitches. I often used Sew Ware decorative borders cartridge #4, stitch #3, narrowed to stitch on each side of the ribbons to look like a textured border and I may add built-in stitch #8 at the edges of the previous stitches (Fig. 11.46). Gold cord is couched down with stitch #8 on cartridge #4 (rickrack), and for other decoration on the velveteen or across the ribbons try cartridge #4, stitch #17 (cross-stitch), #5 (satin-stitched curve), #6 (beads in a row), #7 (triangle border), #13 (feathers), #15 (curved edge triangles). Combine stitches in the Singer memory for variety and stitch over the stocking to give it an elegant Victorian look.

Each stocking I make is personalized with a monogram or initial. I placed this one on the heel.

At the top of the stocking stitch, "Merry Christmas." When the stocking is finished, the message is hidden under the ruffle, but I make a point of embroidering

and decorating under the ruffle as elegantly as the rest of the stocking.

The last decoration is the addition of beads or old buttons. Add them by hand or by machine.

When the stocking front is completed, stitch around it $\frac{1}{4}''$ (6.4mm) from the edge. Next, add the top ruffle (Fig. 11.47). If the lace is not gathered already, zigzag over a cord at the top of the lace and pull up on the cord to gather it. You may want to add another piece of gathered lace at the top for a more finished edge (see color photo). The lace ruffles are placed directly under the stay-stitching and basted in place. The sides of the lower piece of lace are also basted to the sides of the stocking, but the top, short ruffle is rolled at the sides and hemmed by hand (Fig. 11.48). Then add a strip of ribbon to the top (Fig. 11.49) by machine or by hand.

176

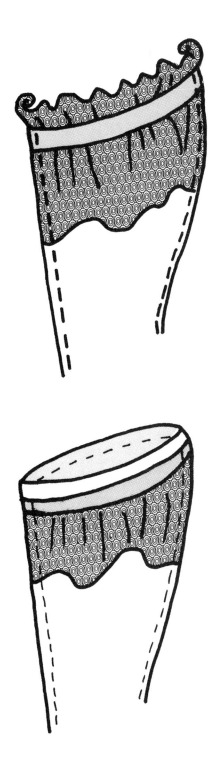

Fig. 11.48 If preferred, add a short ruffle above the stocking before you add the ribbon.

Pin the stocking, right sides together, and stitch the foot first on the stay-stitching line and up the leg to the top. Then go back and do the other side. When I sew it together this way, there is less creeping and the front and back fit together perfectly. Next, turn the stocking right-side-out and fold down the top at the stitching line.

Place the lining pieces, right sides together, and stitch around them, except for the top. Stay-stitch $\frac{1}{4}''$ (6.4mm) down from the edge, around the lining top. Fold down at the stitching to the outside (the lining is still wrong-side-out).

Push the lining down into the stocking (Fig. 11.50A). I use the end of a long water-color brush or dowel. Place the top fold of lining at the folded edge of the stocking. Whip stitch by hand around the top. I usually stitch, also by hand, a strip of lace around the top inside of the stocking to give it an elegant finish (Fig. 11.50B).

Use directions in Chapter 5 to make ribbon roses for the centers of the bows. Also, make a hanging cord either from pearl cotton (see Ch. 10), a short string of pearl beads, or cord from a drapery or fabric store.

Use three different width ribbons to embellish the stocking at the hanger. They can be one to three different colors and widths. Make large loops and tie the loops together with a narrow ribbon or cord, leaving long ends of ribbons to hang at different lengths from below the ruffle of the stocking to just below the calf.

Fig. 11.49 Add ribbon to the top by machine or by hand.

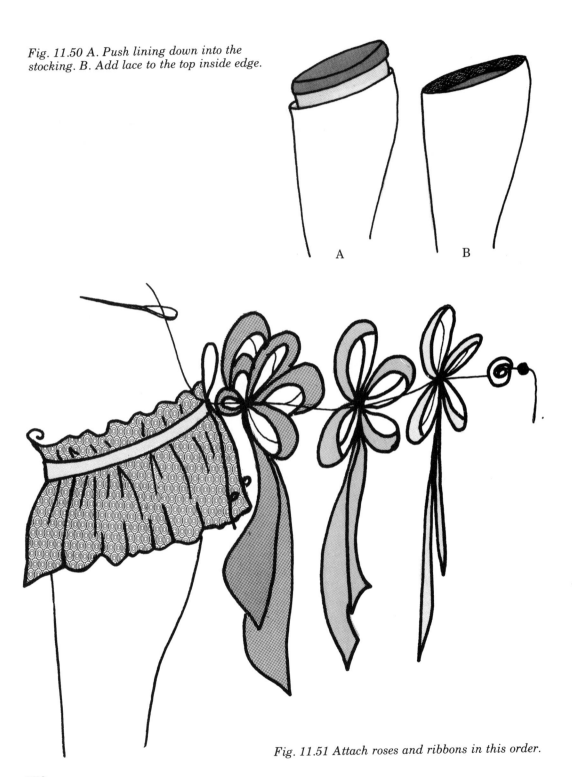

Fig. 11.50 A. Push lining down into the stocking. B. Add lace to the top inside edge.

A

B

Fig. 11.51 Attach roses and ribbons in this order.

178

Fig. 11.52 The finished stocking—voilá.

To assemble the ribbons, hanger and roses, first stitch by hand the hanging cord loop to the right side seam of the stocking. Leave enough cord below the loop to add color or interest to the ribbons. Tie overhand knots at the ends of the cord. Cut back and dot the ends with Fray-check. Or, tie the knots an inch above the ends, then fray out the cord. Next, stitch down the ribbons. The wider ribbon will be the first stitched in place, then any narrower ones in order, ending with the narrowest. Three ribbon roses go on next. Stitch them in place in the center of the ribbon loops. Place a pearl in the center of each rose and stitch through it, the rose, ribbon and stocking for a strong anchor (Fig. 11.51).

Though you've used built-in stitches and Sew Ware when making this stocking and other projects in this book, you can be original in the way you put the stitches together. Just as initials and monograms mark possessions as yours, so do your color, fabric and stitch choices. That's what makes embroidery and sewing on your Singer so creative and exciting.

CHAPTER 12

Making the Tote Bag

The year I became program chairman for an embroiderer's guild, I began to assess previous programs: Why was one a success, another a failure? I remembered the many needlework workshops I had taken, the many projects I had started in those classes and never finished because they were too big or demanded too much of my time. And I knew I wasn't the only one who felt this way, as other members also had boxes of half-finished needlework.

That's when I came up with the idea of the tote bag. I asked the teachers that year to gear their workshops toward making samples small enough to fit in a 6″ (15.2cm) square frame. The fabric squares could then fit into the frames made by the handles on a tote bag I designed. Each new square could easily slip in and out. Not only were the class projects small enough to complete easily, but they were useful and decorative as well.

I'm using the same tote bag for this book (Fig. 12.1). After you've made the tote bag, it can be used to show off the sample squares found in the lessons.

First, I'll explain how to finish the squares you made throughout the lessons in this book. Then I'll explain the tote bag.

Finishing the squares

Specific instructions for each square are included in the lessons. A brief recap: Start with a piece of fabric large enough to fit in a 7″ (17.8cm) hoop, if you will be working with one. I suggest starting with a 9″ (22.9cm) square, as it is better to have extra fabric than not enough. The finished square will be $6\frac{3}{4}$″ (17.1cm). The area that will show in the frame will be 6″ (15.2cm) square. Cut a piece of acetate or cardboard $6\frac{3}{4}$″ (17.1cm) square to use as a template.

After completing the embroidery, quilting, appliqué—whatever the lesson calls for—center the acetate pattern over the

Fig. 12.1 The tote bag, with one of the squares in position on the pocket.

square. Draw a line at the edge of the acetate all the way around with a water-erasable marker or white chalk pencil.

Back the square with stiff fabric, fleece, or iron-on interfacing if it is not stiff enough for the pocket. Stitch along the line you've drawn and cut off the extra fabric to that line.

Slip typing paper or heavy tear-away stabilizer under the square. Finish by satin stitching at the widest setting around the edge. Dab the corners with Fray-Check to keep them from raveling.

Glue or stitch Velcro dots under the corner of each square to correspond to the ones in the pocket frame. (If the square is stiff enough, this will not be necessary.) An alternative to Velcro is an idea from Marilyn Tisol of Hinsdale, Illinois. She backs each square she makes by first cutting a piece of plastic canvas the size of the square; then she attaches the fabric square to it by whipping the edges together. The plastic is rigid enough to keep the square in the frame.

Tote bag construction

My tote bag is made of canvas, but it can be made of any heavy-duty fabric. I used canvas because I wanted a bag that would stand by itself. If the fabric you've chosen is not heavy enough, press a layer of fusible webbing between two layers of material. Whatever you choose, pre-wash and press all fabrics before you cut.

Supplies:
1½ yards (1.4m) of 36″ (0.9m) canvas (includes body of bag, handles, pockets, and bottom of bag)
3⅛ yards (2.9m) of 1″ (2.5cm) wide fusible webbing
Teflon pressing sheet
Four Velcro dots
Sewing thread to match canvas, or monofilament

Fig. 12.2 Layout for the tote b

Rotary cutter and board are timesavers
24″ × 6″ (61cm × 15.2cm) plastic ruler
Water-erasable pen, pencil or sliver of soap
General purpose B or zipperfoot
Jeans needle

My tote (see cover) is made up of many colors and looks as if Dr. Seuss invented it. It includes royal blue for the bottom, yellow pockets, green handles, and red for the body of the bag.

I chose those colors because the striped lining fabric included them all. I backed the lining with Pellon fleece and quilted down each stripe to give my bag even more body. I added pockets to the lining, too.

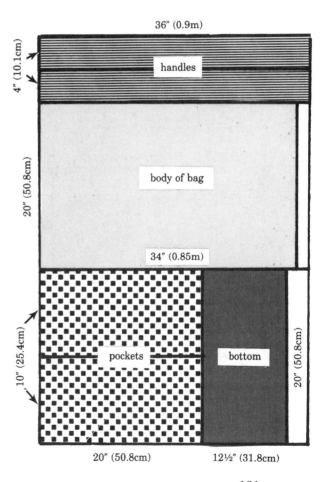

181

Lining is optional, but if you choose to include one, you will need another piece of fabric at least 34″ × 20″ (86.4cm × 50.8cm). Add 20″ × 20″ (50.8cm × 50.8cm) to this if you wish to make pockets for your lining.

The layout of the bag is provided in Fig. 12.2; note that the layout is predicated on cutting all pieces from a single length of cloth, rather than several different colors.

Body of bag:
34″ × 20″ (0.86m × 50.8cm)

1. Cut out fabric. Fold in half and notch bottom on both sides, 17″ (43.2cm) from top. Draw a line between the notches on the inside (Fig. 12.3).

2. Place a 1″ (2.5cm) strip of fusible webbing along both 20″ (50.8cm) edges on the right side of the bag and fuse in place using the Teflon pressing sheet. Fold at the top of the webbing to the backside. Press the fold, using the Teflon pressing sheet on top to protect your iron. Then fold

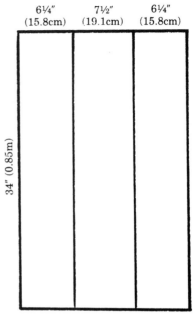

Fig. 12.4 Mark the outside of the bag.

over 1″ (2.5cm) again, using the pressing sheet *between* the fusible webbing and the body of the bag.

3. Mark a line down the length of this piece 6¼″ (15.9cm) from each side, as shown in Fig. 12.4, to use later as guidelines for construction of the bag.

Pockets: 10″ × 20″
(25.4cm × 50.8cm); cut 2

1. Use the ruler and marking pen to indicate stitching lines from top to bottom—6¼″ (15.9cm) from each side. Center area will be 7½″ (19.1cm).

2. Cut slits 1½″ (3.8cm) down from the top on these lines. Make a mark ¾″ (19.0mm) from the top and another ¾″ (19.0mm) down from the first. Draw lines through those marks across the top of the pockets (Fig. 12.5A). It is easier if you mark the middle section on the *back* of the fabric, so you'll be able to see the lines as you fold. Fold on the lines as follows: Each side should

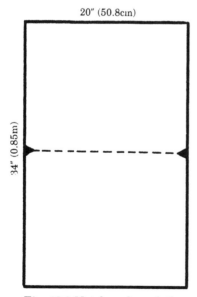

Fig. 12.3 Notch and mark the inside of the bag.

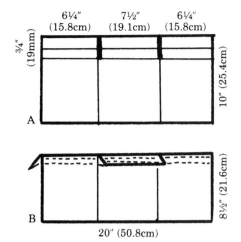

Fig. 12.5 Pocket construction. A. Mark lines to indicate the pockets. Then mark lines across the pockets. $\frac{3}{4}''$ (19.0mm) and $1\frac{1}{2}''$ (3.8cm) from the top. Cut down $1\frac{1}{2}''$ (3.8cm) between the pockets. B. Fold the tops of the side pockets to the back, the top of the middle pocket to the front.

Handles: 4″ × 36″ (10.2cm × 0.9m); cut 2

1. Stitch down one long side 1″ (2.5cm) from edge. Fold. Do the same with the other side. (This stitching is used as a guide to make folding the handles easier and more accurate.) Bring folded edges together and fold again, creating the 1″ (2.5cm) wide handles. Place strips of 1″ (2.5cm) fusible webbing inside the length of the handles and press to fuse. The handle is four layers (plus fusible webbing) thick (Fig. 12.6).

2. Use the zipper foot to topstitch both sides $\frac{1}{8}''$ (3.2mm) from edge. Place the foot on the edge of the fabric and stitch. Change to the general purpose foot B and, using the foot to measure, place the edge of the

be folded twice toward the inside of the bag. The middle $7\frac{1}{2}''$ (19.1cm) should be folded twice toward the front of the fabric. This middle flap creates the top of the frame.

3. Stitch across the top of all three pockets $\frac{1}{8}''$ (3.2mm) from the top edge. Do this on both pocket pieces.

4. Then stitch across side pocket sections through all three layers of fabric at $\frac{1}{8}''$ (3.2mm) from each bottom fold. Finish both side pockets on both pocket pieces this way (Fig. 12.5B).

5. Open out the top of the middle sections on both pocket pieces to enable you to stitch across the folds without stitching them to the pockets. Stitch across the $7\frac{1}{2}''$ (19.1cm) middle sections on both pocket pieces at $\frac{1}{8}''$ (3.2mm) from each bottom fold. This flap will create the top of the frames in which you'll slip the 6″ (15.2mm) squares.

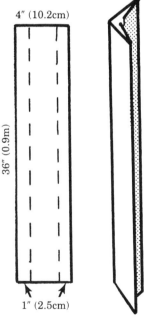

Fig. 12.6 Stitch down the length of the handles 1″ (2.5cm) from each side. Fold down 1″ (2.5cm) at each side, the length of the handle. Then fold the handle in half. Place strip of fusible webbing inside and press in place. Stitch the handles together.

foot on each of the stitched lines and stitch again, $\frac{1}{4}''$ (6.3mm) from the lines on both sides.

Bottom: 12½″ × 20″ (31.8cm × 50.8cm)

1. Fold over 1″ (2.5cm) top and bottom along the 20″ (50.8cm) edges and topstitch across $\frac{1}{8}''$ (3.2mm) from the fold. Draw a line $\frac{3}{4}''$ (19.0mm) from each fold.

2. Fold the bottom in half the long way and notch on the fold on both sides, 6¼″ (15.8cm) from top and bottom (Fig. 12.7).

Assembly

1. First sew pockets to the bag. The pockets will be 3″ (7.5cm) from the top. (Remember that the bag has been folded over 2″ (5.1cm) at the top. Measure from the top of the last fold. Line up the markings, 6¼″ (15.9cm) from each side on bag and pockets and pin in place. Stitch on the lines you've drawn to create pockets and, using a $\frac{1}{4}''$ (6.4mm) seam allowance, stitch down each side and across the bottoms of the pocket pieces.

2. Sew handles next. Find the center of the bag by folding it double the long way. Measure 3″ (7.6cm) from the center to each side of the bag and make a mark with the water-erasable pen; 6″ (15.2cm) will be open in center. Using the 24″ × 6″ (61cm × 15.2cm) ruler, draw guidelines through these marks the length of the bag. Pin handles in place outside those lines. Stitch

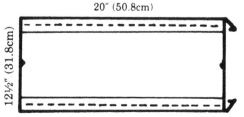

Fig. 12.7 Follow this diagram to fold, mark and stitch the bottom piece of the bag.

across the bottom of the handles and up, $\frac{1}{8}''$ (3.2mm) from the edge, on the existing outside stitching. Extend your stitching all the way to the top of the bag. Do this on the next outside lines as well (you will often stitch on top of other lines of stitching). The top edge of the bag will not be sewn down until later, but sew through the folds as you attach the handles.

3. To make the open frame, stitch only the top of the handles above the pockets on both sides. Leave $\frac{3}{4}''$ (19.0mm) around the frame to insert workshop squares (Fig. 12.8).

4. Attach bottom next. Match notches with those of the bag and pin the bottom in place. Stitch over the $\frac{1}{8}''$ (3.2mm) stitching line to $\frac{3}{4}''$ (19.0mm) from each side of the center pocket (see Fig. 12.8). *Do not* stitch across the center pocket. Then stitch all across the bottom piece on the $\frac{3}{4}''$ (19.0mm) mark. This will create the bottom of the frame. Double check. Is the frame done correctly? Be sure you can slip a fabric square inside.

5. Finish the side edges of the bag with a zigzag stitch (Fig. 12.9). Then put it all together. Fold at center bottom notches with right sides together. Check to see that pockets and bottom meet at each side. Stitch in a $\frac{5}{8}''$ (15.9mm) seam line from top to bottom. Now refold the top edge of the bag and press in place to fuse. Topstitch in place at the top edge and bottom fold.

6. Bag corners should be finished this way: On the inside, pinch the bottom by matching the side seam with the line drawn across the inside of the bottom of the bag (Fig. 12.10). Measure, on the seam line, 2″ (5.1cm) from the point. Draw a line across. Be sure it is exact on each side so stitching is perpendicular to the side seams. Stitch on drawn line for corners. This forms the bottom of the bag. If you wish to cut a piece of $\frac{1}{8}''$ (3.2mm) Masonite or linoleum tile to fit the bottom, do so now before you line your bag.

7. Press one side of four adhesive-backed

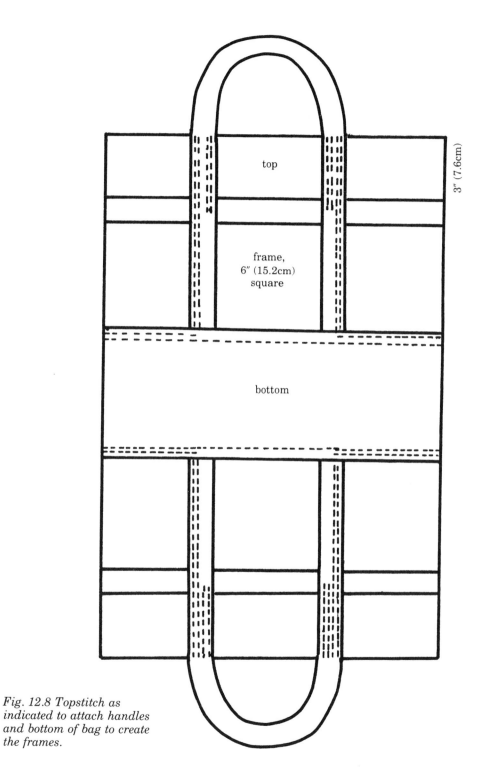

top

frame,
6″ (15.2cm)
square

bottom

3″ (7.6cm)

*Fig. 12.8 Topstitch as
indicated to attach handles
and bottom of bag to create
the frames.*

Fig. 12.9 Finish the edges with zigzag stitches. With right sides together, stitch each side of the tote bag.

Fig. 12.10 Make the tote bag corners by stitching lines perpendicular to the side seams, 2" (5.1cm) up from the points.

Velcro dots into the four corners of the frame.

Lining

If you line your bag, create the lining as if making another bag. Do not include bottom, pockets or handles. However, if you wish to add pockets to the lining, then cut out two pieces of 10" × 20" (25.4cm × 50.8cm) fabric, the same size as the bag pockets. At the top of each pocket piece, turn over 1" (2.5cm) two times and sew down at the top and at the fold. Press up 1" (2.5cm) at the bottom. Place the pocket pieces 3" (7.6cm) from the top of the lining and pin in place. Sew across the bottom of the pocket at the fold and $\frac{3}{4}$" (19.0mm) from the first stitching line. (The double line of stitching will add strength to the pockets.) Then attach the pockets to the sides of the lining by stitching down on each side with a $\frac{1}{4}$" (6.3mm) seam allowance. With a ruler and water-erasable marker, draw lines down the pocket pieces to indicate where you will divide the fabric for pockets. Stitch those in place.

Sew up the sides of the lining, using a $\frac{5}{8}$" (15.9mm) seam allowance) and create the bottom corner. Fold over the top as you did for the bag. I use the double fold for stability.

Whip stitch invisibly by hand around the top to keep the lining and bag together. With heavy canvas, you may prefer to make the lining and then place wrong sides together (bag and lining) and machine stitch around the top.

Afterword

Know Your Singer could go on forever, as there is no way to include, in one book, everything that can be accomplished by your machine.

I hope you're inspired to experiment, to fill your notebook with samples, and to take those long-cuts, choosing decorative over mundane.

A Singer Chronology

1850: Orson C. Phelps of Boston begins manufacturing sewing machines under license from John A. Lerow, a tailor from Boston, and Lerow's business partner, S. C. Blodgett. The Lerow and Blodgett machine is not very practical, however, as the circular movement of the shuttle takes a twist out of the thread with every revolution.

Isaac Merritt Singer, after examining the machine, notes "instead of the shuttle going around in a circle, I would have it move to-and-fro in a straight line. In place of the needle bar pushing a curved needle horizontally, I would have a straight needle and make it work up and down."

With $40, Singer builds in eleven days a sewing machine which has a straight eye-pointed needle and transverse shuttle, an overhanging arm, a table to support the cloth, a presser foot to hold the material down against the upward stroke of the needle, and a roughened feed wheel extending through a slot in the table. Motion is communicated to the needle arm and shuttle by means of gears. This machine is the world's first truly practical sewing machine.

Singer also conceives the idea of using a treadle similar to that of a spinning wheel; all other machines at the time use a hand crank to generate power.

1851: Isaac Singer patents his lock stitch machine and, with a New York lawyer, Edward B. Clark, forms I.M. Singer & Co.

1853: The first Singer machine sells for $100.

1855: I.M. Singer & Co. begins marketing sewing machines internationally.

A Singer sewing machine is awarded first prize at the World's Fair in Paris.

1856: Edward B. Clark originates the hire-purchase plan, prototype for installment or time-payment purchase plans.

The first light machine manufactured expressly for family use is known as the "Turtle Back" because the overhanging arm resembles the back of a turtle. It has a vibrating arm which carries the needle, and motion is given to the machine from the treadle through a driving wheel connected to the mechanism by a flat leather belt.

1889: The Singer Manufacturing Company introduces the first electric sewing machine.

1913: A record 3 million sewing machines are sold.

1927: Singer introduces Singer Sewing Centers for sewing instruction.

187

1975: Singer introduces the Athena, the world's first electronic home sewing machine. The "brain" of the system is a chip that contains more than 8,000 transistors and is less than ¼-inch square.

1985: Singer introduces an entire line of state-of-the-art sewing machines, with models designed to meet individual sewer needs and budgets. The top-of-the-line electronic has the capacity to produce an unlimited number of stitch patterns, over and above its 24 built-in construction, stretch, and decorative stitches, due to its ability to accept interchangeable Sew Ware cartridges; monograms and embroiders electronically and automatically; and sews sideways.

Information courtesy of the Singer Company

Singer Presser Feet and Attachments

Standard and Optional Feet and Accessories Available for Singer Models

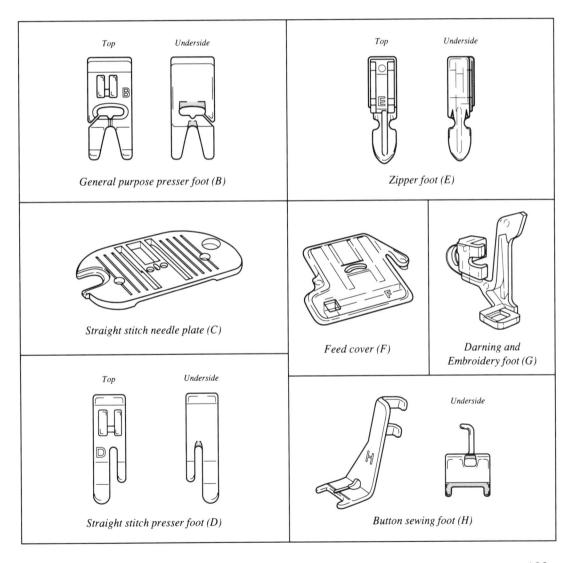

Top   Underside

General purpose presser foot (B)

Top   Underside

Zipper foot (E)

Straight stitch needle plate (C)

Feed cover (F)

Darning and Embroidery foot (G)

Top   Underside

Straight stitch presser foot (D)

Underside

Button sewing foot (H)

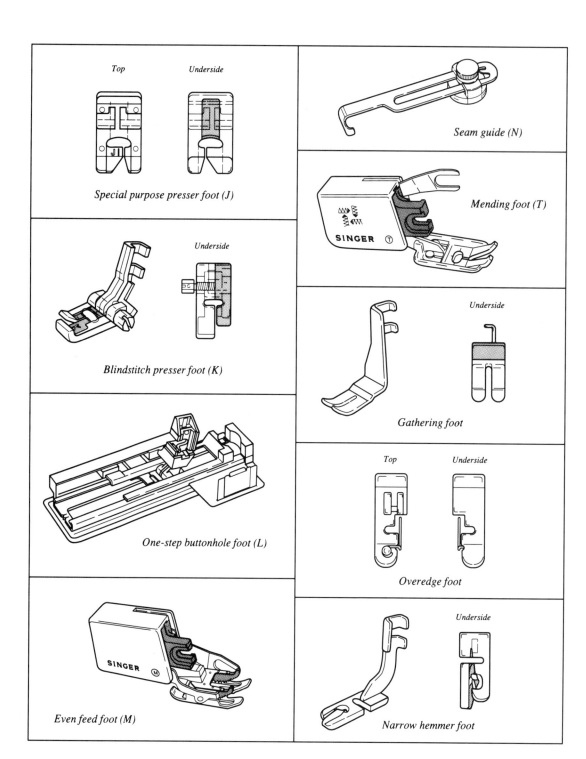

Top　　　　Underside

Special purpose presser foot (J)

Seam guide (N)

Mending foot (T)

SINGER

Underside

Blindstitch presser foot (K)

Underside

Gathering foot

One-step buttonhole foot (L)

Top　　　　Underside

Overedge foot

SINGER

Even feed foot (M)

Underside

Narrow hemmer foot

190

Sources of Supply

Singer Machines and Information

Singer Co.
135 Raritan Center Pkwy.
Edison, NJ 08837

Singer Reference Library
Cy De Cosse, Inc.
Minnetonka, MN 54351

(**Note:** The following listings were adapted with permission from *The Complete Book of Machine Embroidery* by Robbie and Tony Fanning [Chilton, 1986].)

Threads

Note: Ask your local retailer or send a pre-addressed stamped envelope to the companies below to find out where to buy their threads.

Extra-fine

Assorted threads
Robison-Anton Textile Co.
175 Bergen Blvd.
Fairview, NJ 07022

DMC 100% cotton, Sizes 30 and 50
The DMC Corporation
107 Trumbull Street
Elizabeth, NJ 07206

Dual-Duty Plus Extra-fine, cotton-wrapped polyester
J&PCoats/Coats & Clark
PO Box 6044
Norwalk, CT 06852

Madeira threads
Madeira Co.
56 Primrose Drive
O'Shea Industrial Park
Laconia, NH 03246

Mettler Metrosene Fine Machine Embroidery cotton, Size 60/2
Swiss-Metrosene, Inc.
6929 Sunrise Blvd., Ste 200
Citrus Heights, CA 95610

Natesh 100% rayon, lightweight
Aardvark Adventures
PO Box 2449
Livermore, CA 94550

Paradise 100% rayon
D&E Distributing
199 N. El Camino Real #F-242
Encinitas, CA 92024

Sulky 100% rayon, Sizes 30 and 40
Speed Stitch, Inc.
PO Box 3472
Port Charlotte, FL 33949

Zwicky 100% cotton, Size 30/2
White Sewing Machine Co.
11750 Berea Rd.
Cleveland, OH 44111

Ordinary

Dual Duty Plus, cotton-wrapped polyester—
see Dual Duty Plus Extra-fine

Also Natesh heavyweight, Zwicky in cotton and polyester, Mettler Metrosene in 30/2, 40/3, 50/3, and 30/3, and Metrosene Plus

Metallic

YLI Corporation
45 West 300 North
Provo, UT 84601

Troy Thread & Textile Corp.
2300 W. Diversey Ave.
Chicago, IL 60647
Free catalog

Machine-Embroidery Supplies

(hoops, threads, patterns, books, etc.)

Aardvark Adventures
PO Box 2449
Livermore, CA 94550
    Also publishes "Aardvark Territorial
    Enterprise"

Clotilde Inc.
237 SW 28th St.
Ft. Lauderdale, FL 33315

Craft Gallery Ltd.
PO Box 8319
Salem, MA 01971

D&E Distributing
199 N. El Camino Real #F-242
Encinitas, CA 92024

Verna Holt's Machine Stitchery
PO Box 236
Hurricane, UT 84734

Nancy's Notions
PO Box 683
Beaver Dam, WI 53916
    Battenberg tape—free catalog

Patty Lou Creations
Rt 2, Box 90-A
Elgin, OR 97827

Sew-Art International
PO Box 550
Bountiful, UT 84010
    Catalog $2

Speed Stitch, Inc.
PO Box 3472
Port Charlotte, FL 33952
    Catalog $2

SewCraft
Box 1869
Warsaw, IN 46580
    Blank greeting cards;
    Also publishes newsletter/catalog $2

Treadleart
25834 Narbonne Ave.
Lomita, CA 90717

Sewing Machine Supplies

The Button Shop
PO Box 1065
Oak Park, IL 60304
    Presser feet

Sewing Emporium
1087 Third Avenue
Chula Vista, CA 92010
    Presser feet, accessories,
    Olfa circle cutter

Miscellaneous

Applications
871 Fourth Ave.
Sacramento, CA 95818
    Release Paper for appliqué

Berman Leathercraft
145 South St.
Boston, MA 02111
    Leather

Boycan's Craft and Art Supplies
PO Box 897
Sharon, PA 16146
    Plastic needlepoint canvas

Cabin Fever Calicoes
PO Box 54
Center Sandwich, NH 03227

Clearbrook Woolen Shop
PO Box 8
Clearbrook, VA 22624
    Ultrasuede scraps

Different Drummer
Route 5, Box 827
Richland Center, WI 53581
    Interesting frames—free catalog

The Fabric Carr
170 State St.
Los Altos, CA 94022
    Sewing gadgets

The Green Pepper Inc.
941 Olive Street
Eugene, OR 97401
    Outdoor fabrics, patterns—$1
    catalog

Home-Sew
Bethlehem, PA 18018
    Lace—$.25 catalog

Libby's Creations
PO Box 16800 Ste. 180
Mesa, AZ 85202
    Horizontal spool holder

LJ Originals, Inc.
516 Sumac Pl.
DeSoto, TX 75115
    TransGraph

Lore Lingerie
3745 Overland Ave.
Los Angeles, CA 90034
    1 lb. of silk remnants, $9.45

Osage Country Quilt Factory
400 Walnut
Overbrook, KS 66524
    Washable fabric spray glue

The Pellon Company
119 West 40th St.
New York, NY 10018
    Machine appliqué supplies

The Perfect Notion
115 Maple St.
Toms River, NJ 08753
    Sewing supplies

Salem Industries, Inc.
PO Box 43027
Atlanta, GA 30336
    Olfa cutters, rulers

Solar-Kist Corp.
PO Box 273
LaGrange, IL 60525
    Teflon pressing sheet, Fine-fuse

Stacy Industries, Inc.
38 Passaic St.
Wood-Ridge, NJ 07075
    Teflon pressing sheet, Transfuse II

Summa Design
Box 24404
Dayton, OH 45424
    Charted designs for knitting needle
    machine sewing

Susan of Newport
Box 3107
Newport Beach, CA 92663
    Ribbons and laces

Tandy Leather Co.
PO Box 791
Ft. Worth, TX 76101
    Leather

Theta's School of Sewing
2508 N.W. 39th Street
Oklahoma City, OK 73112
    Charted designs for knitting needle
    machine sewing, smocking
    directions and supplies for the
    machine

Magazines
(write for rates)

Aardvark Territorial Enterprise
PO Box 2449
Livermore, CA 94550
    Newspaper jammed with all kinds of
    information about all kinds of em-
    broidery, design, and things to
    order. I ordered the gold rings from
    them and gold battenberg tape

disPatch
107 E. Baseline #6
Tempe, AZ 85283
    Newspaper about quilting and ma-
    chine arts

Fiberarts
50 College St.
Asheville, NC 28801
    Gallery of the best fiber artists, in-
    cluding those who work in machine
    stitchery.

Needlecraft for Today
4949 Byers
Ft. Worth, TX 76109
    Creative uses of the sewing machine

SewCraft
Box 1869
Warsaw, IN 46580
    Newspaper and catalog combination
    containing machine embroidery arti-
    cles, designs and supplies. $2

Sew News
PO Box 1790
Peoria, IL 61656
    Monthly tabloid, mostly about gar-
    ment sewing

Threads
Box 355
Newton, CT 06470
    Magazine on all fiber crafts

Treadleart
25834 Narbonne Ave., Ste. 1
Lomita, CA 90717
    Bimonthly about machine embroi-
    dery

Bibliography

Alexander, Eugenie, *Fabric Pictures,* Mills and Boon Ltd., London, 1967.

Ashley, Clifford W., *The Ashley Book of Knots,* Doubleday & Co., 1944.

Bennet, dj, *Machine Embroidery with Style,* Madrona Publishers, 1980.

Butler, Anne, *Machine Stitches,* BT Batsford, Ltd., 1976.

Clucas, Joy, *Your Machine for Embroidery,* G. Bell & Sons, 1975.

Coleman, Anne, *The Creative Sewing Machine,* BT Batsford, 1979.

Ericson, Lois, *Fabrics . . . Reconstructed* (Lois Ericson, Box 1680, Tahoe City, CA 95730), 1985.

———, *Belts . . . Waisted Sculpture,* 1984.

Fanning, Robbie and Tony, *The Complete Book of Machine Quilting,* Chilton Book Co., 1980.

———, *The Complete Book of Machine Embroidery,* Chilton Book Co., 1986.

Gray, Jennifer, *Machine Embroidery,* Van Nostrand Reinhold, 1973.

Hall, Carolyn, *The Sewing Machine Craft Book,* Van Nostrand Reinhold, 1980.

Harding, Valerie, *Textures in Embroidery,* Watson-Guptill, New York, 1977.

Hazen, Gale Grigg, *Sew Sane* (The Sewing Place, 100 W. Rincon Ave., Ste. 105, Campbell, CA 95008; $14.95 postpaid), 1985.

Hogue, Refa D., *Machine Edgings* (c/o Treadleart, 25834 Narbonne Avenue, Lomita, CA 90717).

Hoover, Doris and Nancy Welch, *Tassels* (out-of-print), 1978.

James, Irene, *Sewing Specialties,* I. M. James Enterprises, 1982.

Lawrence and Clotilde, *Sew Smart,* IBC Publishing Co., 1984.

———, Supplement, IBC Publishing Co., 1984.

Macor, Alida, *And Sew On,* Alida Macor, 1985.

McNeill, Moyra, *Machine Embroidery—Lace and See-Through Techniques,* BT Batsford, 1985.

Nall, Mary Lou, *Mary Lou's Sewing Techniques* (c/o Treadleart, 25834 Narbonne Avenue, Lomita, CA 90717).

Nicholas, Annwen, *Embroidery in Fashion,* Watson-Guptill, 1975.

Ota, Kimi, *Sashiko Quilting* (Kimi Ota, 10300 61st Ave. So., Seattle, Washington 98178), 1981.

Pullen, Martha, *French Hand Sewing by Machine* (518 Madison St., Huntsville, AL 35801), 1985.

Shaeffer, Claire B., *The Complete Book of Sewing Short Cuts,* Sterling Publishing Co., Inc., 1984.

Short, Eirian, *Quilting,* BT Batsford, London, 1983.

Singer Instructions for Art Embroidery and Lacework, Laci's Publications (2982 Adeline St., Berkeley, CA 94703), 1987.

Skjerseth, Douglas Neil, *Stitchology,* Seth Publications (PO Box 1606, Novato, CA 94947), 1979.

Thompson, Sue, *Decorative Dressmaking,* Rodale Press, 1985.

Warren, Virena, *Landscape in Embroidery,* BT Batsford, 1986.

Wiechec, Philomena, *Celtic Quilt Designs,* Celtic Design Co., 1980.

Zieman, Nancy, *The Busy Woman's Sewing Book,* Nancy's Notions Ltd., 1984.

Index

Page numbers in *italic* refer to illustrations

topstitching, 139–140
  presser foot for, 6
topstitching needles, 8, 10, 30
tote bag, 180–186
  construction of, 181–186
  corners of, 184
  handles of, 183–184
  lining of, 186
  pockets of, 182, 184
tote bag squares
  with appliqué and quilting, 106–108
  with cabling, 40–43
  with edge-stitch appliqué, 66
  finishing, 180–181
  with Italian cording, 109–111
  with reverse appliqué, 64
  with straight stitch appliqué, 66–68
transparent fabric
  blurring on, 70
  flower project with, 70–72
  hems for, 130
  layering, 76–77
  sources of, 51
trapunto, 81, 109
triple needles, 10
tunneling, avoiding, 4
typing paper, 11

unique zipper foot, 32
universal-point needles, 9
upholstery, thread and needle for, 9

variegated thread, 22, 27
veiling. *See* bridal veiling
Velcro dots, 181
velvet, thread and needle for, 9

velveteen, quilting hems on, 131
Victorian Christmas stocking project,
  174–179
vine stitch, 126, 127
vinyls, presser foot for, 6

wash-away basting thread, 62
water-soluble stabilizer, 11, 96
  for open-space stitching, 82
waxed quilting thread, 8
wedding gowns, 136
wedding handkerchief project, 120–123
wedge needles, 10
whipped edges. *See* rolled and whipped edges
whipping, 19–20
width, of stitches, 12–13
wire, covered for shaped edges, 136
Wonder-Under Transfer Fusing Web, 10, 169
wool
  quilting hems on, 131
  thread and needle for, 9
woolly overlock, 8

yarn
  on bobbin, 38
  couching, 31–32
  fringing, 43–45
yellow band needles, 9

zigzag stitch, 22
  to fill in designs, 29–30
  multi-stitch, 126–127
  on narrow edge, 135–136
zipper foot, 5, *189*
  for quilting, 106